Library use and User Research

Library use and User Research

M. Ram

RANDOM

RANDOM PUBLICATIONS

NEW DELHI (INDIA)

Library use and User Research

ISBN 978-93-5111-559-5

Published in 2015 in India by

RANDOM PUBLICATIONS

4376-A/4B, Gali Murari Lal, Ansari Road
New Delhi-110 002
Phone : +9111-43580356, 011-23289044, 011-43142548
e-mail: sales@randompublications.com,
info@randompublications.com, randomexports@gmail.com

Reprint 2021

Type Setting by : Friends Media, Delhi-110089
Digitally Printed at : Replika Press Pvt. Ltd.

Preface

Users perceive electronic resources—in particular electronic journals and, for students, the Internet—to hold many advantages. Faculty members at ARL institutions cited convenience, timeliness, and the ability to search text as the most important factors in choosing electronic journals over print. Least important to them was animation of graphics, although others sometimes mention that as an important advantage.

Library will conduct Information Literacy/User Education/Orientation programmes to all in the beginning of the academic year. Besides this, these awareness programmes should be conducted when requested by users from time to time.

Library maintains an inter library loan arrangement with leading local libraries like IIT Mumbai, Homi Bhabha Centre for Science Education and Research 9TIFR), Mumbai University, SNDT University, IGIDR, etc. Apart from this library also has membership with DELNET. Hence, all possible efforts must be made to make available the learning resources needed for the faculty and students.

We concentrate on operational features. The reasons for this are partly technical in that the 'physical' data are more complete than the financial and do not incur the problems of currency conversion and inflation that beset the financial aspects. There are also institutional and accounting problems in compiling financial statistics that are genuinely comparable. (Common examples are whether or not libraries are charged for the cost of premises and staff overheads - which may often be absorbed by the parent institution.) So, for these various reasons, the statistics of operational features are more robust and comparable.

The book will suit to the needs of students, teachers, scholars and general readers.

I would like to thank my team for standing beside me throughout my career and writing this book. My special thanks go to "Random Publications" who have published the book.

–M. Ram

Contents

1

Library User Services

REFERENCE SERVICE

Library houses all important reference sources like Encyclopaedias, Dictionaries, handbooks and Manuals, Statistics, Yearbooks. The collection ranges from general to subject specific sources. All the reference sources are housed in the Ground floor Reference section. Users can also contact staff on duty for any assistance. Library also has access to online reference sources which may be accessed from the library web site.

INFORMATION LITERACY/LIBRARY ORIENTATION

Library will conduct Information Literacy/User Education/Orientation programmes to all in the beginning of the academic year. Besides this, these awareness programmes should be conducted when requested by users from time to time.

INTER LIBRARY LOAN

Library maintains an inter library loan arrangement with leading local libraries like IIT Mumbai, Homi Bhabha Centre for Science Education and Research 9TIFR), Mumbai University, SNDT University, IGIDR, etc. Apart from this library also has membership with DELNET. Hence, all possible efforts must be made to make available the learning resources needed for the faculty and students.

PHOTOCOPYING SERVICES

Presently library maintains two heavy duty photocopying machines. Two operators are appointed to provide photocopying service in shift basis.

ICT SERVICES DIVISION

UGC-INFONET SERVICES

The SDTM Library is one of the members of INFLIBNET UGC-Infonet Digital Library Consortium since 2003. UGC has set up this programme to promote use of electronic databases and full text access to e-journals by the research and Academic community of the country.

Online databases are accessible via the Library Homepage, which provide access to full-text scholarly research articles beyond the physical wall of the library:

- Access to more than 7000 full text scholarly journals online
- 9 online databases in the field of social science
- Project Muse (389 journals); Oxford University Press (202 journals); JSTOR (729 journals); Springer Link (1236 journals); Taylor and Francis (1076 journals); JCCC (Gateway Portal); ISID; Cambridge Journals Online (279 journals); Wiley Interscience (502 journals) available under the UGC-Infonet services
- Library subscribe to Sage Online Journals (240 journals); Emerald Management Xtra (160 journals); ABI/INFORM Complete™ (2950 journals); indiastat.com (statistical database); World Bank Databases (GDF+WDI+e-Library)
- IP Based access to all e-Resources
- Statistical usage reports of e-resources

DOCUMENT DELIVERY SERVICES

TISS Library has been recognized as one of the Twenty Two Document Delivery Centres established by UGC-INFLIBNET, Ahmedabad. The Centre will deliver, on demand, the copies of research papers from 4000 and odd print journals subscribed by these 22 Centres apart from 7000 and odd full text e-journals, conference proceedings and other materials. Access to all these journals has been provided through JCCC gateway portal. Users can also submit an online request in JCCC for the article from both print and e-journals.

DIGITAL LIBRARY SERVICES

A State-of-art Digital Library provides seamless access to various CD-ROM Databases, Electronic Theses and Dissertations, In-house Bibliographic and full text Databases, Institutional Repository, MK Tata Centre Archive etc.

Major CD-ROM database collections includes ProQuest, Wilson Social Science Abstract, Popline, ABI/INFORM etc:

- Access to Electronic version of Indian Journal of Social Work and Sociological Bulletin on Library intranet
- Digitisation of library materials including Rare and Out of Print books but in demand
- Digitisation of Theses and Dissertations submitted to the institute
- External Digitisation projects
- Scanning and printing facility for the students

CYBER LIBRARY

The SDTM Library has set up Cyber Library with over 100 Pentium computers working in a networked environment through connectivity provided by ERNET India using 2 Mbps High Bandwidth Leased Line. It was inaugurated and thrown open to the students on 12th November, 2008 during the ILA International Conference from 12-15 November, 2008 organised by the library in collaboration with Indian Library Association. The Online databases like Project Muse, Springer Link, JSTOR, Blackwell will provide access to full text journals through UGCInfonet E-Journals Consortia. In addition, SPSS and SAS computing facilities will also be accessible to the scholars.

Salient features of SDTM Cyber Library:

- Cyber library in a networked environment with 100 computers using a dedicated 2 Mbps leased line
- Open 24x7 and 365 days a year
- Both reading and computing facilities
- Laser printing facility
- Access to full text online journals through UGC-Infonet E-Journals Consortia and other library e-resources.
- IP based Web Cameras for surveillance to enhance security of the library resources

Cyber Library-Acceptable Use and Code of Conduct:

- Do Not Connect Your Mobile To Computers.
- Do Not Install Any Software Without Prior Permission Of IT Team.
- Do Not Download Movies OR Songs.
- Do Not Remove LAN Cord, Keyboard And Mouse From The Computers.
- Do Not Save Any Document On The Desktop.
- Kindly Scan Your Pen Drive, CDs OR DVDs Before use.
- Keep Your Mobile On Silent Mode.
- Eatables are not allowed inside the Cyber Library.
- Take Care Of Your Own Belongings.
- Turn Off The Computer After Your Work Is Completed.
- All Drives Will Be Formatted After Every 15 Days by IT team Without Any Intimation.
- IT Team Will Not be Responsible For Any Data Loss
- Kindly Co-operate With IT Team For Minimum Downtime Of The Computers.
- Please Inform To IT Team In Case Of Any Computers Problem.
- Please Keep The Cyber Library Clean.
- Keep Silence In Cyber Library.

LICENSES AND FAIR USE OF E-RESOURCES

The INFLIBNET Consortium subscribes to thousands of electronic journals including full-text electronic resources and bibliographic databases for its member institutions. All electronic resources available through the Consortium are governed by license agreements. The terms and conditions for using these resources are spelled out in license agreements that are signed with each publisher by the INFLIBNET Consortium on behalf of its member institutions.

The licenses for electronic resources impose two types of restrictions on its usage, namely:

- Who can use these resources; and
- How the resources can be used.

The first restriction defines authorized users for e-resources, which generally includes students, faculty, staff and onsite visitors of a subscribing institution. The second restriction deals with how these resources can be used. It is the responsibility of individual users to ensure that e-resources are used for personal, educational and research purposes only. Most of the agreements entered into by the Consortium and publishers specify items that users are prohibited to do.

Some of them are as follows:

- Systematic or programmatic downloading, retention, and printing are prohibited. For example, you cannot download entire issue of a journal or print out several copies of the same article.
- Electronic distribution of content is also restricted although the specific restrictions vary from publisher to publisher. It may be permissible to forward an article to another colleague in your own institution by e-mail, however, transmitting an article to someone outside of the institution, or to a large group of recipients, a mailing list, or an electronic bulletin board, is not allowed.
- If you are teaching a class, you can print out a copy of an article from an electronic journal and include it in your course pack. However, do not make multiple copies for circulation. Copyright laws protect published material in any format so that it cannot be copied except in accordance with fair use. Providing access to material for educational purposes falls within the realm of fair use.
- Please ensure that the resource is used for educational and research purposes and not for commercial purposes.
- Providing electronic links on your course web pages to the Library's licensed resources is permitted but you cannot post the PDF of an article on your web site. The publishers' main concern is that people outside of your campus network should not be able to access resources licensed by your institution. However, a researcher can post a pre-print of an article written by himself.
- As with any kind of scholarly communication, a researcher can use phrases or quotes from other articles and cite the source of information. However, a researcher is prohibited from using large chunk of information from an article or from a chapter in a book.

What Happens if the License is Violated

Publishers track the use of their electronic resources in terms of number of downloads made by subscribing institution. Misuse, if any, is notified to the subscribing institution with details of kinds of violations and institution is expected to take action.

The publisher also suspends the access to e-resource pending suitable action by subscribing institution. The access is stopped not only for journals where license agreement was violated but for all journals by the same publisher. Moreover, the access is suspended not only for the individual violator but for the entire institution.

Conditions of Use and Licensing Restrictions for Electronic Resources

The Consortium subscribes to thousands of electronic journals and bibliographic databases for use by authorized users in member institutions. The terms and conditions for using these resources are spelled out in electronic resource license agreements with each publisher. It is the responsibility of individual users to ensure that the use of electronic resources does not breach the terms and conditions specified in the license agreements.

Licenses vary from publisher to publisher; however, the general principles are as follows:

- Permitted:
  - Viewing, downloading, copying, printing and saving a copy of search results
  - Viewing, downloading, copying, printing and saving individual articles
  - Using e-resources for scholarly, educational or scientific research, teaching, private study and clinical purposes
  - Sending a copy of an article to another authorized user (*i.e.* current faculty, students or staff)
  - Posting the URL to the publisher's version of the article on a class web site (publisher links will allow only authorized users access)
- Not Permitted:
  - Use of robots or intelligent agents to do systematic, bulk or automatic downloading is not permitted
  - Systematic downloading or printing of entire journal issues or volumes, or large portions of other e-resources is not permitted
  - Using e-resources for commercial gain is not permitted (*i.e.* reselling, redistributing or republishing licensed content)
  - Transmitting, disseminating or otherwise making online content available to unauthorized users (*i.e.* sending to mailing lists or electronic bulletin boards) is not permitted

- Posting the publisher's version or PDF of an article to an open class web site is not permitted (instead, post the URL to the article which will allow only authorized users access)

Breaches of the license agreement with publishers could result in the suspension of access to the resources for the member institutions. Generic license agreements for all publishers specifying all the terms and conditions of the following databases are available at their respective web site.

e-Resources under UGC-Infonet Digital Consortium:

- Project Muse (389 journals)
- Oxford University Press (202 journals)
- JSTOR (729 journals)
- Springer Link (1236 journals)
- Taylor and Francis (1076 journals)
- JCCC (Gateway Portal)
- ISID (Industrial Development Bibliographic Database)
- Cambridge Journals Online (279 journals)
- Wiley Interscience (502 journals)

e-Resources Subscribed by SDTM Library:

- Sage Publications (240 journals)
- Emerald Management Xtra (160 journals)
- ABI/INFORM Complete™ (2950 journals)
- indiastat.com (statistical database)
- World Bank Databases (GDF+WDI+e-Library)

Computer Access-Acceptable Use and Code of Conduct

Only registered members of the Library are authorized to use the Computers, Internet facility or to access e-Resources. Prior to such authorization, the students must sign and return the Library Registration Form acknowledging their responsibilities and the consequences of violation. Students are expected to observe network etiquette by being polite. Students are prohibited from pretending to be someone else; transmitting obscene messages or pictures; revealing personal addresses or telephone numbers-either their own or another person's; or using the network in a way that would disrupt use by others. The following policy for acceptable use of computers, networks, and system resources, including the Internet and e-resources, shall apply to all TISS administrators, faculty, staff, and students. All technology equipment shall be used under the supervision of the site administrator. Any user who violates any condition of this policy is subject to disciplinary action or administrative sanctions.

In addition to any other disciplinary action taken, the Technology Department reserves the right to terminate access to system resources for any user who violates these guidelines:

- Every user in whose name a system account is issued will be responsible at all times for its proper use.
- Users shall not let other persons use their name, logon, password, or files for any reason
- Users shall not use others' system accounts or try to discover another user's password.
- Users shall not erase, rename, or make unusable anyone else's computer files, programmes or disks.
- Users shall not use Computers for any non-instructional or non-administrative purpose, including, instant messaging, online shopping, or personal use of streaming media such as online radio stations or video broadcasts.
- Users may not install, download, copy, or distribute copyrighted materials such as software, audio or video, files, graphics, and text without the written permission of the administrator.
- Users shall not use the Computers for illegal purposes, in support of illegal activities, or for any other activity prohibited.
- Users shall not write, produce, generate, copy, propagate, or attempt to introduce any computer code designed to self-replicate, damage, or otherwise hinder the performance of any computer's memory, file system, or software. Such software is often called a bug, virus, worm, Trojan Horse, or other name.
- Users shall not use Computers to purposefully distribute, create, or copy messages or materials that are abusive, obscene, sexually oriented, threatening, harassing, damaging to another's reputation, or illegal.
- Users shall not use Computers to purposefully access materials that are abusive, obscene, sexually oriented, threatening, harassing, damaging to another's reputation, or illegal. In the event that accidental access to prohibited materials occurs, users are expected to immediately discontinue such access and report the incident either to Library staff or to the administrator.
- Users shall not intentionally damage the system, damage information belonging to others, misuse system resources, or allow others to misuse system resources.
- Users shall not alter or vandalize computers, networks, printers, or other associated equipment and system resources. Alteration or vandalism includes, but is not limited to: removal of parts, intentional destruction of equipment, altering system settings or software, installing unauthorized or unlicensed software or programmes, attempting to degrade or disrupt system performance, or attempting to make system resources unusable.

- Users shall not use Computers for the forgery or attempted forgery of e-mail messages. Attempts to read, delete, copy, or modify the e-mail of other system users, deliberate interference with the ability of other users to send/receive e-mail, or the use of another person's e-mail account is prohibited.
- Users should not use library network for sending and receiving a large number of personal messages, including using group e-mail distribution lists to send non-administrative or non-instructional messages to other users.

NATIONAL CENTRE FOR SOCIAL SCIENCES INFOR MATION AND DOCUMENTATION

The TISS library with its valuable collections both in terms of quality and quantity in the field of social sciences, social work, health sciences act as a nodal centre of major source of information in the field of social sciences in India as well as abroad. This Centre's vision is to bring world class information services to the academic community of India in the field of social science.

The main mandate is to provide full range of documentation and information services in the area of social sciences apart from the core subject of Social Work, which will accept request from other user libraries via post, telephone, e-mail or fax and delivers the information. The centre is also providing 50 research students space for retrieving information, analysing data with all IT infrastructure from India and abroad with residential facility from the institute.

Salient features of the Centre are:

- Provide seamless, network access to worldwide scholarly information resources of relevance to the academic community, facilitating improved learning, teaching, research, collaboration and information sharing
- Provide orientation and training to the academic community in making effective use of electronic information sources, tools and services
- Dedicated Data Centre for e-journals, full text CD-ROM databases in the field of social sciences
- Training Centre for Research Scholars from NGO's, Institutions who are involved in Social Science Research and dissemination of information

PHYSICAL AMBIENCES

- *Cleanliness:* Library is a central resource department that is the backbone of all academic programmes of the institute. Students and faculty would be spending their considerable time in library premises pursuing their research and studies. Hence it is very much essential that library has a checking system in place to monitor the cleanliness and hygiene of the library premises like regular sweeping, cleaning and mopping of all floors, and washrooms.

- *Electricity and Water and Ventilation:* Library will ensure that these essential things are working at all times and users would not be put to any inconvenience.
- *Floor Plan and Direction/Guideposts:* Library shall have floor plans designed and proper directions/guideposts for people to move around the library looking for resources/services.

MANAGING THE PERFORMANCE OF LIBRARY TEAM

TISS library is managed by a professionally qualified and competent team. It is suggested that the performance of the team can be optimized by taking the following measures.

CLEARLY DEFINED JOB DESCRIPTIONS AT ALL LEVELS

Each member of the library team shall have a clearly defined, unambiguous job description that facilitates and gels with the library's and then Institute's Mission and Vision Statements. The organization chart with a clear reporting structure be developed for having effective span of control within the library.

QUARTERLY WORK PLAN AND PREDEFINED, AGREED TARGETS FOR ACHIEVEMENT

Each section in the library shall have a Quarterly Work Plan. Here, the works to be carried in the next quarter and the predetermined, agreed targets for achievements will be decided. There will be a review process after the every quarterly for assessment.

GENERAL CONDUCT

Every member of library team shall exhibit the highest level of professional conduct in discharging their duties. Staffs are expected to be in their sections unless otherwise their work takes them away from the desk. Providing polite and efficient service shall be the motto of the library.

DEPARTMENT PERFORMANCE AUDIT BY YEARLY USER FEEDBACK SURVEYS

Library will initiate a annual department performance audit wherein the performance of each section of library will be evaluated based on the feedback surveys, user satisfaction surveys. This feedback and evaluation will certainly help library to overcome any lacunae in the facilities and services being provided.

BIMONTHLY REPORTS ABOUT LIBRARY FUNCTIONING

Library shall compile, analyse and submit a performance report every two months. IN this, the performance and productivity of each section of the library shall be reported with descriptions as to how many targets were achieved, difficulties faced and how they were overcame.

GENERAL RULES AND REGULATIONS

- All the students/scholars and outsiders entering the Library shall deposit their bags and other belongings at the entrance and sign in the Register at the checkpoint. Only notebooks and the Library books to be returned will be allowed inside. Do not to leave any valuables at the Check Point. Library is not responsible for any loss of personal belongings. All files, books and notebooks must be presented to the security guard at the checkpoint for inspection while leaving the Library. Library does not permit any exception in the observance of this rule.
- Identity Card is compulsory for getting access to the library.
- Books removed from the shelves by students, if not required for reference, should be kept on the book trolley or on table nearest to them. Please do not try to shelve them yourself. *Please remember that a book misplaced is a book lost.*
- The newspaper(s) should be folded properly after reading and kept back in the designated place.
- Readers should not deface, mark, cut, mutilate or damage library resources in any way. If anyone is found doing so, he will be charged the full replacement cost of the resource. Books Borrowed should be protected from RAIN, DUST, INSECT, etc.
- All the students/scholars are required to bring three copies of their recent photographs (Passport Size) along with the Fee Receipt while applying for Library membership.
- All the students are advised to bring their own Reading Cards while using the Library.
- The Reserve Shelf book must be returned on the due date between 9.00 am to 10.00 am. And General Shelf books on or before the due date. General Shelf books are issued upto 8.00 pm.
- Claim for Reserve Shelf books should be made in the Register maintained at the counter between 8.30 am to 2.00 pm and they should be collected between 3.30 pm to 7.00 pm.
- Books are issued to students for overnight during the examination time only.
- Compendiums should be issued on reserve shelf card only.
- Those students who do not return the books, issued for overnight use, in time, will not be issued any book for a period of 7 days.
- *All the students who want to return the books issued on their names are advised to wait until the books are shown as cancelled against their names.*

- The "PASS OUT" slip should be handed over to the security guard at the checkpoint before taking out the issued book/s.
- There will be a fine of ₹ 1.00 per General Shelf book and Reserve shelf book, ₹ 2.00.
- For the loss of Readers Ticket, a fine of ₹.10/- each will be charged.
- Students are advised not to issue Books to others on their names.
- A fine of ₹ 75/- will be charged for the loss of compendium, files and such other reading materials. For book three times of the original price charged.
- Coupon for Xeroxing is available at the cash counter in the A/C Section up to 3.00 P.M. The Xeroxing charge per exposure is 0.50 p. After 3.00 P.M. payment can be made by cash in the library.
- Conversation and discussion disturbs library ambience. Therefore, all are requested to maintain dignified silence. If discussion is necessary, the common room should be utilized for the same.
- Smoking is not permitted in the Library.
- All users are requested to keep their mobiles switched off or in silent mode in the Library.
- Beverages and Eatables are not allowed inside the library.
- No visitor or guest is permitted to use the Library without the prior permission of the Librarian. He/She is required to produce a proper introduction letter from the concerned Institution/Organization to which he/she is attached. A fee of ₹.15/- per day is charged for a visitor who wishes to use the Library facility.
- No photograph of the Library shall be taken without the prior permission of the Librarian.
- Library reserves the right to call back any issued book/item at any time.
- All research scholars are advised not to keep Library books/journals (loose and bound) inside their cupboard without getting them issued.
- Librarian reserves the right to check the Ph.D. & M.Phil tables and cupboards, whenever necessary.
- All students are advised to come to the Library in decent dress as they are in the classrooms.
- Demand and suggestion slips are available at the circulation desk for your use.

LIBRARY SERVICES: CHALLENGES AND OPPORTUNITIES

The provision of appropriate and meaningful reference and instructional services to e-learners is fraught with both challenges and opportunities.

E-learners require more than access to e-resources. Traditionally, a reference librarian acts as an additional resource, someone who can be counted upon to provide expertise in making sense of library systems and research tools, and to offer a helping hand along that often slippery path known as the research process.

Virtual library users face additional challenges in mining relevant information out of a computer system that "obstinately" returns zero hits in response to a query that does not match the character strings in its database files.

The most common means of providing electronic reference services to remote users has been e-mail, the advantages and disadvantages of which have been well documented in the literature. The around-the-clock and around-the-world accessibility of e-mail enables e-learners to connect with librarians beyond the walls of library buildings and outside the usual hours of operation.

E-mail provides a written record of requests and responses, permits the electronic transmission of search results, and allows librarians time to reflect on requests. One of the most serious concerns about e-mail reference services is their impact on traditional face-to-face reference interviews, particularly the absence of verbal and non-verbal cues, which typically assist a librarian in effectively responding to a question.

A well designed reference web form, such as that provided on the Athabasca University Library's "Ask about a Research Topic" web page, encourages e-learners to include full identifying and course information.

This web page encourages users to clearly describe their research problem and search terminology, and to state the parameters of their assignment. The feature also clarifies requests for librarians and reduces the need for e-mail. Automated e-mail replies sent out in response to the receipt of a message reassure e-learners that their messages have been received and lets them know what to expect in terms of service.

E-mail reference service can be enhanced and supplemented with additional technologies that raise the level of interaction via real-time communication. Chat technology allows e-learners and librarians to send text messages back and forth instantly, using a form of communication that is familiar to most Internet users.

A number of issues surround the use of chat in the provision of reference services to remote users. Choosing the appropriate programme for the library's specific needs and resources is essential if the virtual reference initiative is to be successful.

Available programmes range from vendor-based systems that offer features such as "co-browsing, patron queuing, sharing files, and the ability to keep more extensive statistics", to instant messaging programmes, which are freely available. Some chat programmes require downloads on the part of users, which can be problematic and may also discourage e-learners from using the service.

In an effort to reach more e-learners, some libraries have begun using instant messaging programmes such as AOL's *AIM* product, MSN's *Messenger*, and *Yahoo! Messenger,* primarily because many e-learners are already using these systems.

More recently, libraries have begun experimenting with programmes such as *Trillian* and *Pidgin,* which log into a number of instant messaging accounts simultaneously and allow librarians the flexibility to respond to instant messaging questions coming into the library, no matter which system the e-learner is using.

This reduces the need to monitor several different instant messaging programmes at the same time. Virtual reference consortia have the potential to expand the library's abilities to serve its community of users effectively.

Libraries in the consortia answer questions from e-learners in other parts of the consortium service area. Traditionally, chat reference services are only available during specified hours, so virtual reference consortia are beneficial for e-learners in different time zones than their home institution, because they increase the likelihood of a librarian being available to answer questions immediately.

Even if the initial reference transaction is received through chat, however, it may ultimately prove difficult to provide a complete answer using this method. If a user requires assistance in learning how to use a particular library resource, it may be possible to provide a complete response via chat.

However, if the user is requesting assistance to find information on a complex topic, the librarian may need time to determine appropriate search strategies before responding. In these cases, the follow-up response is often done by e-mail. Providing e-learners with a toll-free telephone number remains an effective and convenient reference services strategy, particularly for intricate enquiries. The telephone reference interview works best when both librarian and e-learner are working in front of computers connected to the Internet.

Instruction

E-learners are frequently silent and invisible as they search and explore a library's online resources, and they do not have the same access that oncampus learners have to formal library instruction sessions.

With the array of digital resources available to them, the many different interfaces and search tools, and the need for evaluation and critical thinking when using the Internet for research, information literacy skills are essential. Information literacy has been defined in relation to competencies, with information sources in a variety of formats. According to the Association of College and Research Libraries, an information-literate student

- Determines the nature and extent of the information needed.
- Accesses needed information effectively and efficiently.
- Evaluates information and its sources critically and incorporates selected information into his or her knowledge base and value system.

- Individually, or as a member of a group, uses information effectively to accomplish a specific purpose.
- Understands many of the economic, legal, and social issues surrounding the use of information, and accesses and uses information ethically and legally. Supporting the integration of information literacy skills training into the core curriculum has become an important issue for libraries.

A discussion is also emerging around the need to promote critical reflection in relation to information and knowledge, to conceptualize a *critical information literacy* that goes beyond a focus on competencies.

Critical information literacy draws on scholarship in critical theory and critical education to provide librarians with a theoretical framework that acknowledges their responsibility to help students see that knowledge is not neutral but socially constructed and contested.

Teaching the value of incorporating peer-reviewed journals in research papers, for example, need not preclude a discussion about how alternative voices may be silenced by the peer-review process and how to find alternative literature.

As an extension of their traditional role in providing library instruction sessions and developing instructional materials, librarians design online tutorials and courses that promote information literacy and encourage active learning. Particularly fine examples are the University of Texas System Digital Library's TILT – Texas Information Literacy Tutorial; and Utah Academic Library Consortium's Internet Navigator, a multi-institutional online course developed by a team of librarians and web developers.

The Open University Library created SAFARI, a freely available interactive tutorial, as well as an information literacy course called Making Sense of Information in the Connected Age or, more commonly, MOSAIC. Athabasca University offers the undergraduate course, Information Systems 200: Accessing Information. Many libraries provide instruction to e-learners by making information available on their web pages, including research guides and "how-to" pages. for example, Athabasca University Library's Help Centre.

An awareness of the importance of context-specific help has grown and it is quite common to find links to tutorials at the point of need. Software packages for developing animated tutorials, such as ViewletBuilder, Camtasia, and Captivate enable librarians to demonstrate effective database searching techniques asynchronously.

Brief tutorials that incorporate voice-over and demo-nstrate database features within the context of real searches are particularly effective. Joining an existing, collaborative initiative reduces workload and removes the need to "reinvent the wheel." The Council of Prairie and Pacific University Libraries (COPPUL), a consortium of twenty university libraries located in Manitoba, Saskatchewan, Alberta, and British Columbia, is responsible for the *Animated*

Tutorial Sharing Project (*ANTS*).

Participating libraries, including libraries outside of COPPUL, access a wiki where they can adapt databases for tutorial development, upload tutorials, and download tutorials developed by other libraries. Online tutorials usually operate on a model in which the e-learner interacts in isolation with a computer. Their effectiveness can be enhanced by the addition of more interactive forms of instruction. The librarians at the Florida Distance Learning Reference and Referral Centre, for example, have experimented with chat software to simulate a virtual classroom and open a "live" group instruction to e-learners. Librarians can be incorporated through the learning management system, participating in online courses as teaching assistants, co-instructors, or co-designers.

This 'embedded librarian' approach increases learner awareness of the value of the library in research and scholarship, and improves access to the expertise of librarians within the context of course needs and assignments. In addition, podcasting and video clips have become a popular choice in the delivery of instructional materials to remote users, as libraries recognize the popularity of mobile devices such as the *iPod.*

According to a Pew Internet and American Life survey, "more than 22 million American adults own iPods or MP3 players, and 29 per cent of them have downloaded podcasts". These methods allow e-learners to access the materials "anytime, anywhere," while still providing them with the type of instruction that their on-campus counterparts may receive.

Tutorials range from a simple orientation to the library and its services to more in-depth tutorials on the research process or searching specific databases. For example, Mount Allison University Library makes audio *libcasts* available. These libcasts can be downloaded or subscribed to and listened to, using *iTunes* or a similar product.

PARTNERSHIP AND COLLABORATION

In reviewing definitions of the virtual library, Sloan identifies an emphasis on the technological and informational building blocks, and a neglect of the human components, such as the service tradition and human interaction.

The continuing changes in technology have been truly astonishing, and the scope for building new information services and new ways of representing content seem unlimited. Although technology is the key infrastructure of the virtual library a tool used to support library goals human factors are the most important determinant of the success of the virtual library.

As noted by Colgate, Buchanan Oliver, and Elmsly, technology could cause problems in building relationships because of the difficulty in developing a successful rapport between people via remote contact.

One of the major challenges that virtual libraries face is the lack of opportunity for face-to-face reference service and communication. Combine this with a lack of awareness of library services and the end result is poor communication between library staff and e-learners.

The digital library serves mainly as a facilitator in organizing and providing knowledge and resources to its users. Sharing knowledge and information among library staff, researchers, faculty, students, and other departments within the institution encourages them to work together, develop their skills, and form strong and trusting relationships.

One method which can be effective in the development of strong relationships with faculty is the librarian-liaison role, where a librarian liaises with specific departments regarding resources, library services, and the provision of instructional support for students in those departments. When the liaison focuses on building effective channels of communication and understands the effects of technology on communication, it becomes easier to share knowledge and information among institutional stakeholders.

In addition, the focus on collaboration between the library and the faculty promotes a responsive approach to course design and supports teaching and learning objectives, particularly when this collaboration incorporates student contributions and feedback.

This approach considers the library as an active partner of the learning community, helping e-learners to become "information literates" by integrating information literacy skills into the curriculum.

The library can help e-learners to think critically about information, offer reference and instructional support, mentor their work by offering one-to-one communication and interaction, and work collaboratively with them to achieve a deeper level of understanding of what e-learners need.

A number of models can be involved in creating an environment that is responsive to the scholarly information needs of a diverse group of e-learners. Librarians select, describe, and ensure access to quality digital resources, providing e-learners with content from a wide range of resources and publications, including peer-reviewed journals.

Within this framework, the library works with faculty, researchers, scholarly societies, and publishers to develop and manage a collection of enriched online scholarly resources. Such a partnership enables researchers to interact with others, exchange experiences, and publish their works online.

The library role is thus transformed from simply providing library resources to meeting the ongoing support needs of the parties involved. The library also fosters research skills by encouraging e-learners to search, investigate, discover, and take advantage of these valuable online resources.

Further, senior management support and involvement is as much a key to success in developing the virtual library as in any other project.

They need to work closely with the library staff to understand the nature of services, values, and support the library should be offering, and to adopt successful communication and interaction strategies.

An institution providing distance and online education has an ethical obligation to ensure that its learners have access to appropriate library support. The Canadian Library Association *Guidelines* categorize responsibilities in terms of funding, administration, personnel, facilities, resources, services, publicity, and professional development of librarians.

The *Guidelines* note as essential advance planning by the library in consultation with faculty, programme administrators, and other appropriate campus personnel, and with librarians at unaffiliated libraries. The *Guidelines* also advocate that leadership should come from all levels of the institutional administration, but particularly from the library. All staff involved in providing library support to e-learners must be included in the partnership. Technological changes have been the dominant force reshaping library services.

Instilling a culture of sharing, motivation, equity, and active partnering encourages library staff to respond positively to the changing roles, responsibilities, and skills that the integration and use of technology requires.

A well-designed, ongoing training programme enables library staff to upgrade their skills to their new assignments, and helps them to understand and control fear of change. The home institution has primary responsibility for library support, but can benefit from external partnerships, collaborative efforts, and consortia in supporting e-learners.

Within Canada, university libraries extend in-person borrowing privileges to students, faculty, and staff from across the country, through the *Canadian University Reciprocal Borrowing Agreement.*

There are also initiatives to share virtual reference desks, such as the Library and Archives Canada's Virtual Reference Canada, through which e-learners benefit from the range of information resources and staff expertise available at a variety of participating institutions. Consortia approaches to database subscriptions enable libraries to expand the scope of the electronic resources they are able to offer their e-learners in a time of shrinking budgets and escalating journal costs.

The Lois Hole Campus Alberta Digital Library (LHCADL) initiative, through funding provided by the Government of Alberta, provides participating post-secondary institutions in Alberta with digital information resources for teaching, learning, and research.

LHCADL includes an information literacy and awareness component dedicated to sharing expertise and training resources with participating libraries.

In summary, library services are an essential component of a quality online learning experience. As access to online courses grows, an increasing number of e-learners are dispersed around the globe, often in parts of the world where physical access to the collections of large academic and research libraries is impossible or severely limited.

These learners are largely dependent on the quality and academic usefulness of services that the library can offer electronically. The strength of virtual libraries and digital collections depends on the relationships libraries develop and maintain with the creators, publishers, and aggregators of e-resources, as well as with those who use, learn from, and evaluate these resources. Providing ongoing technical, reference, and instructional support to e-learners requires that libraries redefine their values and services, collaborate with their users and other partners, and approach their tasks creatively.

TECHNOLOGICAL INNOVATIONS IN IMPROVING LIBRARY SERVICES

Once librarians were considered only the custodians of the library collection, but the change in information media from print to electronic has shown the new sunrise in the life of librarians. The basic aim of a library is to meet the teaching, learning, scholarly-research and other information needs of its faculty, students and research scholars and that too effectively and with efficiency. Medical library and information professionals ensures that health care providers have access to reliable, relevant, accurate, up to date and timely information that enhances the quality of health care.

The migration of information from paper to electronic media has changed the whole nature of research. With the easy availability of office computers and the transformation of media, the popularity and usage of digital and virtual libraries has been increased. World Wide Web has totally changed the meaning of a library. Physical presence has been decreased rapidly with the invention of virtual library. There is a universal assumption that man was born innocent or ignorant and should actively seek knowledge. "Information seeking is thus a natural and necessary mechanism of human existence". Information seeking behaviour is the purposive seeking for information as a consequence of a need to satisfy some goal. In the course of seeking, the individual may interact with manual information systems or with computer-based systems.

Information seeking behaviour involves personal reasons for seeking information, the kinds of information which are being sought and the ways and sources with which needed information is being sought. Information seeking behaviour is expressed in various forms, from reading printed material to research and experimentation. Scholars, students and faculties actively seek current information from the various media available in libraries, *e.g.* encyclopaedias, journals and more currently, electronic media. In this era of 'E', a sea change can be seen in the information-seeking behaviour of the users of library.

In the phase of print media, users had no choice except going to the library and search for the material in books, journals and archives for hours. Search was very time consuming in print phase. Changing needs of users have changed the role of a librarian, which has transformed a librarian into information professional. Librarians have always acted as a link between knowledge source and its users.

In this era of 'E', librarians are playing the role of an electronic middleman. They are now helping the readers in the best possible way by using the latest technology and searching techniques. Users are being connected to the information resources via Internet for hyper-links and for many more options and choices for advance search. The change in the information-seeking behaviour is the result of the invention of E-resources. Readers felt relaxed with this invention and inclination towards these resources was natural.

There are many types of E-resources like Ebooks, E-journals, various open sources, gateways and databases. Chronologically we can divide these resources specifically journals as, in-print journals, on-line journals free with print, only on-line journals, on-line databases. In the era of 'E', readers demand has become significant as they ask for an article or topic in place of a book or journal and at the same time they prefer to search online databases to fulfill their needs. With the invention E-resources quantity and quality of research both have been affected. Different search techniques are undertaken by library users to search and locate relevant information. To understand how users of libraries search and locate relevant documents, we librarians, need to understand the search techniques and what resources and sources of information they generally use and require. Information professionals and users both suffer from the problem of exhaustive information, from a wide range of sources and shortage of time to find, manage and evaluate.

Sometimes users search internet indiscriminately without knowing the facts. Here librarian plays an important role by making the users aware of the importance of the evaluation of the retrieved information by guiding them, how to retrieve, what to retrieve and how to further use that retrieved information, which is called evaluation of information. The challenge posed by the information explosion is being successfully met by electronic information sources. Further this information explosion, diversity of user need, financial crunch and impossibility of self-sufficiency has led to the formation of consortia at local, regional, national and international level.

OBJECTIVE

The main objective of this study is to know the changing needs and information-seeking behaviour of the users and further various methods and resources being adopted by the librarians to fulfil these needs, which is the result of various technological innovations. Information seeking is a fluid and situation dependent activity where a seeker's actions are influenced by access to information, perceived quality and trust in the information source. This reminds the necessity of regular study and development of information system and management information services in North Indian Medical Institutes.

This work intends to study followings in libraries as a prototype of North Indian Medical Institutes:

- To examine information seeking behaviour of library users of North Indian Medical Institutes.
- To study the problems faced by the library users of North Indian Medical Institutes while seeking and using information.
- To explore the role of the library consortia's for providing service to the library users.
- To review the use of E-databases in this era of information explosion.

HYPOTHESIS

In this study it is hypothesized that:

- Physical visit to the libraries has been declined.
- Preference of users has been shifted to online documents from print one.
- Lack of knowledge about IT is the main problem the user face in the information searching process.

METHODOLOGY AND SCOPE

There are many ways to get information. The most common research methods are: literature searches, talking with people, focus groups, personal interviews, telephone surveys, mail surveys, e-mail surveys and internet surveys.

A survey has been conducted on North Indian Medical Libraries through a questionnaire to know the changes in the information-seeking behaviour and needs of the users in this era of 'E'. So the medical professionals who were enrolled as member in the various medical libraries of Chandigarh and adjoining areas were considered for the study in hand. Further it can be stated that there were about 720 active library users of these libraries, so these users were taken as the subject for the study.

Through the stratified random sampling technique 72. Questionnaire method was used as it can be completed in one of the two basic ways. Firstly, respondents were asked to complete the questionnaire with the researcher not present and thus data was collected from 72 medical professionals, out of which 33 were students and 39 were senior residents, Assistant professor and professors.

Secondly, respondents were asked to complete the questionnaire by verbally responding to questions in the presence of the researcher. This variation is called a structured interview and this method was applied on 28 librarians to know their observations.

FINDINGS (USERS)

Visits to the Library

Twenty-nine respondents (40 per cent) reported frequently visiting a medical library, 18 (25 per cent) rarely visited and 24 (33 per cent) never visited; one respondent did not answer this question. Respondents in their first year reported frequent visits to the library more often than those did in their second year. In the overall group, those who never or rarely visited a library indicated that E-resources are not sufficient; documents that they needed were not available or libraries were not needed because of the Internet.

So the main observation regarding visit to the library is that students visit library more frequently in their initial years of college/ institute. Overall group of users prefer to search Internet as they are not satisfied with the available E-resources in their library. They only visit the library after making sure that this required information is available in the library. This service is being provided through WEB OPAC in most of the libraries today. So hypothesis 1 stands proved.

Preference of Information Sources

Most respondents reported performing database searches independently. Among those who did their own searches, MEDLINE and PUBMED was the bestknown and most frequently used database: only 1 of 72 respondents did not know of MEDLINE. HINARI is being used by some users but the main problem with this database is that site is very slow. When asked about criteria for selecting references, the most important feature was free full-text availability with the demand of online database and formation of consortia. Regarding access to the full text, few respondents said they visited a library to check document availability and ordered articles through a library. More than half of respondents preferred electronic tools for literature searching. Yet most indicated they preferred to print documents rather than read them online. Respondents were further asked about their preferences about the form of the document. An online database is the most preferred format (39 per cent) in contrast to the print only format that is the least preferred one (10 per cent). This observation directly shows the shift of the preferences of the users from print to the online formats. It is strongly supported by the findings in which online journals and databases have become the most preferred form of document as 75 per cent users need only online resources in form or the other. Further users prefer taking print of the required information as they feel discomfort in reading directly from the screen. So hypothesis 2 stands proved.

Problems in Information Seeking

Several problems were identified in the information searching process. Many respondents found difficulties in choosing among the large number of documents retrieved in searches and lack of time was also noted as a problem. Common obstacles in the information-seeking process identified by respondents include lack of time, doubt about the existence of relevant information, retrieval of too much information and difficulties with navigation and searching. Since latest innovations have made the search easier with the latest options like E-mail alerts, send articles etc., but problem in information searching still persists due to the lack of knowledge of I.T. So the hypothesis no. 3 also stands proved.

OBSERVATIONS (LIBRARIANS)

According to the librarians, Internet search engines, E-print services, author Web sites, full-text databases, electronic journals and print resources are all used to some extent by most of the users. Convenience remains the single most important factor for information retrieval. Speed of access, ability to download, print and send articles are top advantages of electronic journals for all groups. All these services and facilities are possible with the application of IT.

These observations reaffirm that important opportunities remain for librarians and libraries in providing both access to information resources and educating clinicians in how to effectively utilize such tools. Determining the relevance of a document or source is solely an individual's perspective, so the library or librarian is not a determining factor in differentiating sources. It would, however, be advantageous for a library to know and have the relevant material available for use. Library users expect their libraries to obtain new electronic resources while simultaneously maintaining or growing traditional print collections until the electronic resources are fully stable. Libraries are expecting to do this with no additional funding. Research has also concluded that information sources like electronic databases are of fundamental importance in a clinical environment giving their direct contribution to decision making in health issues, often making the difference in patient survival. Increasing demand of E-databases can be met with the formation of consortia only, as E-databases are the main feature of consortia these days. Important observation is that these databases have become addiction for the users.

Library Consortia

Information explosion, diversity of user need, financial crunch and impossibility of self-sufficiency has led to the formation of consortia at local, regional, national and international level. A library consortium is an association of a group of libraries to achieve mutually the common objective. Working in an atmosphere, which is fully affected by *Information Communication Technology* (ICT), librarians are mastering the use of electronic resources to better understand and meet the information needs of the users and further train them in using new searching tools for better search.

Consortia provide the following common benefits to the libraries involved:

- Access to otherwise un-subscribed reading materials.
- Scope for electronic archives.
- Getting deep discounts through joint pricing negotiations.
- Developing common resources databases.

- Effective document delivery system.
- Enhanced search facilities
- Better scope for developing a union catalogue among participating libraries.
- By forming consortia, librarians are contributing to the economy of their country by saving Government revenue to a great extent. Following are some of the big and successful consortia's of India.

E-DATABASE

Understanding the user needs play an important role in growing the libraries and librarians; otherwise the library profession may grey in future. To meet the increasing and advanced demands of the user, consortia are playing an important role. Secondly to avail full fruit of consortia a very sincere suggestion to library professionals is to be in touch with whole of the new technology, bridging the libraries through I.T and ICT. One should know the inside out of all the E-databases and involved I.T application.

An E-database is an organized collection of information, of a particular subject or multidisciplinary subject areas; Information within an Edatabase can be searched and retrieved electronically. Edatabase can be full-text or bibliographic. Full-text databases contain the whole content of an article such as citation information, text, illustrations, diagrams and tables. Bibliographic databases contain only citation information of an article, such as author name, journal title and publication date and page numbers. There are many Edatabases and all these databases have various features of searching techniques and tools, which are being used by the librarians to help the users in finding best information in less time.

Some of the popular medical E-databases are mentioned below:

- Academic Search Premier:
  - BMJ
  - MEDLINE
  - OVID
  - PROQUEST
  - PUBMED
  - SCOPUS
  - WEB OF SCIENCE
  - HINARI

Almost all the reputed publishers have come up with the Edatabases like Oxford University Press, American academy of Pediatrics, Cambridge University press and many more. All these e-databases can be considered as the latest technological innovation in the field of information.

USE OF PUBLIC LIBRARY SERVICES

Expert assessment of the nation's health care system suggests that it is slow in translating knowledge into practice and that patient care is not keeping abreast of advances in basic research. The American Medical Informatics Association recently proposed a plan for improving health care delivery. The plan focusses on clinical decision support, which "encompasses a variety of approaches for providing clinicians, staff, patients or other individuals with timely, relevant information that can improve decision making, prevent errors, and enhance health and health care."

The National Library of Medicine (NLM) can make a substantial contribution to improving national health by making a wide range of biomedical resources readily accessible to advanced information technology. There is a large, and growing, amount of online health-related information. Some resources are in the form of text readily accessible only to humans; examples include MEDLINE/PubMed and ClinicalTrials.gov. Other information is structured and includes biomedical vocabularies, clinical and molecular biology knowledge bases, and model organism annotation databases. Within NLM, examples include the Unified Medical Language System and Entrez Gene.

There are also several specialised biomedical databases, for example the BIND database and PharmGKB, as well as commercially curated drug databases, such as Micromedex DRUGDEX and DrugDigest. The growth of online information resources for biomedicine is outstripping access applications that could allow users to maximally exploit those resources. In order to take full advantage of available resources, the Library needs to provide services beyond traditional information retrieval.

Emerging research provides the underpinnings for developing applications that accommodate the growth in online information. Advanced applications manipulate information, not just text, and provide visualisation of results and interconnections among multiple sources. Some research concentrates on extracting information from text. Other emerging systems focus on using the information extracted; examples include automatic summarisation, question answering, and knowledge discovery.

METHODS AND PROCEDURES

We discuss issues involved in constructing a Biomedical Knowledge Repository and illustrate an emerging Web application that exploits a preliminary version.

The SemRep and Sem Gen natural language processing systems will be used to extract information in the form of semantic predications consisting of arguments and a predicate that represent relations between concepts asserted in text. Information in biomedical structured resources will be converted into a common format and all information will be integrated into the repository. Finally, a significant aspect of this project is the development of applications that exploit the Biomedical Knowledge Repository.

Extracting Predications from Text

Two programmes developed at LHNCBC will initially be used to extract semantic predications from ClinicalTrials.gov narrative and MEDLINE/PubMed citations for the repository. SemRep was devised to apply to the clinically oriented research literature, while SemGen addresses the genetic etiology of disease.

SemRep

SemRep is a rule-based symbolic natural language processing system developed for the biomedical research literature. As the first step in identifying semantic predications, SemRep produces an underspecified syntactic analysis based on the SPECIALIST Lexicon and the MedPost part-of-speech tagger. The most important aspect of this processing is the identification of simple noun phrases. In the next step, these are mapped to concepts in the Metathesaurus using MetaMap. Syntactic analysis in table, for example, contains Metathesaurus concepts and semantic types for the sentence in table.

Table. SemRep Analysis

Sentence	Phenytoin induced gingival hyperplasia	(1)
Syntactic analysis	[[head(noun(phenytoin)), metaconc('Phenytoin' :[orch,phsu]))], [verb(induced)], head(noun(['gingival hyperplasia')), metaconc(' Gingival Hyperplasia':[dsyn]))]]	(2)
Semantic Network	'Pharmacological Substance' CAUSES 'Disease or Syndrome'	(3)
Semantic Predication	Phenytoin CAUSES Gingival Hyperplasia	(4)

SemRep relies on structures to translate syntactic structures into semantic predications. One aspect of this processing is 'indicator' rules which map syntactic elements to predicates in the Semantic Network. Argument identification rules then find syntactically allowable noun phrases to serve as arguments for indicators.

If an indicator and the noun phrases serving as its syntactic arguments can be interpreted as a semantic predication, the following condition must be met: The semantic types of the Metathe-saurus concepts for the noun phrases must match the semantic types serving as arguments of the indicated predicate in the Semantic Network.

For example, in the structure given in table, the indicator *induced* maps to the Semantic Network relation in table. The concepts corresponding to the noun phrases *phenytoin* and *gingival hyperplasia* can serve as arguments because their semantic types match those in the Semantic Network relation. In the semantic predication produced as output, the Metathesaurus concepts from the noun phrases are substituted for the semantic types in the Semantic Network relation.

SemGen

SemGen was adapted from SemRep in order to identify semantic predications on the genetic etiology of disease. The main consideration in creating SemGen was the identification of gene and protein names as well as related genomic phenomena. For this SemGen relies on ABGene, in addition to MetaMap and the Metathesaurus. Since, the UMLS Semantic Network does not cover molecular genetics, ontological semantic relations for this domain were created for Sem Gen. The allowable relations were defined in two classes: gene-disease interactions and gene-gene interactions.

Other Systems

The information submitted to the repository by SemRep and SemGen could be supplemented with output from other natural language processing technologies that produce relationships. Phenotypic information from clinical narrative could be made accessible with the NLP system described by Friedman *et al.*. For molecular biology phenomena, several systems use syntactic templates and shallow parsing to produce a variety of relations, including gene and protein functions, protein interactions, and protein modifications such as phosphorylation. Friedman *et al.* use extensive linguistic processing for relations on molecular pathways, while Lussier *et al.* use a similar approach to identify phenotypic context for genetic phenomena.

Converting Structured Data into a Common Format

Since, relations in structured resources are already represented in some kind of formalism, their conversion to a common format is somewhat easier than extraction from text. However, the challenges in normalising such knowledge are not unlike those encountered with textual data. In both cases, knowledge extraction involves syntactic issues and semantic issues.

Various formalisms are used to represent structured data, including relational databases, tables, graphs, etc. Currently, no universal conversion mechanism is available. Moreover, the semantics of the data is often implicit or limited, for example, to short column names in a database schema. The objective of the conversion is the creation of 'normalised knowledge'. This effort, in the context of knowledge management, is somewhat equivalent to term normalisation. Knowledge normalisation ensures that the same entity referred to in different resources is ultimately identified in such a way that it is recognised as a unique thing. Knowledge normalisation forms the basis for information and data integration.

Description of Resources

Over the past twenty years, NLM has developed many knowledge resources, from various perspectives. Terminological resources such as the

Unified Medical Language System (UMLS) result from the integration of many existing terminologies and ontologies, represented in a common formalism–UMLS' Rich Release Format—and partially normalised. While synonymous terms are grouped together as names for a given concept, synonymous relationships are typically not identified as such.

Nevertheless, with some 8 million relations, the UMLS Metathesaurus constitutes an important resource, providing mostly hierarchical relations and co-occurrence relations. Another source of structured knowledge is represented by the many databases available under the umbrella of the NCBI's Entrez system. While some databases such as MEDLINE/PubMed and *Online Mendelian Inheritance in Man* (OMIM) are mostly textual resources, many other NCBI databases contain predominantly structured information.

Entrez Gene, for example, is a gene-centric resource in which a record provides gene properties such as names, associated diseases, function, sequence, etc. While numerous links have been created across the resources in the Entrez system for navigation purposes, such links typically require human interpretation and therefore cannot be used for knowledge discovery purposes in high-throughput systems. Finally, structured databases and knowledge bases are also available outside NLM.

One example of large, publicly available genomic resource is represented by the genome annotations for the major model organisms. Here, the existence of a controlled vocabulary—the Gene Ontology—has contributed to developing unified functional annotations, integrated in systems such as the Mouse Genome Database and the Saccharomyces Genome Database. In the clinical domain, the various knowledge bases of drug information constitute important resources about drug-drug interactions, drug kinetics and metabolism, and indications and contraindications. DRUGDEX, produced by Micromedex, is an example of such a resource.

Representing Normalised Knowledge

One of the strengths of the World Wide Web is that it relies on textual information, easily created and interpreted by humans. This is also one of its principal limitations. The absence of explicit semantics prevents agents from being able to make sense of the information on the Web. This is the motivation of the Semantic Web, which aims at creating a vast collections of integrated and interoperable resources.

There is an obvious parallel between the Semantic Web and the Biomedical Knowledge Repository we propose to create. The technologies developed for the Semantic Web offer possible solutions to some of the challenges we face, including selecting a formalism for normalised biomedical knowledge and identification issues for biomedical entities. It is worth noting that some of these issues are still actively being debated in the Semantic Web community, especially in the Semantic Web Health Care and Life Sciences Interest Group.

Formalism

Many of the resources produced by NLM and other organisations are available in XML, the eXtensible Markup Language. However, the semantics of XML is limited. In addition to XML, the World Wide Web Consortium (W3C) has produced the specifications of other formalisms for representing resources.

Collectively know as Semantic Web technologies, these specifications define the building blocks of the Semantic Web. Of particular interest to us is the Resource Description Framework. RDF extends the capabilities of the extensible markup language XML as it enables many-to-many relationships between resources and data.

The resulting structure is a graph in which the nodes are resources or data and the edges are relationships.

The basic unit in RDF is therefore the equivalent of a triple, similar to a relation in the UMLS Metathesaurus or a predication extracted by SemRep. RDF integrates limited inference rules, enabling, for example, the definition of subclasses and subproperties.

Some extensive resources such as UniProt have already been converted to RDF. The BioRDF task force of the W3C Semantic Web Health Care and Life Sciences Interest Group currently investigates methods whereby existing biomedical resources can be converted to RDF.

Such methods include XSLT, GRDDL and DB2RDF, among others. The *eXtensible Stylesheet Language Transformation* (XSLT) uses a stylesheet approach to converting XML to RDF. GRDDL specifies associations between markup languages–including XLM–and RDF. Finally, DB2RDF is used to convert databases to RDF.

Identification Issues

In order for RDF triples to form a graph–and for integrated knowledge to be interoperable-entities and relationships must be identified consistently and unambiguously.

For example, if the disease *Neurofibromatosis 2* is identified by the code *SNOMEDCT:92503002* in one resource and by the code *MESH:D016518* in another, the RDF triples involving *SNOMEDCT:92503002* and *MESH:D016518* will not come together as expected unless both resource are converted to the other annotation system or mappings are created between the two systems.

For example, the UMLS Metathesaurus could be used to convert or bridge between MeSH and SNOMED CT, in this case through the concept *C0027832*. The predications extracted from the literature by SemRep already use UMLS codes to identify biomedical entities. From a technical perspective, several technologies have been developed by various communities to implement identification mechanisms for RDF.

There are three major identification mechanisms:

- LSID (Life Science Identifier), promoted by the Life Sciences community. Examples of applications using LSID include Taverna and resources created by the BioPathways Consortium;
- Solutions based on the HTTP protocol, promoted by the W3C; and
- ARK (Archive Resource Key), promoted by the Digital Library community.

There are important differences among three mechanisms regarding location independence, backward compatibility, resolution mechanism and versioning. It is unclear at this time what mechanism would suit our needs best.

Pilot Project: Converting Entrez Gene to RDF

As a proof of concept, we converted the Entrez Gene database into RDF. The entire Gene database in its native ASN.1 format was downloaded by FTP from the NCBI web site and later converted to XML using the programme gene2xml provided by NCBI. Using the *eXtensible Stylesheet Language Transformation* (XSLT) approach, we mapped the element tags of the XML representation to more intuitive relationship names manually, and used them during the automatic conversion to RDF. Finally, we stored this RDF version of Entrez Gene in the Oracle 10g relational database management system, which provides support for storing and querying native RDF data. The conversion process is illustrated in figure.

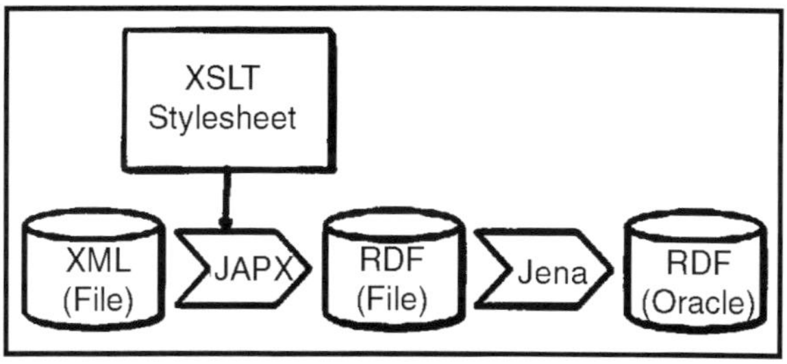

Fig. Overview of the Conversion of Enrez Gene from XML to RDF

Mapping XML Element Tags to RDF Properties

While XML data can be mechanically converted to RDF, the resulting RDF graph would be of limited interest because the semantics of the properties is most often implicit in XML and needs to be made explicit. Starting from one typical Entrez Gene record, we identified all its XML element tags, corresponding to the properties of the gene, as described in the Gene record.

Examples of such properties include *<Genetrack_geneid>* and *<Genetrack_update-date>*, indicating the identifier and the update date of the gene record, respectively. A total of 124 unique elements tags were identified. Because XML element tags represent gene properties, they were transformed into predicates in RDF. For example, <*Genetrack_geneid*> becomes *has_unique_geneid* and relates the gene record to its unique identifier in the Gene database. Note that the RDF property now conveys the notion–implicit in the XML representation–that the identifier is a unique identifier, corresponding to a primary key in a relational database. Converting XML elements to RDF properties requires familiarity with the structure and content of the original record structure and is a key component to the mapping process. After eliminating redundant and superfluous XML element tags, 106 unique RDF properties were created. The mapping of Entrez gene XML element tags to RDF properties is specified formally using the XPath language and constitutes a stylesheet. This stylesheet is specific to the conversion of the Entrez Gene database.

Converting XML to RDF through XSLT

Once the stylesheet is created, it can serve as an auxiliary file for existing programmes realising the XML to RDF conversion. In other words, the major interest of this approach is that no specific code is required for the conversion, because the transformation logic resides entirely in the stylesheet. We used JAXP, the Java *Application Programming Interface* (API) to XML, to implement the conversion. The resulting 411 million RDF triples were then loaded in a store using Oracle 10g using the Jena API.

Lessons Learned, Issues and Challenges

This experiment confirmed the feasibility of converting a large resource from XML to RDF. It also showed that the issues are not technical, but rather lie in the necessity of making explicit the relationships represented implicitly by element tags in XML. This step requires the manual intervention of a domain expert. In our experience, it took less than a week for one person familiar with both bioinformatics and stylesheets to formalise the mapping between XML element tags and RDF properties.

Although the stylesheet created is specific to the Entrez Gene database, it is expected that part of the expertise acquired during this transformation can be applied to transforming other NCBI resources. The major unresolved issue concerns entity identification. If the RDF graph resulting from the conversion of Entrez Gene is to be integrated with clinical or bibliographic information, the diseases associated with genes must be represented not as literals as they currently are, but by their identifiers in the corresponding clinical and bibliographic controlled vocabularies, or with the *concept unique identifier* (CUI) in the UMLS Metathesaurus. Only after such mapping will the RDF graph integrating Entrez Gene and, say, the Metathesaurus, support queries such as *Find all genes associated with neurodegenerative diseases*. The knowledge required in this cases comes in part from Entrez gene and from UMLS.

Integrating Predications: Biomedical Knowledge Repository

The Biomedical Knowledge Repository can be understood as a specialised version of the Semantic Web. It consists of an extensive collection of predications, represented in a common format, processable by computers. Biomedical terminologies and ontologies provide the concepts involved in the facts. Logical reasoners extend the capabilities of the repository by inferring new knowledge. Each fact in the repository is annotated with metainformation regarding its origin, making it possible for applications exploiting the repository to select facts of interest in a given context and for a particular task. Once it is fully populated, the Biomedical Knowledge Repository is expected to comprise several hundred million facts, collected from hundreds of sources.

Origin of the Predications

The Biomedical Knowledge Repository (BKR) comprises predications form three major sources: extracted from the biomedical literature by NLP programmes such as SemRep, converted from existing structured knowledge bases, and contributed by users.

In our vision of the BKR, NLM not only contributes to populating the BKR, but also makes it available to the community as a framework for researchers to deposit their predications.

Predications resulting from experiments, from alternative processing of the literature, and inferred from other predictions, for example, can be contributed by members of the community and made available to others. One measure of success of the BKR would be for it to become a standard repository for the knowledge created through biomedical research experiments. In order to maintain the consistency and integrity of the BKR, its developers would have to follow guidelines regarding formalism of the predications and identification mechanism for biomedical entities.

Metainformation Associated with the Predications

Just as few users need all the vocabularies in the UMLS Metathesaurus for a given purpose, it is unlikely that all predications will be equally useful for a given task, such as question answering. Instead, a mechanism supporting the selection of relevant sets of predications is needed.

The metainformation associated with each predication enables this selection and may include the source of the predication, the method of extraction, the date of extraction, in addition to the usual metadata associated with MEDLINE/PubMed citations for predications extracted from the literature. Researchers contributing predications to the BKR will be requested to annotate them with similar metainformation. Another form of contribution to the repository is to provide not predications, but annotations to existing predications. Such a contribution represents a form of collaborative curation of the repository by the community, similar to the framework developed by the SWAN project for the Alzheimer research community.

Storing the Predications

Several technological solutions, called RDF stores, have been developed for storing information in RDF format, generally implemented on top of some storage system. One such open source RDF database is Sesame. More recently, traditional database management systems have started offering direct support for native RDF triples. For example, version 10g of the Oracle system supports RDF in addition to the relational model. Since, we need to store large amounts of both RDF and traditional information, we started experimenting with Oracle 10g while converting Entrez Gene to RDF last summer. Preliminary results are encouraging although we might face optimisation issues.

Querying the Predications

Analogous to SQL for relational databases, SPARQL is the language for querying RDF. Like SQL, SPAQRL queries have a SELECT and a WHERE clause. However, in a SPARQL query, the WHERE clause follows the pattern of a RDF triple in which at least one element of the triple is replaced by a variable. In the BKR, the predications to be queried would first be selected based on their annotations.

For example, a typical query supporting multidocument summarisation would be as follows.

Select all predications from MEDLINE/PubMed returned by a PubMed query on *metabolic syndrome*, restricted to citations from *JAMA*, *Am J Cardiol.* and *J Hypertens.*, published between 2004 and 2005. Additionally, select those predications from the UMLS Metathesaurus and Entrez Gene having at least one node in common with those from the literature.

Integrating Predications

The query example presented above illustrates the interest of integrating knowledge under a unique framework. First, there is a unique namespace for all knowledge in the BKR. As suggested, largely rely on the UMLS for identifying biomedical entities.

Second, once integrated into a graph, the predications can serve as a basis for inferencing, creating additional knowledge along the way. This represents an advantage over traditional database and information retrieval approaches. Finally, complex rules can be written to implement additional reasoning. For example, it is possible to restrict queries to those redundant predications asserted in more than 2 sources and for which the frequency of occurrence is above a certain threshold.

Estimated Size of the Repository

Once fully instantiated, the Biomedical Knowledge Repository is expected to comprise several hundred million predications extracted from the literature, terminological resources and structured knowledge bases. Assuming an average of ten predications is extracted from the title and abstract of each MEDLINE/PubMed citation, we can expect about 150 million predications from MEDLINE/PubMed.

The UMLS Metathesaurus records about 9 million relations, either symbolic or statistical. Some seven million functional annotations for the major model organism databases are recorded in the Gene Ontology database. Finally, our conversion experiment with Entrez Gene yielded over 400 million RDF triples. In this experiment, the objective was to systematically represent in RDF all the information present in the original XML file. In fact, part of this information would become metainformation in the context of the BKR, resulting in a significantly smaller number of triples to be actually contributed to the repository.

Exploiting the Repository: Semantic Medline Web Portal

As a pilot project to exploit a preliminary version of the Biomedical Knowledge Repository, we are developing a Web portal, called Semantic Medline, for managing the results of PubMed searches. The portal is designed as a Java-based Web application that seamlessly integrates PubMed, SemRep processing of the results of the search, automatic summarisation, and, finally, visualisation of the results, with links to the underlying citations and relevant additional knowledge in the UMLS Metathesaurus, the Genetics Home Reference, and Entrez Gene. Realtime access is achieved by pre-processing text from MEDLINE/PubMed abstracts and other sources with SemRep/SemGen and storing the results in a database.

Background

Several recent systems visualise the results of information identified in text as a way of providing users with enhanced access to the information retrieved. Results are often represented as a graph of interrelated relationships. The Telemakus project is based on relationships identified by hand and is meant to enable knowledge discovery through interactive visual maps of linked concepts among documents. Jensen *et al.* constructed literature networks of genes found relevant in gene expression data analysis.

Analysis is based on co-occurrence of genes in MEDLINE/PubMed abstracts. Van der Eijk *et al.* use various relations for literature-based discovery. The relationships represent co-occurrence of MeSH headings associated with MEDLINE/PubMed citations by a mapping programme. Feldman represent several gene-related relations in a graph. The relations were extracted with a type of underspecified natural language processing. Finally, Tao *et al*. visualise genomic information across both structured and textual databases.

Implementation

Semantic Medline is implemented as a three-tier, Java EE-based Web application. The three-tier architecture allows for the separation of user interface, application logic and data storage, providing improved performance, easier maintenance and scalability. We leverage mature open-source technologies in the development to the extent possible. The prototype runs in a Tomcat servlet container on an Apache Web server. It has been developed using the Apache Struts Web application framework. This framework encourages the use of *Model-View- Controller* (MVC) paradigm to provide a clean separation of application model, navigational code, and page design code through the use of Java Servlet API.

The controller is a Java servlet that mediates the application flow; the model comprises Java classes that represent the functionality of the semantic tools and the view is JSP pages that contain dynamic content. A MySQL database is used to store Semantic Medline data, which includes semantic predications extracted from MEDLINE/PubMed abstracts and ClinicalTrials.gov clinical study texts as well as a subset of UMLS Metathesaurus data.

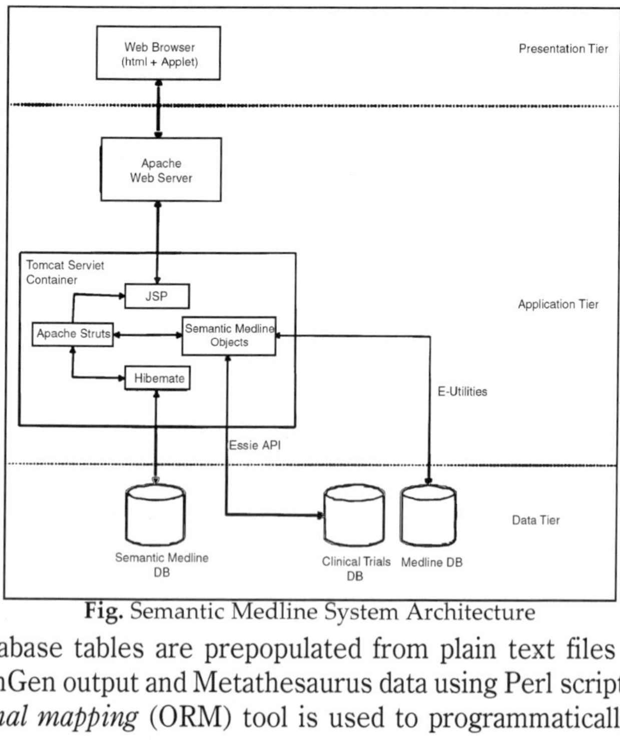

Fig. Semantic Medline System Architecture

The database tables are prepopulated from plain text files that contain SemRep/SemGen output and Metathesaurus data using Perl scripts. Hibernate *object/relational mapping* (ORM) tool is used to programmatically access the database. We use such Hibernate features as database connection pooling and query caching for increased performance.

Using Semantic Medline

MEDLINE/PubMed contains more than 16 million citations drawn from nearly 4,600 journals with biomedical relevance. Searches often retrieve large numbers of items. For example, the query 'diabetes' returns 207,997 citations. Although users can restrict searches by language, date and publication type, results can still be large. For example, a query for treatment for diabetes, limited to articles published in 2003 and having an abstract in English finds 3,621 items; limiting this further to articles describing clinical trials still returns 390 citations. It is difficult for a user to effectively exploit the information in this many citations. Semantic Medline addresses this difficulty by allowing users to summarise the results of searches focused on one of several points of view, including diagnosis and treatment of disorders, drug interactions and adverse events, genetic basis of disease, and pharmacogenomics.

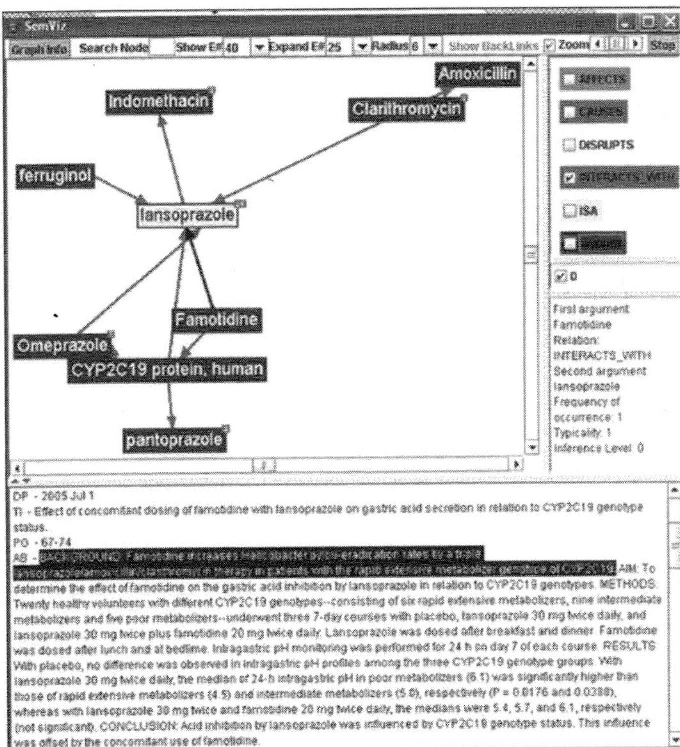

Fig. Summary of 564 MEDLINE/PubMed Citations for Lansoprazole

A clinical scenario based on a summary focused on drug interactions illustrates the potential use of Semantic Medline for taking advantage of the research literature in clinical practice. In a hypothetical situation, a patient presents with peptic ulcer and tests positive for *Helicobacter pylori*. The clinician has tried several standard regimens including two different triple regimens: and; however, the patient still tests positive for *H. pylori*.

In order to gain insight from recent research, the physician uses Semantic Medline to issue a PubMed search for lansoprazole. SemRep extracts 5,971 predications from 564 citations returned by this search, and automatic summarisation for drug interactions involving lansoprazole condenses the final list of predications to 182, which are visualised by the system as the interactive graph in figure. Figure provides an informative overview of recent research on lansoprazole represented as predications asserting INTERACTS_WITH. Each predication is linked to the MEDLINE/PubMed citation that generated it.

Table. MEDLINE/PubMed Citations

PMID	Title
15963082	Effect of concomitant dosing of famotidine with lansoprazole on gastric acid secretion in relation to CYP2C19 genotype status
15710002	Concomitant dosing of famotidine with a triple therapy increases the cure rates of Helicobacter pylori infections in patients with the homozygous extensive metaboliser genotype of CYP2C19

Of interest for this case are two predications in the graph: 'Lansoprazole INTERACTS_WITH Famotidine' and 'Famotidine INTERACTS_WITH CYPC19 Enzyme.' SemRep extracted the first predication from a citation with title seen in the first line of table and the second from a citation with in the second line.

Both citations discuss the salutary effect of combining famotidine with lansoprazole. In the second citation, which reports on a randomised controlled trial, the authors realised between 63 per cent to 100 per cent eradication of *H. pylori* with the addition of famotidine to a standard triple therapy and conclude that this is a promising option for patients who phenotypically are extensive metabolisers. If the patient in this hypothetical scenario falls under this category, it would be a potentially valuable regimen to pursue.

EVALUATION PLAN

We intend to follow a multifaceted evaluation plan, focusing evaluation activities on specific aspects of the project.

Evaluating Extraction

For this project, effectiveness of information extracted from text crucially depends on the accuracy of SemRep and SemGen. We have performed linguistic evaluation across a wide variety of predicates that includes the clinical as well as the genetic domain.

Among the predicates evaluated were Treats, Prevents, Location_of, Causes, Isa, Interacts_ With, Affects, Disrupts, Process_of, Part_of, Manifestation_ of, Associated_With, Inhibits, Stimulates and PREDISPOSES. Recall on the extraction of semantic propositions with these predicates has ranged from 41 per cent to 74 per cent and precision from 68 per cent to 84 per cent. Previous evaluations have been reported in and as suggested, continue this evaluation paradigm.

The framework for evaluating knowledge extraction from terminological and structured knowledge bases is not as well established as the evaluation of relation extraction from text. However, several aspects are particularly important. The rules used for the conversion need to be reviewed independently by several experts for a given knowledge base and integrated across databases in order to ensure consistency of the extraction of the relationships. Key to the consistency of the graph is also the mapping of literals to concepts–the nodes in the RDF graph and their consistent representation by identifiers from authoritative sources.

Evaluating Integration

Ideally, the graph resulting from integrating knowledge from several sources is consistent both structurally and semantically. Therefore structural techniques based on graph theory and semantic approaches similar to reasoning services created for description logics are expected to play a central role in evaluating the quality of knowledge integration in the repository.

However, the UMLS Metathesaurus, while resulting from the integration of a much smaller body of terminological knowledge, is already not always structurally or semantically consistent. Like the Metathesaurus, the Biomedical Knowledge Repository will allow contradictory predications to be represented as long as they occur in the original information sources. However, consistency is expected to be found at both structural and semantic levels on limited subsets of the repository.

Evaluating Applications

When evaluating applications such as automatic summarisation, it is useful to compare results against curated resources. Standard measures of performance can be calculated with respect to the reference standard chosen. For treatment of disease, the British Medical Journal clinical evidence concise is one alternative. For drug interactions and adverse events, Micromedex DRUGDEX, DrugDigest, and the First DataBank's National Drug Data File can be used. A more ambitious method, requiring human experts, is task-based evaluation. Ultimately, user-centred evaluations such as the one described by McKeown must be considered.

PROJECT SCHEDULE

- *Year 1:* Pilot study, processing all of MEDLINE/PubMed, integrating Entrez Gene
- *Year 2:* Integrating UMLS and other NCBI resources

- *Year 3:* Annotating predications, opening the BKR to collaborative development and use
- *Year 4:* Fully integrated ALS system available

PROJECT RESOURCES

This project relies on a range of existing competencies and resources and has the potential to federate research energies throughout the Lister Hill Center. In addition to the efforts of the two core component projects, Semantic Knowledge Representation and Medical Ontology Research, the success of this project relies on collaboration with the Indexing Initiative, the Lexical Systems Project, and ClinicalTrials.gov.

The effectiveness of applications drawing on the repository could be strengthened by providing links to Visible Human images where appropriate. In order to accomplish the goals of this project additional staff and equipment are required: staff for creating and populating the repository and servers for providing effective access to the repository. Initially, PubMed and ClinicalTrials.gov will be processed by SemRep and SemGen and the predications extracted will be stored in the repository. Dedicated servers are required to process PubMed for this project.

2

Library Use and Perception

THE DCRB CORE STANDARD

Bibliographic control of rare book collections has always been a time-consuming and specialized process. The materials in special collections are there for particular and compelling reasons. Catalogers of such collections have traditionally identified those special attributes in catalog records with full-level bibliographic description, extensive notes, and as many access points as are deemed appropriate by both catalogers and curators. The bibliographic standards for cataloguing rare books, with the principles of *Anglo-American Cataloguing Rules*, (AACR2) underlying them, have evolved over a number of years, first in 1981 in *Bibliographic Description of Rare Books* and most recently in *Descriptive Cataloguing of Rare Books* (DCRB), published in 1991. A new edition, with the title *Descriptive Cataloguing of Rare Materials*, is now in preparation by the Association of College and Research Libraries, Rare Books and Manuscripts Section (RBMS), Bibliographic Standards Committee.

The new edition will include rules for the various formats of materials. The documentation for books will be known as DCRM(B). While the current standard of DCRB is written primarily for books printed before 1801, it can be used for post-1800 imprints as well. The Programme for Cooperative Cataloguing (PCC) has defined and approved core standards for many of the bibliographic formats, beginning with the standard for books in the mid-1990s. All the core standards, written for use by the participants in the Bibliographic Records Cooperative (BIBCO) programme, are intended to encourage "faster, better, cheaper" cataloguing. They ensure the same reliability in description, authorized headings, and call numbers as full-level records, but they do not require as many notes or subject headings.

In January 1999, the PCC approved the Core Standard for Rare Books. Called DCRB Core because it is based on the full standard of DCRB, the standard is intended for use in cataloguing books with imprint dates between 1500 and 1800. The text of the standard was written and proposed by the Task Group for Developing a Standard for Core Treatment of Rare Books, a group that was charged with the creation of the core standard by the PCC Standards Committee and that included several members of the RBMS Bibliographic Standards Committee. The expected use of the DCRB Core standard is for cataloguing books that have been chosen more for their need of accessibility than for their full bibliographic details.

LIBRARY OPERATIONS AND USE

We concentrate on operational features. The reasons for this are partly technical in that the 'physical' data are more complete than the financial and do not incur the problems of currency conversion and inflation that beset the financial aspects. There are also institutional and accounting problems in compiling financial statistics that are genuinely comparable. (Common examples are whether or not libraries are charged for the cost of premises and staff overheads - which may often be absorbed by the parent institution.) So, for these various reasons, the statistics of operational features are more robust and comparable.

TRENDS

STAFF

We estimate that about 374,000 staff were employed in libraries, an increase of 3.7 per cent since 1991. This increase in staffing numbers is weighted towards the professional staff whose numbers increased by 4.9 per cent over the period. The increase in Trained staff occurs mostly in EU States.

The number of trained librarians in all sectors of libraries (206,000) is higher than previous estimates for the mid-1990's (175,800 for 1991). However, the number of other support staff is substantially lower than previous estimates. Proportionately the returns for 'Other Staff' are appreciably lower in the CEE than in the EU.

Table. Staff FTE * (thousands)

	Qualified	Other	Total
1991	196	165	361
1992	195	163	357
1993	191	164	355
1994	195	163	357
1995	199	162	361
1996	201	159	360
1997	206	160	367
1998	206	168	374

Note: *Full Time Equivalent, *i.e.* part time staff count as fractions in proportion to hours worked.

MATERIALS

The overall position and trends are summarised in this table:

Table. Trends in Materials Provision (millions)

Resources	1991	1998	% change
Book stock	2,778.0	2,944.0	6
Audio Visual stock	104.0	127.0	22
Periodical subscriptions	19.5	21.3	9
Manuscripts	29.5	32/0	8
Microforms	316.0	313.0	-1
Annual Movements:			
Book Additions	171.0	171.0	=
A/V Additions	9.7	12.1	25
Inter Library Loans (received)	15.2	29.0	91

The trends in annual additions to stock appear to vary between sectors. National libraries report a growth in their annual additions in books and audio-visual materials. Public libraries book acquisitions fell between 1991 - 1995 but have since stabilised, while their audio-visual materials have increased steadily. With a large increase in the population served by Tertiary Education, so have their book acquisitions grown hugely: but there has been a decline in audio visual additions. Current periodical subscriptions in the tertiary sector have remained surprisingly constant during the period 1991 to 1998. The largest number of subscriptions are in special libraries. The statistics show that holdings of Manuscripts and Microforms continue to be significant. Inter Library Lending has almost doubled: much of this is concentrated in the activity of national libraries - particularly the large scale operations in the UK and Germany - but it is also important in the smaller states.

USE AND USERS

The count of Registered Members increased in total from 126 million to 139 million - an increase of 10.5 per cent. As this count includes those who use several libraries the proportion it represents out of the total population (484 million) - 29 per cent - is disappointingly low. But the trend is moving upwards. Estimates for Loan Transactions at 3,543 million and Visits at 3,468 million are close and show only a small difference in trend: + 5.2 per cent against - 1.3 per cent. When taken together the ratio for Loan Transactions per Registered Member point to high intensity of use - moving from 26.8 to 25.5.

MODERNISATION

Several questions were introduced into the survey in order to assess aspects of service development and automation. The response to these was generally poor, though better in the CEE states than elsewhere. Typically they are not yet found in established statistical series. It will take some time before the efforts of LIBECON 2000, ISO and IFLA rectify this position, but a valuable start has been made and the information compiled here is invaluable in pointing to important trends.

Overall total estimates show the following:

- Workstations for users increased more than fourfold from 74,000 in 1991 to 310,000 in 1998. The stock of CD ROMs went up exponentially during the second half of the period, going from an estimated 456,000 in 1991 to 2,500,000 in 1998. These developments are well publicised in the profession and will come as little surprise.
- Less well known are two aspects relating to the automation of traditional materials and services. The Percentage of Catalogue Records Automated is estimated to have gone up from 36 to 46 per cent while the Percentage of Stock on Open Access increased only from 60 to 61 per cent. These figures show some progress but also point to a large deficit of automation development still required to update services and operations.

SERVICE POINTS

Including all sectors, it is estimated that in 1998 there were 224,000 service points throughout the study area. There has been a considerable contraction since 1991, averaging 7.1 per cent, but this has taken place particularly in the Central and Eastern European countries (CEE) where the proportionate drop was 14 per cent and where the main closures took place in public libraries.

THE IMPORTANCE OF THE LIBRARY SECTORS

One would expect, even over a lengthy period, to find little change in the relative size of the various library sectors. Estimates in previous surveys showed that, between 1981 and 1995 public libraries and higher education libraries increased their share of total spending on libraries - with the share of other sectors largely unchanged. In this survey we find a very different result - as illustrated in this table:

Table. Library Sector Shares

	By Total Expenditure		By Total Staff	
Sector	Previous Estimate		Present Estimate	
	1981 •	1995 §	1998	1998
National	6.0%	5.9%	5.4%	4.1% Higher Education
15.3%	16.9%	19.9%	16.5% Public	47.3% 49.5% 45.0%
45.2% Special	8.6%	8.6%	21.3%	16.7% Other Major 4.9%
4.5%	0.8%	2.2% School	17.8%	14.7% 7.7% 15.5%

Note: * EU States only § estimated from The Historic Libecon Database

The main reason for these changes is the new methodologies adopted to evaluate the size of the Special Library sector. This springs from two separate initiatives. First, there has been substantial research activity (chiefly but not exclusively in the UK and Germany) to apply statistical sampling techniques. As a result, what many had always suspected has been demonstrated - namely that the various types of library designated under the Special Library label are very much more numerous than had previously assumed in the absence of any systematic statistical evidence. These new estimates are still subject to error which could be substantial - but the work has been conscientiously done. Second, the exercise launched in connection with the revision of ISO 2789 has already had an effect on these statistics in that many countries (but by no means all) have gone along with the LIBECON suggestion to return libraries in the Miscellaneous sub category under Special Libraries rather than under 'Other Major'.

The sub division of Special Libraries into sub categories has also prompted in some countries more analytical estimates. In view of this major change table also includes a column to show how different the sector proportions appear when analysed by the numbers of staff employed rather than by expenditure. (The high proportions for School and Other sectors are influenced by some unusually high returns on staffing from Poland - which may be exaggerated.).

DIAGRAMS/ ILLUSTRATIONS

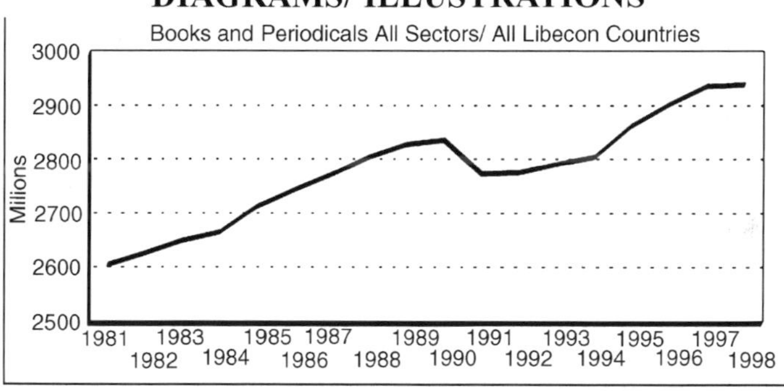

Fig. Book and Peribdicale All Scitirm/All Libecon Countries

Please note that the left hand scale in each of the charts is scaled to describe the trend shown. For this reason there is no comparability between each chart, and the actual movement that is displayed in each may appear exaggerated.

COUNTRIES AND SECTORS

We now move from consideration of Trends to look at the relative strengths of countries and sectors. The LIBECON 2000 data are well suited for this.

The analysis is intended to serve several purposes:

- To point to the size and stage of development of library services in different countries;
- To point to the relative importance of sectors within each country;
- To point to the features that distinguish each sector from the others;
- To show the relative importance of sectors;

- To suggest possible bench marking exercises;
- To give practical examples to demonstrate the 'grossing' methodology;
- To allow the reader to evaluate conclusions and the quality of grossed up totals according to the number of responses and non- responses in relation to each feature: for example, information on Staff Numbers is fully provided for Public and Tertiary libraries, but it is sparse for Special and School libraries;
- To show in summary form the gaps in data not provided.

For this purpose we present 'Cross Sector Total' tables for the main resource and use features - for the year 1998. The tables shown here mainly give absolute data uncorrected for size of country (population) and their value lies partly in emphasising the differences between large and small states. Each table consists first of the 1998 data entered onto the database for each country. Three dots (...) show that we have no information provided for that feature in that country. The grossed up estimates for All States and for regions and geographical areas. The 'Response per cent' gives the proportion of the All States grossed up figure that is represented by actual data. Finally percentages are calculated to show, for this feature, the relative strength of each sector overall.

STAFF NUMBERS

Table contains, in a comparative sense, very complete data. It is particularly pleasing to see so many estimates for the Special Library sector - which give rise to an estimate of 16.7 per cent of all staff employed in Special Libraries.

Table. Total Staff (FTEs)

	National	Tertiary	Public	Special	Other	School	1998 Total
Bulgaria	329	...	...	...	...	...	
Czech Republic	444	608	4,344	...	0	...	
Estonia	525	498	1,466	157	130	534	
Hungary	540	960	3,881	875	...	...	
Latvia	448	330	1,900	194	100	...	
Lithuania	618	646	4,116	435	152	1,855	
Poland	907	6,601	17,828	4,063	1,338	26,000	
Romania	351	...	5,014	...	0	...	
Slovak Rep	349	493	1,927	...	...	105	
Slovenia	...	372	775	243	0	780	
Austria	308	941	1,588	...	...	...	
Belgium	200	710	3,940	...	...	...	
Denmark	316	894	5,199	390	0	1,160	
Ireland	68	750	1,300	350	0	...	
Finland	180	1,103	4,193	250	...	...	
France	...	3,884	20,545	...	...	...	
Greece	486	...	1,834	57	...	...	
Iceland	...	...	...	...	0	44	

Italy	595	...	...	...	...	...	
Liechtenstein	...	...	...	...	0	...	
Luxembourg	...	...	...	...	0	...	
Netherlands	250	1,870	...	2,890	0	...	
Norway	341	901	1,901	443	0	...	
Portugal	317	941	1,449	1,281	91	...	
Spain	520	4,600	5,500	3,170	1,470	...	
Sweden	291	1,567	5,228	328	...	...	
Switzerland	103	...	...	...	0	...	
UK	2,903	13,000	25,829	18,000	0	5,200	
Germany	2,190	9,266	18,900	6,375	...	...	
All States	15,235	61,848	169,169	62,668	7,509	57,934	374,363
CEE	4,595	15,058	44,865	10,365	4,188	46,416	125,488
EU	10,184	44,401	119,091	51,124	3,321	10,796	238,917
EFTA	456	2,389	5,213	1,178	0	722	9,958
Northern Europe	1,139	4,518	16,701	1,438	440	4,431	28,667
Central Europe	7,583	31,901	80,114	38,460	880	6,038	164,977
Southern Europe	1,918	10,370	27,489	12,404	2,001	1,049	55,231
Baltic States	1,591	1,474	7,482	786	382	2,875	14,591
Eastern Europe	3,004	13,584	37,383	9,579	3,806	43,541	110,897
Response total	13,580	50,934	138,658	39,502	3,281	35,678	281,633
Response%	89	82	82	63	44	62	75
Sector proportions	4.1	16.5	45.2	16.7	2	15.5	100

In contrast the estimates for Schools libraries continue to be sparse - and the high figure for Poland is derived from a special survey conducted as long ago as 1991. Almost certainly this has distorted the grossing up estimating so that the sector proportion of 15.5 per cent may prove to be an exaggeration. But the difficulty of obtaining data on Schools libraries has long been UNESCO experience and this gap needs urgent rectification in Europe as in other parts of the world. Complete data for all sectors have been provided by Estonia, Lithuania, Poland, Denmark and the UK. (The absence of positive data from most of them for the 'Other' sector does not indicate incompleteness, rather compliance with the intention of the survey.) Note: In all these tables there is a line to show data provided in actual responses and the percentage this represents of the total estimate. For example, in table National Libraries reported 13,580 staff: this was 89 per cent of the 15,235 estimated total. This total included estimates for Slovenia, France, Iceland, Liechtenstein and Luxembourg.

BOOK ADDITIONS

Statistics of Book stock and acquisitions are traditionally the other most popular series in countries' statistics - and Table demonstrates their anticipated completeness.

Table. Book Additions 000s

	National	Tertiary	Public	Special	Other	School	1998 Total
Bulgaria	45	103	251	59	133	175	
Czech Republic	72	246	1,816	...	0	562	
Estonia	38	99	544	28	27	180	
Hungary	26	...	...	...	...	...	
Latvia	25	79	445	1,208	46	...	
Lithuania	75	220	969	52	46	753	
Poland	...	1,843	3,794	343	188	5,401	
Romania	16	...	984	...	0	...	
Slovak Republic	45	95	356	...	...	199	
Slovenia	...	110	366	98	0	239	
Austria	48	457	...	...	...	...	
Belgium	50	393	1,602	...	...	...	
Denmark	56	242	2,242	124	0	1,246	
Ireland	22	261	650	...	0	...	
Finland	34	436	1,569	206	...	...	
France	...	1,041	6,206	...	...	...	
Greece	74	...	278	9	...	...	
Iceland	...	...	80	...	0	32	
Italy	...	2,778	...	...	...	...	
Liechtenstein	...	...	...	...	0	..	
Luxembourg	...	...	...	...	0	...	
Netherlands	...	...	...	...	0	...	
Norway	105	339	936	108	0	445	
Portugal	33	296	528	195	49	352	
Spain	199	1,228	1,836	737	308	...	
Sweden	92	560	1,858	54	...	...	
Switzerland	33	...	...	...	0	...	
UK	308	2,906	10,980	4,300	0	9,404	
Germany	795	3,718	...	1,288	...	...	
All States	3,327	20,519	62,703	15,310	1,518	67,765	171,142
CEE	553	4,210	10,542	3,344	516	11,174	30,339
EU	2,633	15,413	49,625	11,681	1,002	55,402	135,756
EFTA	141	896	2,536	285	0	1,189	5,047
Northern Europe	290	1,596	6,686	499	38	3,812	12,921
Central Europe	1,766	10,016	35,050	8,694	423	35,739	91,688
Southern Europe	719	4,697	10,424	2,774	541	17,040	36,195
Baltic States	138	397	1,958	1,288	119	1,182	5,082
Eastern Europe	414	3,813	8,585	2,056	397	9,991	25,256
Response total	2,191	17,447	38,292	8,808	798	18,987	86,523
Response%	66	85	61	58	53	28	51
Sector proportions	1.9	12	36.6	8.9	0.9	39.6	99.9

Here there are more data from Schools and less from Special libraries. Of course these data give only the numbers of items acquired and take no account of value. There the financial figures for Tertiary and Special libraries give much higher proportions - in line with very much higher unit prices paid per unit acquired. The low figure for National Libraries will be influenced in some cases by the exclusion of legal deposit acquisitions from this count.

LOAN TRANSACTIONS

Again the data in Table is relatively complete.

Table. Loan Transactions (000s)

	National	Tertiary	Public	Special	Other	School	1998 Total
Bulgaria	11	5,282	16,197	1,662	4,857	6,877	
Czech Republic	201	2,034	62,003	...	0	...	
Estonia	37	1,651	15,352	1,295	490	4,444	
Hungary	...	1,788	36,724	435	...	8,548	
Latvia	244	3,050	17,902	847	2,174	...	
Lithuania	36	6,813	21,991	2,016	20	9,690	
Poland	132	11,597	189,035	17,705	3,309	87,044	
Romania	1,090	...	37,893	...	0	...	
Slovak Republic	5	2,498	25,800	...	...	1,777	
Slovenia	...	3,565	15,600	471	0	5,768	
Austria	345	3,643	16,066	...	...	...	
Belgium	248	1,293	68,475	...	...	...	
Denmark	...	4,789	75,514	586	0	29,151	
Ireland	...	3,049	12,485	...	0	9,203	
Finland	8	7,637	100,332	510	...	...	
France	...	12,266	280,197	...	...	...	
Greece	484	...	1,829	57	...	...	
Iceland	...	...	2,000	...	0	441	
Italy	1,081	5,556	...	...	...	...	
Liechtenstein	...	...	...	...	0	...	
Luxembourg	...	...	...	...	0	...	
Netherlands	...	...	...	...	0	...	
Norway	...	3,051	19,029	604	0	4,443	
Portugal	423	1,468	1,681	1,531	2	773	
Spain	...	13,817	21,417	3,714	5,356	...	
Sweden	151	5,305	80,479	469	...	17,000	
Switzerland	...	...	...	...	0	...	
UK	5,781	79,742	497,889	10,000	0	90,819	
Germany	...	...	324,555	5,552	...	...	
All States	21,154	254,227	2,337,545	78,137	27,747	824,577	3,543,387
CEE	1,984	50,511	438,496	38,660	12,715	186,244	728,610
EU	18,711	195,643	1,846,583	37,880	15,032	626,148	2,739,997
EFTA	458	8,073	52,467	1,597	0	12,185	74,780
Northern Europe	605	20,966	277,355	2,205	569	59,689	361,389

Central Europe	14,584	156,902	1,306,743	26,026	6,340	389,244	1,899,839
Southern Europe	3,981	25,848	314,952	11,246	8,123	189,400	553,550
Baltic States	317	11,514	55,244	4,159	2,684	18,291	92,209
Eastern Europe	1,668	38,997	383,251	34,502	10,031	167,953	636,402
Response total	10,277	179,894	1,940,445	47,454	16,208	275,978	2,470,256
Response%	49	71	83	61	58	33	70
Sector proportions	0.6	7.2	66.0	2.2	0.8	23.3	100.1

This is the measure by which Public library activity is most commonly assessed - and the suggested comparisons with Schools libraries are interesting. The low proportion for Special Libraries corresponds with ways in which they are typically used and is not surprising. The low figure for the Tertiary sector is probably not a good indicator of use: typically they have heavy use of material on the premises - which, when taken from open shelves, is frequently not included in the statistics of transactions. Ways to overcome this weakness are being actively explored in many places - not least in the context of the revision to ISO 2789. Table 'Loan Transactions per member of Staff' provides an indication of productivity.

Table. Loan Transactions Per Member Of Staff

	National	Tertiary	Public	Special	Other	School	1998 Total
Bulgaria	35	...	...	...	...	...	
Czech Republic	452	3,346	14,274	...	...	...	
Estonia	70	3,313	10,469	8,230	3,769	8,320	
Hungary	...	1,863	9,462	498	...	...	
Latvia	545	9,242	9,422	4,368	21,740	...	
Lithuania	58	10,547	5,343	4,635	133	5,224	
Poland	146	1,757	10,603	4,358	2,473	3,348	
Romania	3,106	...	7,557	...	...	...	
Slovak Republic	14	5,067	13,388	...	...	16,924	
Slovenia	...	9,584	20,129	1,938	...	7,395	
Austria	1,119	3,873	10,116	...	...	...	
Belgium	1,239	1,821	17,379	...	...	...	
Denmark	...	5,357	14,524	1,503	...	25,130	
Ireland	...	4,065	9,604	...	...	...	
Finland	44	6,927	23,929	2,040	...	...	
France	...	3,158	13,638	...	...	...	
Greece	996	...	997	996	...	...	
Iceland	...	...	...	...	...	10,071	
Italy	1,817	...	...	...	...	...	
Liechtenstein	...	...	...	...	...	...	
Luxembourg	...	...	...	...	...	...	
Netherlands	...	...	...	...	...	...	

Norway	...	3,387	10,008	1,362	...	...	
Portugal	1,335	1,560	1,160	1,195	22	...	
Spain	...	3,004	3,894	1,172	3,644	...	
Sweden	518	3,386	15,394	1,431	...	...	
Switzerland	...	...	...	...	...	...	
UK	1,991	6,134	19,276	556	...	17,465	
Germany	...	...	17,172	871	...	...	
All States	1,389	4,111	13,818	1,247	3,695	14,233	38,492
CEE	432 3,354	9,774	3,730	3,036	4,012	24,338	
EU	1,837	4,406	15,506	741	4,526	57,998	85,015
EFTA	1,006	3,380	10,064	1,356	...	16,882	32,687
Northern Europe	531	4,640	16,607	1,533	1,292	13,471	38,076
Central Europe	1,923	4,918	16,311	677	7,205	64,466	95,500
Southern Europe	2,076	2,493	11,457	907	4,060	180,553	201,545
Baltic States	199	7,810	7,383	5,288	7,027	6,362	34,069
Eastern Europe	555	2,871	10,252	3,602	2,636	3,857	23,773
Response total	**	**	**	**	**	**	**
Response%	**	**	**	**	**	**	**
Sector proportions	3.6	10.7	35.9	3.2	9.6	37.0	100.0

DEFINITION OF THE DCRB CORE STANDARD

Two documents define the core record for rare books: Core Standard for Books and the DCRB Core. The Books Core requires authorized headings, a call number from a standard classification system, full fixed-field data, descriptive fields 245-4XX but fewer notes only one or two subject headings, and as many added entries as the cataloger judges to be appropriate. Significantly, notes for justification of added entries are not required. The frequently occurring bibliographical references note is also not required.

With the requirements of the Books Core as a base, the DCRB Core standard specifies additional or differing elements. Figure presents the DCRB Core elements arranged in MARC tag order, with an indication of how or why the elements should be used. The code "dcrb" in field 040 $e is mandatory because the bibliographic description is based on the full standard of DCRB.

Differing from the Books Core, the DCRB Core does not require a standard call number. Many libraries do classify their rare books, but other libraries use local call numbers. The DCRB Core standard does not require that catalogers who use local call numbers go an extra step and assign a standard call number as well.

The title, edition, imprint, physical description, and series areas are all required if appropriate to the item being cataloged, just as they are in the Books Core, but their inclusion follows the descriptive method prescribed by DCRB and may apply the options for shortening the bibliographic record. The DCRB Core standard specifies two note fields in addition to those required by the Books Core. If the cataloger transposes the elements on the title page in the transcription in the title field of the bibliographic record, the transposition must be acknowledged in a 500 field.

The citation/references note field provides, in standard form, reference to bibliographic sources. In a fulllevel DCRB record, the 510 field may provide justification for information included in the catalog record. In a DCRB Core record the same reference may lead the user to information that has been omitted from the record, but DCRB Core requires only the five sources listed in DCRB rule 7C14 for post-1500 imprints. The final element of the DCRB Core standard, the index term field that employs genre, form, or physical characteristic terms from standard thesauri, is encouraged but not required. DCRB Core defines the minimum requirements for the bibliographic record. At the discretion of the cataloger, more note fields and more access points may be added to a given record. This flexibility means that a core record may contain more than the minimally required fields without attaining the level of a full record.

Examples of a full-level DCRB bibliographic record and its corresponding DCRB Core record illustrate significant differences between the two standards. A DCRB Core record can be recognized by the encoding level code "4" and "dcrb" in the cataloguing source field 040 $e. The examples used here have the appearance of OCLC records, and the full-level record has been adapted from an existing OCLC record. Other examples illustrating the differences between the two standards can be found on the Web pages of the RBMS Bibliographic Standards Committee.

The difference in the length of the two records is immediately noticeable. The core record has been created by using the options in the full DCRB standard for shortening the bibliographic description in several areas and by omitting fields not required by the core standard. In the publication area, the cataloger has followed the option in rule 4C6 in the full standard to shorten the field. Instead of transcribing all six names of the printers of the book, the cataloger has given the name of the first printer and a bracketed statement that there are five other printers.

The DCRB Core standard does not require any of the thirteen notes used in the full-level record, including the notes that justify the main and added entries. The thirteen note fields in the full-level record have been reduced to one note in the core-level record, the 510 field. While the 510 is not one of the five citations required by the full standard, the cataloger has chosen to include the 510 that gives the reference to the bibliography of Daniel Defoe because the bibliography contains substantially all of the information in the other notes in the full-level record.

Even though this work is a multipart title, the contents note as taken from the title page does not reflect distinct titles of the individual volumes. The contents note, therefore, has been left out of the core record. The DCRB Core record contains only one of the subject headings and one of the added entries used in the full-level record. While the examples are coded as BIBCO records, any library that is not a participating BIBCO member may also create core records. The 042 will be absent from a non-BIBCO record. Creating a core bibliographic record would obviously take much less of the cataloger's time. The time savings and therefore the cost savings may be significant factors for some libraries.

To implement the standard, however, may alter the past practice of describing a book to the fullest to help users find the edition or issue of a title that they are looking for. The DCRB Core standard was written to give catalogers the option and discretion of using a less-than-full standard when collections have been identified as more important for access than for fuller bibliographic details. The flexibility of adding more to the core record and the dependence on the cataloger's judgement in choosing to add more are two key principles of all the core standards. These two characteristics may make use of the DCRB Core, in particular, an attractive alternative to the time-consuming full-level record.

TEXT APPRAISAL

Although a number of articles have been written about the Books Core and other core standards, little has been published about the DCRB Core standard. When the standard was being written, discussion and reports at the RBMS Bibliographic Standards Committee meetings were recorded in the minutes of the committee. The work of the DCRB Task Group was documented in its final report. During the time of the task group's work on the standard, discussion and comments were solicited on the Exlibris list.

All of those exchanges are available in the archives of the list. After the standard was written and approved, discussion concerning issues of its actual implementation and use was not initiated on Exlibris or Autocat, two lists to which many rare book catalogers subscribe. Much of the literature treating the core record describes its development within the context of the history of the PCC, its purpose in encouraging "faster, better, cheaper" cataloguing that can be relied on for quality of description and authorized headings, and its potential contribution to the success of the national programme. There are, however, some studies and reports that investigate particular issues that are relevant to the DCRB Core. Several studies have been done to evaluate the time savings and cost-effectiveness of the core record. Thomas notes that an unpublished study done at Cornell University by Boissonnas found that core records could be created 25 per cent faster than full-level records.

The UCLA/OCLC Core Record Project, conducted from December 1994 to April 1995 with the same group of catalogers creating core- and full-level records, confirmed the assumption that core-level cataloguing is faster than full-level cataloguing and further confirmed that fewer subject headings and added entries are used in the core records. Other libraries' subsequent use of those core records in the OCLC database with little additional editing attested to the reliability of the records. Hyslop discusses an unpublished study of experimental core cataloguing done at the Library of Congress in 1996.

The experiment underscored the efficiency and productivity of cataloguing using the core standard. Cataloguing statistics at Colorado State University over several years indicated that the use of the Books Core to catalog government publications primarily in the backlog was successful in making a greater number of books accessible more quickly than before the core standard was used. Two recent studies explore the sufficiency of the core record. The first study analyses the access points and notes in the core- and full-level records and finds statistically significant differences in the two levels of records. While the authors indicate the fields that catalogers may want to augment, they acknowledge that catalogers may want to accept basic corelevel requirements unless the need for additional fields outweighs the time savings in the creation of core records.

The second study is a pilot study of library users' opinions about the usefulness of the various elements in the core and full records. Although the study finds the need for further research to confirm the preliminary indications about users' preferences concerning the usefulness of the various access points in the bibliographic records, it does indicate that even though users prefer fulllevel records, they still feel the core record is sufficient for finding the materials they need. In a study conducted by interview of cataloger and cataloguing manager attitudes towards the BIBCO core record, Banush found that both groups of participants, while generally satisfied with the core record, expressed varying opinions about its problems and benefits.

The cataloguing managers expressed more satisfaction with the core record than did the catalogers. Banush notes that this attitude of satisfaction with the core record is in contrast to the reduced percentage of core records actually created by the BIBCO participants during 2000 and early 2001. He also reports that there is a distinction between those accepting core records created by other libraries as copy cataloguing and those creating original core bibliographic records. Even though libraries readily use other libraries' core contributions to the shared cataloguing databases, often without revision, they are more reluctant to create them, preferring instead to create fulllevel records. Cromwell reports that even before the Books Core standard was implemented as part of the BIBCO programme, Stanford University used a similar standard with varying success.

She suggests that the use of the core record cannot achieve the level of cost-effectiveness that is expected without the acceptance and understanding of the catalogers themselves about its purpose and its concomitant emphasis on catalogers' judgement and flexibility. The published and reported studies of the efficiency and cost-effectiveness of creating core records point to an encouraging potential for the application of all the PCC core standards. The research about access points, users' perceptions, and practitioners' opinions tempers the findings of the efficiency of the core record while producing some statistical and qualitative data that encourages further study.

While the DCRB Core standard bears the approval of the PCC to be used by the libraries participating in the BIBCO programme, it may be applied by any library, whether a BIBCO participant or not. In the three years since the approval of the DCRB Core standard by the PCC, however, there has been little evidence that the standard is being widely used. This study investigates the trends in the use of the DCRB Core by means of a survey designed to investigate catalogers' use and perceptions of the standard.

METHOD

To reach catalogers and special collections librarians who would be able to provide information about their experience with the DCRB Core standard, a query was posted to three lists: Autocat, Pcclist, and Exlibris. Although many people subscribe to all three lists, the profile of subscribers is different for each. Autocat is a list of several thousand people worldwide who are interested in cataloguing issues; Pcclist is a list whose subscribers are from participating PCC libraries; and the subscribers to Exlibris are those who have an interest in the field of rare books and special collections.

In November 2001, the query was posted to the three lists, asking three questions:

- If anyone has cataloged using the DCRB Core standard;
- If not, has a decision been made not to use the standard; and
- If either is the case, would the recipient be willing to participate in a longer survey about the use and perceptions of the DCRB Core.

The questions were posed in this way to find catalogers who have given some thought to the use of the core standard, whether or not they actually use it. The intent was not to seek responses from catalogers who do not use the core and have never considered doing so. Within a reasonable amount of time, only 15 libraries had sent responses, and of those, only 4 indicated that they use the DCRB Core standard. Thirteen, however, said they were willing to participate in a survey.

A few respondents to the query to the three lists indicated that they were responding because someone else had forwarded the query to them. Several more focused groups of potential respondents, therefore, were polled by e-mail: the liaisons at the BIBCO libraries, the members of the RBMS Bibliographic Standards Committee for the past several years, and the heads of cataloguing, heads of special collections or special collections catalogers at member libraries of the Association of Research Libraries (ARL). Using this second method, 135 queries were sent to the three groups. Sixty-five libraries responded and, of those, 30 indicated that they would participate in a survey. By using these two methods, posting to the lists and soliciting individual libraries, 43 libraries were identified that were willing to participate in the survey.

In March 2002, the 43 surveys were distributed to the participants as Word and rich-text-format attachments to e-mail messages. All participants were assured that their names and the names of their institutions would be kept confidential. Thirty-seven surveys were returned. Since most of the solicited libraries are large research institutions, the majority of the returned surveys are from that category of library. The responses to the list postings, however, came from a broader range of libraries. The overall group of respondents therefore has more diverse representation and includes public, private, university, government/national, and special libraries.

The geographic distribution of the respondents includes libraries from the United States, Canada, and the United Kingdom. Fifteen libraries participate in the BIBCO programme of the PCC. Twenty participants are OCLC member libraries, 2 are exclusively RLIN libraries, and 14 contribute catalog records to both utilities. One library catalogs solely in its own system. Although the initial query was designed to identify willingness to participate in a survey and some responses indicated only yes or no to the three questions, 54 respondents supplied additional comments about the DCRB Core standard or characterized their cataloguing practices or their collections. Of the 54 initial respondents, 24 did not wish to participate further.

In addition, the six libraries that received the survey but did not return it provided some information about their reasons for using or not using the core standard. Their comments will also be included in the following discussion as indicators of perceptions about the DCRB Core standard.

THE SURVEY AND RESULTS

The survey document contained 12 questions, most of which included multiple parts. The first two questions sought information about the type of library, the rare book collection, and the catalogers of the collection. Succeeding questions asked about the original cataloguing policies of the library, whether the DCRB Core standard has been considered, what decision has been made about its use, and whether any DCRB Core cataloguing records have been created. Questions in the next part of the survey suggested reasons for either using or not using the core standard.

Further questions asked how DCRB Core records created by other institutions are handled and whether any studies of users' perceptions have been done. Space for other comments was provided in question 12. While it was expected that the institutional data would vary from the responding libraries, questions 1 and 2 were asked to determine ranges of information to characterize the participants. No clear conclusions can be drawn about the relevance of the type of library, the size of the collection, the number of volumes cataloged or in the backlog, the number of rare book catalogers, or the reporting hierarchy within the institution. Both large and small collections are represented among the responses, ranging between a few hundred rare volumes in a collection to close to or more than one million rare volumes, with dozens to more than 175,000 volumes in the backlog.

The number of original rare book catalogers ranges from.25 full-time equivalents (FTE) to 9 FTE. Only 8 of the 37 libraries have more than 1 FTE rare book cataloger, 11 have less than one FTE, and 2 did not specify a number; the remaining 16 have only a single full-time cataloger. The questions about the size of the collection and the degree to which it is cataloged fully, minimally, or not at all seemed to pose more problems for the respondents than any other questions. Several respondents indicated they would be delayed in returning the questionnaire until they were able to determine the statistical information about their collections. Rare book catalogers report to cataloguing or technical services departments in 19 of the responding libraries, to special collections departments in 12 libraries, and to both departments in 6 libraries. The survey asked about the cataloguing policies of the libraries to determine how many libraries use full-level DCRB or full-level AACR2 for cataloguing pre-1801 books.

The answers were not as straightforward as expected. In responding to how much original cataloguing follows the full DCRB standard, 11 libraries responded that they do all their pre-1801 cataloguing using that standard, and 13 libraries responded that they catalog none of their books using the standard. When answering the reverse question of how much original cataloguing of pre-1801 books follows the AACR2 full standard, 14 libraries indicated all and 15 libraries indicated none.

One library catalogs none of its books according to either standard, but instead creates bibliographic records that are fuller than either DCRB or AACR2. Among libraries that do not adhere strictly to one standard, 12 libraries answered that they catalog some of their sixteenth- to eighteenth-century books using the full DCRB standard, and 7 indicated that they use full-level AACR2 for some of their books.

The differences can only be attributed to the complexity with which catalogers of rare material view their work and to exceptions in cataloguing practices. To begin the enquiry about the use of DCRB Core by the responding libraries, four questions were asked: have you considered using the DCRB Core standard, have you decided to use it, have you decided not to use it, and have you actually used it? Eighteen of the 37 libraries have considered using the DCRB Core, 14 have decided not to use it, and 6 have decided they will use it. Six libraries have, in fact, created records using the standard.

The 6 libraries that have decided to use DCRB Core are not the same 6 that actually have used the standard. One library said that the decision has been made to use the standard, but implementation has been hindered by staffing difficulties. Another library has applied the core standard without having made the policy decision that it expects to make in the near future.

Two other libraries expressed their intention to use the standard in the future, one as soon as appropriate collections have been identified. Depending on the answer to the question of use of the DCRB Core, respondents were asked to indicate why and how they use the standard or why they do not. In each case, a list of reasons was given for potential responses with additional space for other comments. In the discussion that follows, the responses of those libraries that use the DCRB Core standard will precede the responses of those libraries that do not use the standard.

Each of the 6 libraries that use the DCRB Core did not answer all the questions; and since the number is small, only the positive responses will be noted. One library uses the DCRB Core standard to catalog all of its sixteenth- to eighteenth- century books. Four use DCRB Core for some of their cataloguing; 1 among them uses the standard as the default, but enhances the record if there is a compelling reason. The sixth library uses the DCRB Core to catalog its rare books even though none are pre-1801 imprints. Three of the 6 libraries use the DCRB Core for particular reasons: for a specific collection or when lack of expertise or want of a significant reference work would make it impossible to catalog at the full level.

All 6 have applied the standard at cataloger discretion. and 2 of the 6 also have applied it at curator discretion. In response to why and how they use the DCRB Core standard, four libraries answered that they use it to save time, three to increase production, four to gain faster control over their backlog, and three because it is more costeffective. In addition, one librarian whose institution does not hold any pre-1801 imprints replied that they use the DCRB Core because it is "better to capture the uniqueness of what we own in the archival and special collections department," and another respondent noted that they upgrade to the level of the DCRB Core standard some of the brief records for early imprints that can be found in the OCLC database.

Only 1 library uses the standard as it is written, "since it is written to be flexible"; 2 other libraries sometimes use it as written. Four libraries add more fields than the standard requires. The additional fields include: notes for contents, immediate source of acquisition, and ownership and custodial history; genre, form, or physical characteristic terms; added titles; and local information required by the library's online system or cataloguing policies. Five of the libraries encourage cataloger's discretion to determine whether to include additional fields and what the fields should be.

The 6 libraries indicated the percentage of bibliographic records created using the DCRB Core standard to be less than 1 per cent, 1 per cent, less than 5 per cent, less than 10 per cent, and 100 per cent, with one library reporting that no statistical records had been kept for DCRB Core records. In actual numbers 4 libraries reported they have created the following numbers of records: 10, 10–15, 18, and ca. 4,400. The fifth and sixth libraries were unable to give figures. The library that catalogs all its sixteenth- to eighteenthcentury books using the DCRB Core standard does not add bibliographic records immediately to OCLC, and there may be a period of time before they appear in the utility's database.

The library that said it starts with the DCRB Core record as the default and enhances as necessary, creates its original catalog records locally without an 040 field because the generic 040 with the library's holding symbol is added automatically when the records are sent to OCLC. This library has not kept records of the number of DCRB Core records created. Given that these 2 libraries may create a considerable number of DCRB Core records without a way to track them in OCLC and that other libraries, that they have created a minimal number of DCRB Core records, it would be surprising if the national databases have a significant number of DCRB Core records.

The initial responses of the 2 libraries that said they have used the DCRB Core but did not return the survey indicate that they probably have created few catalog records using the standard. When 1 of the 2 libraries applies the DCRB Core, it does so only for seventeenth- and eighteenth- century books, not for fifteenth- and sixteenth-century books, and it never omits notes justifying added entries.

The other library applies the standard in limited instances because it feels that rare books should be given full-level cataloguing. Since the DCRB Core does not require a standard call number, this second library can contribute BIBCO records for broadsides and pamphlets that it does not classify. Adding these 2 libraries that did not participate in the survey to the 6 that did participate brings the total of known users of the DCRB Core standard to 8.

The 31 libraries that do not use the DCRB Core standard indicated their reasons in response to a ten-part question that suggested 9 possible reasons and asked for others in the tenth part. Each of the reasons was affirmed by some of the libraries.

That the DCRB Core standard is inferior was the reason cited by most of the libraries, 19, that have not used it in their original cataloguing records for rare books. Fifteen respondents said that the description is not accurate enough and that there are not enough access points with the use of the standard. Eleven stated that they have not used the DCRB Core because it would require learning a new standard, and 8 said they do not use the standard because they are unfamiliar with it. Six respondents reported shortages or changes in staff that have kept them from using the standard.

Table. Thirty-one Survey Respondents'Ranked Choices for Not Using the DCRB Core Standard (from Question 9)

Reasons	Yes	% Yes	No	Unanswered
Core is inferior	19	61.3	11	1
Description not accurate enough	15	48.4	14	2
Too few access points	15	48.4	16	–
Requires learning new standard	11	35.5	18	2
Unfamiliarity with standard	8	25.8	22	1
Shortages or changes in staff	6	19.4	24	1
Use would disrupt workflow	5	16.1	24	2
Training is unavailable	5	16.1	25	1
Material not appropriate	4	12.9	27	–
Additional reasons	18	58.1	–	13

Five libraries said that training is unavailable, and 5 also indicated that the use of the DCRB Core standard would disrupt the established workflow. Only 4 said they do not have material appropriate to catalog using the standard. The opinion and perception of nearly two-thirds of the libraries responding that they do not use the DCRB Core standard is that the DCRB Core record is inferior to the full record. Almost half think that the standard does not provide enough access points and that the description is not accurate enough. Clearly these three most prevalent perceptions indicate that the survey respondents have not been willing to give up fuller bibliographic treatment for their rare books.

This opinion of the lesser quality of the DCRB Core record as a reason for non-adoption by most of the respondents is reminiscent of a similar kind of negative perception and resistance to acceptance that were noted for the Books Core by Cromwell in her observation that cataloger's attitude and acceptance are needed for the success of the Books Core. The six other reasons that the respondents affirmed for not using the DCRB Core standard are all operational obstacles within their libraries more than opinions or perceptions. Changes in libraries' current personnel, procedures, or materials issues might create more acceptable conditions for the adoption of the DCRB Core standard. Catalogers could learn the new standard or become familiar with it, changes or shortages in staff could be overcome with time or more money, a new workflow could be established, training could be sought, and appropriate materials might be acquired.

The participants gave a number of other reasons, however, for not undertaking use of the DCRB Core. In response to the possibility that a library may not have appropriate materials for using the core standard, some libraries qualified that reason noting the small quantity of rare books they catalog. Seven libraries said that they do not catalog many rare books, that they do so little original cataloguing, especially of rare books, or that they have so few pre-1801 imprints that it is easier to apply the full standard and not worth applying a different standard when they encounter a title that may be eligible for core-level cataloguing.

One librarian replied that the categories of materials that would be candidates for DCRB Core-level cataloguing are generally cataloged to their own minimal-level standard. Administrative or departmental policy to catalog all books at full-level DCRB was cited by 6 libraries as the reason for not applying the DCRB Core standard. Although 13 libraries answered that they do not use full-level DCRB for cataloguing any of their sixteenth- to eighteenth- century books, 4 specifically reiterated that they use only AACR2 full for cataloguing rare books.

Two libraries emphasized their production goals and decisions to apply certain standards as reasons for not taking time to learn a new standard. One librarian thinks "the introduction of a DCRB Core standard runs contrary to the whole intent of DCRB to provide fuller description than AACR2."

Another librarian said that not justifying access points is confusing to users and that if the cataloger starts to add more fields, it would be easier to create full-level records. Two respondents said their reference collections are not comprehensive enough to provide references in a 510 field to allow the abbreviated description of the DCRB Core standard.

Two other libraries indicated that their backlogs are not large enough to need to implement DCRB Core cataloguing. Four librarians each offered one of the following reasons: use of the Core does not increase production, it would create more inconsistencies in the catalog than are already there from so many changes in standards over the years, there is little time for the catalogers to assimilate the new standard, and catalogers prefer one standard not choices.

These additional reasons and comments express strong opposition to the use of the DCRB Core standard. For the most part, they are internal or operational issues that pose obstacles to the adoption of the standard. Remarks from the 24 libraries that did not wish to participate in the survey provide further insight into why some libraries do not use the DCRB Core. Their reasons are categorized in table.

Table. Categorized Reasons for Not Using DCRB Core from Twenty-four Non-participants in Survey

Reasons	No.
Not enough of a collection to make it worthwhile	11
Not informed enough or aware of DCRB Core	6
Cataloger is retiring or have a change of staff	5
Do not use DCRB full	4
Have a shortage of staff	4
Do not use any core standard	3
Policy is to catalog at full level (including BIBCO records)	3
Other libraries would not be able to enhance records to full level	2

Feels the need to justify added entries	1
Feels limitation in training	1
Feels limitation in knowledge	1
Does not do BIBCO for books	1
Has not cataloged rare books in a while	1
Does not create BIBCO records for rare books	1
Only a few catalogers are trained in DCRB	1
Too little time to discuss issues related to DCRB Core	1
Has a large backlog	1
Uses Books Core	1
Catalogs few original records for rare books	1
Differences between core and full are minor	1
Using core does not save much time	1
Doubts can convince Special Collections of value of core records	1
E-resources are becoming priorities	1

Some of the reasons are identical to those of the survey participants:

- The rare book collection is not sufficiently large to warrant learning to catalog by any standard other than full-level DCRB (11 libraries);
- The library is not familiar with or even aware of DCRB Core (6 libraries);
- There are changes (5 libraries) or shortages (4 libraries) in staff;
- The DCRB full standard is not used (4 libraries);
- The policy is to catalog at the full level (3 libraries); and
- Training poses a problem (1 library).

In addition to these commonly held reasons for not applying the DCRB Core, 3 libraries indicated that they do not use any of the core standards, and 2 libraries hesitate to use the DCRB Core because it might prohibit a non-BIBCO library from enhancing the core record to a full-level record in OCLC. Each of the following reasons was cited by a single library for not employing the DCRB Core standard: added entries should be justified in a note; knowledge is too limited to apply the standard; BIBCO books records are not created; BIBCO rare books records are not created; rare books have not been cataloged recently; only a few catalogers are trained to use DCRB; too little time is available to discuss DCRB Core and issues related to it; the backlog is large; the Books Core is used instead; too few original records for rare books are created; the differences between core and full level are minor; the core standard does not save much time; the value of DCRB Core records cannot be sold to Special Collections; and, finally, e-resources are becoming more of a cataloguing priority than printed special collections materials.

Common emphases and implications that run through many of these reasons are the little availability of time and the desire for adherence to fuller standards, two characteristics that have long been in competition in technical services processes in libraries. One library, however, intends to use the DCRB Core standard, and two others are considering using it. How well cataloguing copy is viewed and used by other libraries is one way of evaluating the efficacy of a cataloguing standard. Responding to question 10, 9 participants in the survey said their copy catalogers accept DCRB Core records without changing them, although 1 library said there was room for cataloger's judgement and 2 libraries indicated that they might add subject headings or local notes. Nineteen respondents said their copy catalogers edit DCRB Core records locally.

In response to the question of whether original catalogers enhance DCRB Core records to full level locally, 29 libraries answered in the affirmative; 5 do not enhance core records to full level locally. At 16 libraries, original catalogers enhance DCRB Core records to full level nationally; at 16 libraries they do not enhance nationally, although 2 libraries said they may do so in the future. Four of the respondents noted that their catalogers have never seen a DCRB Core record; 1 of them would edit if a core record were encountered. Since there is so little evidence for the creation of DCRB Core records, it is surprising that not more libraries commented that they have not seen them in the bibliographic utilities.

Further research in the databases of the bibliographic utilities is needed to confirm that the DCRB Core standard has as yet found little acceptance and use among rare book catalogers and curators. The final question on the survey asked if any use studies of DCRB Core records have been conducted. Not surprisingly, none of the respondents has done such a survey. In their additional comments, however, three librarians said they think the purported time savings of core cataloguing records are not worth the cost to the users in locating materials they need. These opinions are greatly supported by many special collections departments' preferences for using the DCRB full standard.

WRAPPING UP

Clearly, the preponderance of the evidence indicates that most libraries surveyed have not used the DCRB Core standard and prefer to catalog their rare books using a full standard, whether DCRB or AACR2. The DCRB Core standard was not written as a replacement for full-level cataloguing for all rare books. The standard states that the expectation is that materials cataloged using the DCRB Core will be chosen more for their accessibility than for full bibliographic treatment. Eight libraries have identified appropriate collections to catalog using the DCRB Core standard.

Among the responses received both in the initial query and in the survey itself, six additional libraries indicated that although they do not now use the DCRB Core standard in their cataloguing, they are expecting to do so in the future or seriously want to consider using it. The total of fourteen libraries that either do use the DCRB Core or almost assuredly will use it in the future indicates the beginning of acknowledgement of the value of the standard and a more positive attitude among some catalogers towards the standard. A recent survey of the special collections departments of the ARL libraries finds that large portions of the collections are uncataloged.

Although formats other than books form the bulk of the uncataloged collections, an average of 15 per cent of the book collections have no access through any form of bibliographic description, and 49 per cent have access only through a card catalog. Many non-ARL libraries may also have large proportions of their special collections in uncataloged backlogs. According to the minutes of recent meetings of the ARL Task Force on Special Collections, one primary issue under discussion is the question of providing increased access to those backlogged materials through bibliographic control.

Many of the books in backlogs may have existing bibliographic records in OCLC and RLIN that can be used by copy catalogers. For those books that do not already have catalog records in the bibliographic utilities, however, the application of the DCRB Core standard in creating original bibliographic records has potential. To begin a project to catalog backlogged material using the DCRB Core standard, a primary task for special collections librarians is to identify specific collections that will be appropriate for DCRB Corelevel cataloguing. One library among the survey respondents is considering cataloguing its early French pamphlets using the DCRB Core. Other pamphlet collections or subject collections, such as political or religious tracts, may be candidates for DCRB Core cataloguing.

One librarian said that using a cataloguing template for materials issued by the same publisher would make DCRB Core cataloguing even more efficient. Several libraries indicated that they are looking for appropriate collections. One respondent noted that sometimes the DCRB Core standard is applied to enhance a brief cataloguing record to bring it up to a higher level without the necessity of enhancing to the full level. In addition to identifying collections that are candidates for DCRB Core cataloguing, libraries will need to encourage cataloger's judgement to help overcome the resistance to using core standards. Because the flexibility of the core standard permits a wide range of additional elements in the core record, the cataloger is not limited to the bare minimum requirements. Not every book in a backlog will be a candidate for core-level cataloguing, but identifying the proper collections and undertaking DCRB Core-level cataloguing projects can help increase accessibility to those materials that users do not know exist in rare book collections.

3

Culture and Conflicts Faced by Users in Library

MANUAL AND ELECTRONIC SEARCH

Searching for manual sources required scanning catalogue cards or indexing and abstracting sources. As cross-references often increase the number of cards or pages, there was a difficulty in being very exhaustive. Conducting selective dissemination of information (SDI) services had been extremely difficult as the document profiles must be matched with user profiles with the aid of semi-mechanical systems. Most of these limitations are easily eliminated in the electronic environment due to the very nature of information processing and organisation in electronic form.

The inherent advantages of indexing electronic information help the user to search for any or all the fields in a timesaving manner. Since, document profiles are already stored in the database and search software supports creation of user profiles, current awareness services (CAS) and SDI services are achieved more easily. The concern for end-user searching was dominant right from the beginning of early CD-ROM database systems since, the time spent for searching does not involve communication costs as is the case with online searching. Also with the universe of knowledge getting increasingly complex as a result of continuing advances in research in intra and inter-disciplinary areas, vitiating the search conducted by a generalist like a librarian may not be effective in amassing the user's information requirements completely or not achieving the desired results expected by the user.

The convoluted information requirements of present day researchers require sufficient knowledge of their disciplines and since, the users are increasingly exposed to the computerised work environment, they feel very confident to conduct information searching on electronic systems. The professional ethos and egos also plays a part as users find more satisfactory results from electronic systems than manual systems, and in a relatively easy and convenient way. The librarians should recognise the confidence and maturity of users to conduct searches on their own as they have better knowledge of their disciplines, more exposure to the different keywords and their relationships and because of the inherent advantages of locating related sources serendipitously while scanning the retrieved results.

There should be closer interaction and effective communication between library professionals and users to understand each other's views about information needs and use. Library user meetings, orientation sessions for new users, special help for research scholars, training programmes about usage of print and electronic resources, a help desk at reference counter, holdings locator services, interacting with users through phone and e-mail, encouraging users to approach the librarian, ask a librarian, and user friendly web sites are some options practiced in libraries in India.

INFORMATION USE

Information services provided by a library are primarily based on subjective input from users and hence, justify users commenting about misses or noise in electronic information service outputs. An information need is what an individual ought to have; an information want is what an individual would like to have; an information demand is what an individual asks for; an information use is what an individual actually uses; and an information requirement denotes what is needed, what is wanted or what is demanded.

Information needs are affected by a variety of factors such as the range of sources available, the uses to which information will be put, individual characteristics of the user, social, political and economic systems surrounding the user, and the consequences of information use. Accessibility of information resources is usually assumed to depend on a range of cognitive, social, and physical factors, such as whether a person is aware of a resource, has the knowledge and skills needed to access it, and has the resource close at hand. Scientists spend 50–60 per cent of their time communicating. The computerised environment has increased the quantum of information available nearby, but it has not enhanced a person's information consumption skills.

There is a burden of effort in information storage and retrieval that may be shifted from author to indexer to index language designer to searcher to user. Though the user is exposed to more microfilms, Xerox copies, and electronic information on desktop/ Intranet/Web, ready to display at the touch of a button, the more time one spends in searching and collecting information, the less time s/he gets to use the information. Scholarly articles are identified for reading in five basic ways: browsing, automated searches, citations found in the litreature, mentions by other people, and current-awareness tools. How much information one requires to work on a particular problem is also subjective as human beings observe the 'principle of least effort'. Perhaps one may easily deal with an information crisis by identifying a part of the total references and by using few of what is identified.

USER BYPASSING

Though libraries in India are progressing well on the automation and information access front, there is a definite case of fewer users present in the library due to different reasons. The real question is whether electronic services of libraries have in any way affected the user interests or have the users found more confidence in an information superhighway beyond the library. The same proportions of scientists still browse to identify scholarly articles to read, but more are using online searches and the proportion of readings identified through online searches appears to be increasing. Library acquisitions suffered a serious setback in recent years unable to withstand the price rise and these budgetary constraints forced users to look beyond the library for their varied information requirements.

Hence, research publications in some disciplines now cite more Web resources. Librarians are not yet acting as true consumers and hence, cannot blame predatory publishers for taking advantage of the situation. Another issue involves the very large and rapidly increasing number of articles obtained through photocopying, interlibrary loan, document delivery, preprints, and reprints. The right step in assessing whether there is a depleted user interest in libraries is to study use patterns over the years and, in a populous country like India, just going by the numbers will not address the qualitative aspects.

There has not been much reduction in book issues in an academic library, but are the new acquisitions being used to the same extent? But what is seen is the fall in library attendance, as observed and reported by many library managers. It is evident that fewer users actually visit the library, and very few still spend more time, a lot of others use the library through lending, photocopies, electronic access through networks, etc. It becomes difficult to quantify use as the library has statistics only about explicit use, but there are also implicit uses through browsing or reading inside the library, which are difficult to quantify.

There are also vital questions about whether mere issuing a book or taking a photocopy of a journal article attribute to use and hence, comes the need for a qualitative assessment of use. Perhaps professionals are afraid to look at these issues as the results of such assessment may force the authorities to examine critically the investments in a service institution like the library. Like Reenen's comment about false consumers, it seems that librarians fear self-assessment of library usage or to undergo a performance audit.

THE LIBRARIAN'S IDENTITY CRISIS

EDUCATION AND TRAINING

The students, faculty, curriculum and training methodology at the library schools have to be visibly improved to meet the challenges posed by electronic information and impatient, highly demanding users. There are also problems of infrastructure and a directionless attitude in the teaching and research sector often forgetting the interdisciplinary aspect of the subject. Working librarians have good exposure to new databases, their acquisition and use, pragmatic implementation of various routines, etc., which are not accessible to library schools. Thus apart from teaching faculty, expert practitioners in the discipline would also be involved in education programmes to bridge the gap between preaching and practice.

The existing courses must always look at the sweeping changes in the library workplace and adapt well to enable the students to face the challenges with confidence, giving ample opportunities for improving reasoning, communication skills, general awareness, and other characteristics identified for a multi-tasking service organisation. The age-old teacher-centric teaching has to be circumvented by student oriented and professional (job)-centric teaching.

JOB OPPORTUNITIES

Though the major employer, the government, is not recruiting many, more and more universities/institutions are offering library courses in the regular and distance modes. And this upheaval in quantity does not contribute in any way to the quality of these courses. For a prospective student/parent, the job advertisements provide an impression of plenty of jobs in the field, as library jobs at different levels in different institutions do not follow standard designations. But only when one finishes the course and looks for job openings, does the actual state of affairs come to light. Actually the increase in library-related jobs is merely additive, and not multiplicative, like computers, management or engineering, and should not show an exponential rise at any point of time.

CONTINUING EDUCATION

Since, the mode and rate at which information is generated, organised and used is witnessing sweeping changes in the perfectly wired information age, a continuously evolving discipline like LIS is meant to tackle the intricacies of information for societal development; thus it shall not be learned effectively and practiced perfectly by exposing students to a framed curriculum in formal education only. The discipline has changed drastically from being based totally on print sources; aware of the increasing richness of information in electronic forms and available over networks thus is leading to embracing vigourously other disciplines like computers, management, and information and communication technology.

It is imperative for the information practitioners to continuously monitor and augment their professional skills through continuing education (CE) to discharge their duties to users, employer and profession. The present initiatives on CE are generally being made by national institutions and suffer limitations such as: they are of short duration, generally infrequent, claiming comparatively high fees, working professionals finding it difficult to get sponsorship from their institutions, involve travelling to far off destinations hampering their regular work, etc.

CULTURES AND CONFLICTS FACED BY LIBRARIANS

Gone are the days of close-minded librarians and the quality of candidates entering the profession is continuously improving. As technology-intensive librarianship is gaining ground in the country, working librarians are getting much exposure to new technology tools for providing better information products and improved information services. Working librarians in at least the major academic and research institutions have better computer infrastructure and possess better expertise on the latest information products and services.

It is quite natural in the emerging print plus electronic hybrid library scenario that a library professional right from first job is expected to be conversant with the electronic apart from the manual means of information collection, processing, management and servicing. But there are also apprehensions about the level of technology appropriate to conducting well in the challenging and demanding academic and research setup.

A library professional must be distinct from a computer professional due to the very nature of their profession and the expected deliverables. But the acute emphasis on technology has created a situation that a professional can hide many of his/her professional ignorance by a little computer knowledge which is not going to be good either for the profession or for the libraries. Google cannot and will not be replacing libraries because both can co-exist with their diverse functionalities catching the attention of users at different occasions.

The professional nature of the librarian's job always motivates him or her to help the users unlike administrative staff in the institution who are always rule-based; sometimes this may lead to not so proper upkeep of administrative procedures and records, and in some cases cause unnecessary rivalry with the administrative staff. There are also personnel problems as the librarians fail to command a leadership role in many institutions thereby eclipsing their role in strategic planning.

Institutions attach prime importance to libraries but are they doing the same towards the personnel in their libraries? It is a strange case of all the virtues are of the system and the problems are due to the staff. Largely a service wing in many institutions, not enjoying the power, visibility, service conditions, and career prospects of the research and teaching staff, the status of library professionals in many of these institutions is not a morale booster, leaving many of them underperforming. It is not uncommon to see non-professionals heading many libraries, maybe just because they are senior teachers or good administrators or researchers and not because they are good as librarians.

There are also problems of the lack of a peer group in the profession resisting such attacks on the profession as many senior professionals have become self-centred, and professional associations compete for minor issues. The professional staff members working in many libraries in developing countries are totally engrossed in administrative and routine jobs related to library operation and administration. Many institutions do not demand their library professionals to pursue an offensive role. The users always need quick services and they never respond to any of the reasonable operational or managerial delays.

The real situation is that the libraries have very little control over their suppliers whereas their consumers have too much control over them. Users are not patient enough to interact constantly with the library staff to tune their profiles to improve the relevance of information services, maybe due to time constraints on their parts. Again by a rough assessment, it seems that less than 10 per cent of the users usually respond to SDI results and the remaining are either using it as it is or rejecting it straightaway. Out of those responding, only a few show their willingness to give feedback to modify their keywords to improve the utility of such services. Users may sometimes get so arrogant with the helpful nature of library staff and doubt it as their weakness.

USING MULTIPLE VIEWPOINT SYSTEMS

SEARCHING

Except in systems exclusively designed for user-directed browsing, a method is needed to guide the system in finding data relevant to the initial query. This may be as simple as consulting all viewpoints in parallel, or, in a system with a well-understood and specific purpose, it might be a complex algorithm for choosing various subsets of viewpoints, and adjusting the query over and over again depending on characteristics of those results found so far, such as the size of the result set, ranking of results in it, and on time elapsed in the search so far.

The degree of viewpoint parallelism in a multiple viewpoint system describes to what extent the same query (under various transductions) is used to consult more than one viewpoint (these consultations may occur serially in time; so long as the same query is being used, we regard this as viewpoint parallelism). Viewpoint parallelism both allows one viewpoint to make up for other viewpoints' mismatches with the user's vocabulary, providing results that the other viewpoints would not have supplied, and allows viewpoints to reinforce each other on results judged relevant in more than one viewpoint.

The way in which the results are actually combined depends on the merge method; merging that works on the same principles as voting algorithms is an appropriate way to take advantage of viewpoint parallelism. The notion of boosting is a method of improving learning algorithms by combining several rough, inaccurate predictive rules into a more effective predictive strategy; viewpoint parallelism is the analogue of the idea of boosting in the realm of information retrieval.

Reducing the degree of viewpoint parallelism through collection selection is appropriate when there is a gain in efficiency to be won from only consulting a subset of possible viewpoints (the most highly trusted, perhaps, or those with the highest bandwidth, or those located in a certain geographical area), either for considerations of speed, or to improve the precision of results by eliminating results from irrelevant viewpoints entirely.

Collection selection may also be appropriate when there are identifiable classes of viewpoints in the system, some appropriate for one purpose in searching, and some for another.

Query progression is any adjustment to the query made based on the results from one viewpoint consultation (possibly, from the results of several viewpoints consulted in parallel), before the new version of the query is used to consult another viewpoint (or viewpoints). This may take the form of making adjustments to the wording of the initial user query before transducing it to another viewpoint, choosing the representation of a document to stand as the query, changing the required threshold of similarity for the query, or any combination of these.

Typically, the use of a transition mapping is immediately preceded by a query progression, as when the first result of a consultation is chosen as the new query, and then this result is used as input to the transition mapping. Simply using a transition mapping in itself is not considered query progression, because although it may change the form of the query entirely, the result of following a transition mapping is the best approximation of the query in the context of the new viewpoint. Relevance feedback is a form of user-assisted query progression.

INTERACTION STYLES

A searcher may be involved in a multiple viewpoint search to greater or lesser extent. The tightness of the user interaction loop expresses how frequently input from the user is elicited. How much input the user can have is limited by the degree of viewpoint transparency in the system. A user unaware of the existence of different viewpoints in the system cannot directly choose which ones are to be consulted, although choices made by a user in a viewpoint transparent system may be used by the system in making such a choice.

A user could be asked for input at every decision point—a tight interaction loop—and yet never be aware that there is more than one viewpoint in use. A loose user interaction loop, in which the user supplies only the initial query, may still take place in a non-view point transparent system if, for instance, the system results are organized or annotated so that the viewpoints from which they arose are made clear.

The user 's judgement might be solicited with regard to the relevance of an intermediate result, to change or augment the query, to choose when to transition and what viewpoint to transition to, and when to stop a search. To some extent, our definition of a "search session" will impact the observed level of user input.

For example, the difference between a system that allows the user to change the query entirely during a search, and does not store state information, and a system that returns a result and then takes a new query, is partly a matter of where we draw the boundaries of a search session.

A tight interaction loop with many degrees of freedom for the searcher is probably best suited to information exploration and browsing tasks. Maintaining both context and a sense of purpose in such an interaction remains a major HCI research problem.

Other Possible Elements of a Multiple Viewpoint System

The addition of such tools as *lenses*, and special-purpose viewpoints, further extends the use (and complexity) of multiple viewpoint systems. the set of possible documents it may include in a result set, but also, auxiliary data items, from related documents that are inappropriate as results to the keywords used to index documents in various viewpoints.

This universe of all data items can be decomposed into categories in several ways, such as separating keywords from valid results, or distinguishing fiction from non-fiction.

Such data decompositions are suitable for broad, rigid categorizations, but lack the fluidity of description available with viewpoints. A lens is a filtering process that intersects some such data category with another subset of the universe of data items; for instance, a lens for non-fiction books could be applied to the result of a library search so that only non-fiction books satisfying the search are shown.

Malone, Grant, and Turbak use the phrase "information lens" to refer to another type of information filter. While ours is a simple and static organization of the universe of data items, theirs filters incoming e-mail using detailed representations of message content and of a user's interests.

Wilensky and Phelps describe a "lens" for viewing individual documents, rather than dividing a collection; here, multivalent documents have more than one representation, and through different lenses, different representations are displayed. An *auxiliary viewpoint* is one that is concerned only with auxiliary data items. These may be very useful during a search, but none of their results are included in the final system result.

Typically, these are used for the purposes of query progression, as when a thesaurus viewpoint is used to change the wording of a query to make it more compatible with vocabulary used across the viewpoint of a system. Auxiliary viewpoints may also be used for purposes of collection selection. An example of this is a meta viewpoint, which, given a query, determines which of the viewpoints in the system the query is most appropriate to.

Designing a Multiple Viewpoint System for a Problem Domain

The first step in designing a multiple viewpoint system is identifying the problem area of interest, which typically corresponds to the universe of artifacts; we must identify the potential set of results and any useful auxiliary data items. In the case where we have the luxury of designing a system from scratch, we will need to consider conceptual sources for viewpoints on this data, what representational schemes are appropriate for our various viewpoints, and how we can obtain information about different attributes of our data items.

Attributes may be calculated directly from the data, using automatic methods of extracting information from a document collection; for instance, extracting terms used in text documents, or histograms from images. Secondary descriptions of the data, such as external keywords or descriptions, may also exist. For relatively small collections of data it may be possible to get experts' opinions about the relationships among data items, or to extract such relationships from observed user interaction with the data.

Two systems with the same underlying viewpoint structure might arrive at their results in entirely different ways. One system might search in parallel from a user query and infrequent feedback to create single ranked list of novelists while another, using the same viewpoints, is browsed in user-driven sequence, to produce an arrangement of book titles organized by year of publication. Although we generally view viewpoints as mapping artifact descriptions to sets of artifacts, it is important to note that the represented "artifact" may just as well be an informative number, boolean value, or index term as a document identifier. Furthermore, the method by which a viewpoint arrives at a result from a given query need not be simple, nor even deterministic. It is, however, important that the characteristics of its component viewpoints be taken into account when designing a multiple viewpoint system.

If a viewpoint in the system can give as a result a range of values, then these values are part of the system domain, and are explicitly a part of the universe of data items that are of interest. A system including a viewpoint that gives non-deterministic viewpoint results will, if that viewpoint is consulted and its results used in the course of a search, give non-deterministic system results.

Encapsulating a complex algorithm within a single viewpoint in the system is quite possible under our definition of viewpoints, but is probably only appropriate if the algorithm itself represents a viewpoint on the domain of interest. Otherwise, it should be included as a part of the search strategy instead.

EXAMPLES

Earth Science Data

The application that led to the exploration of these ideas was the searching of Earth Science data. The controlled vocabulary used to index these datasets provides one viewpoint on the datasets. An additional viewpoint can be created based on the terms used in a set of auxiliary text descriptions of the datasets. We call these, respectively, the controlled vocabulary viewpoint, and the text term viewpoint. We have built a prototype multiple viewpoint system using these two viewpoints.

When the user chooses a query, either by entering a free text query or by selecting a dataset as a new query, the user can also choose which viewpoint will be consulted with that query. The viewpoints are made absolutely explicit to the user, and the user controls every adjustment made to query and viewpoint, so this system is not viewpoint transparent, and is tightly user interactive.

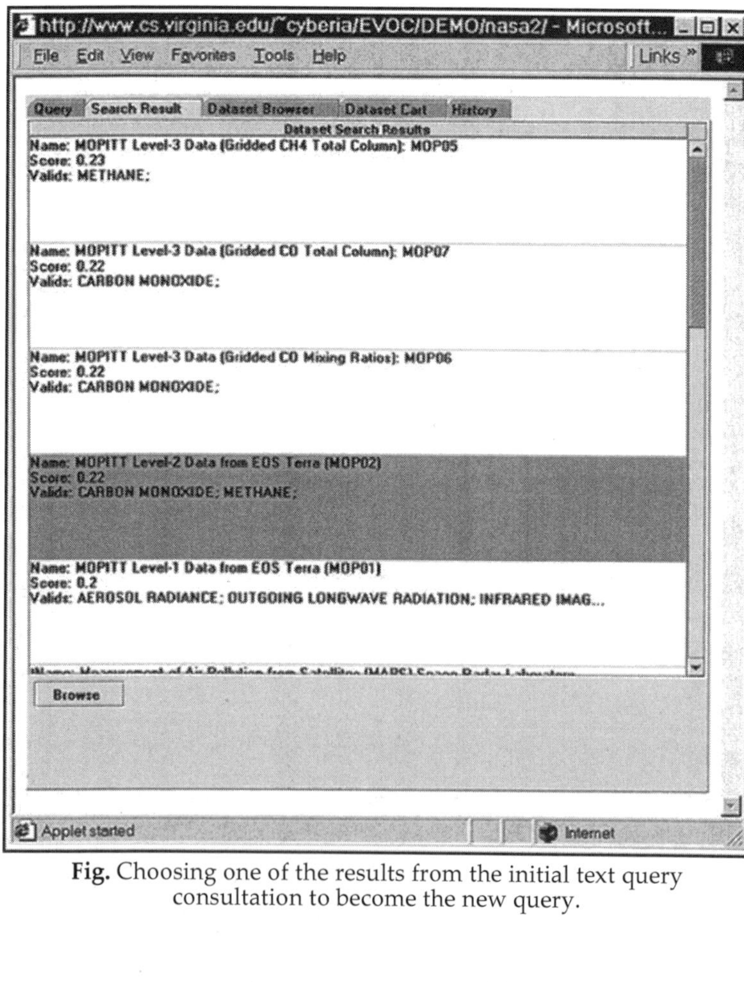

Fig. Choosing one of the results from the initial text query consultation to become the new query.

Query progression occurs in this system whenever the user chooses a new query from among the results of the previous viewpoint consultation.

Viewpoint parallelism only occurs in this system when the user explicitly chooses to use the same query to consult both viewpoints, first one, and then the other. Here we give an example illustrating a case in which information can be found using more than one viewpoint, but not otherwise.

Figures show the search tool at various points during the search. We begin by entering the phrase "atmospheric pollution" in the free text search interface—a standard text-input box, not shown—and consulting the text term viewpoint.

The results are those data sets that are most similar to the query in the text term viewpoint.

We can transition to the controlled vocabulary viewpoint to see the associated controlled vocabulary terms for each of the result datasets.

In this system, the transition mapping simply maps between different representations of the same documents. Of the result data sets that appear relevant, many are associated with the controlled vocabulary terms "CARBON MONOXIDE" and "METHANE."

For the purposes of further searching, we choose one of these data sets (the fourth, MOPO2), which contains both terms, to be our new query. The next set of results are those that are similar to MOPO2 in the controlled vocabulary viewpoint. Among these, we find the ATMOS (Atmospheric Trace Molecule Spectroscopy Data From Spacelab-3) dataset.

According to the ATMOS dataset summary: "The Atmospheric Trace Molecule Spectroscopy (ATMOS) experiment was flown on the Space Shuttle STS-51B as part of the Spacelab-3 laboratory to demonstrate the capability to monitor environmental quality by surveying the atmosphere for trace constituents and by identifying their sources, flow patterns, and decay mechanisms."

Inspection of the controlled vocabulary associated with the ATMOS dataset together with this summary clearly indicates that the ATMOS dataset has potential to be relevant to a query on atmospheric pollution.

To search further, we now choose to remain in the controlled vocabulary viewpoint, but choose the ATMOS data set as a new query. The results of this consultation, particularly the first four are data sets relevant to atmospheric pollution.

It would at first seem that we have simply used our first query "atmospheric pollution" to discover that the appropriate query terms would have been "carbon monoxide methane." However, if this query formulation is entered directly, the system does not find the ATMOS data set. It is the multiplicity of viewpoints that allowed us to find the relevant data.

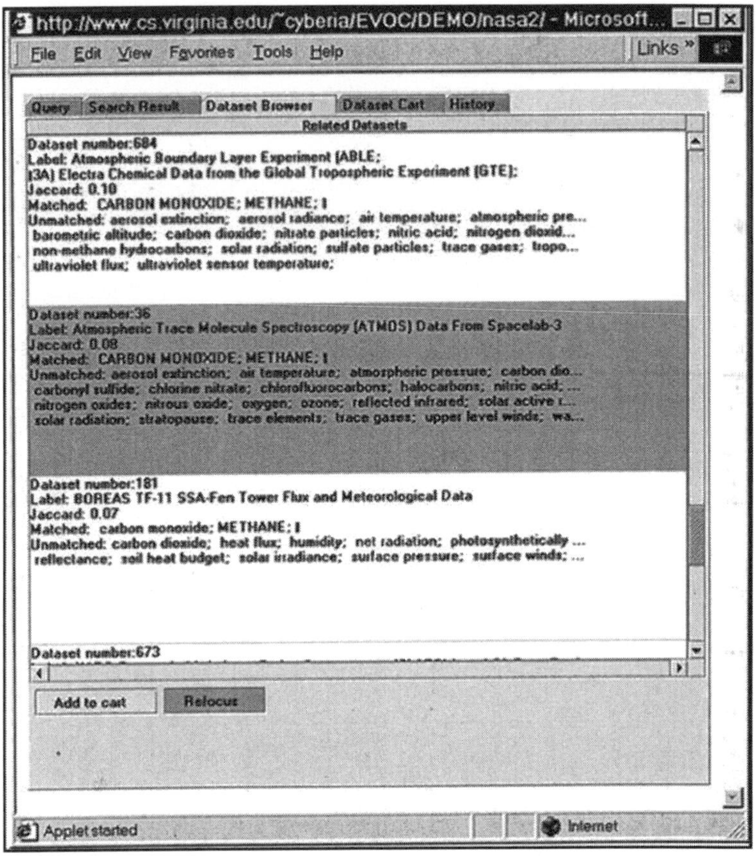

Fig. Choosing one of the Results of the Second Consultation to become the New Query.

This system provides a “shopping cart” into which documents judged relevant by the user can be saved during the search process, and also a history listing, for each text query, the dataset queries that were used subsequently in the search. This kind of user-driven merge method is well suited to this highly transparent, tightly user interactive system, although an additional merged list of results from all consultations thus far might also be useful.

CONTENT BASED IMAGE RETRIEVA

Content-based image retrieval (CBIR) systems use features that can be extracted from the images themselves inorder to index collections of images.

In image retrieval systems that are queried “by example,” the searcher submits a query image that the searcher has judged relevant to his information need, and the system searches based on features it extracts from this image.

But unless the searcher is very familiar with the behaviour of the system, or the image retrieval task is very specifically defined, it is unlikely that the features the user identifies as important in judging the query image relevant to the information need will be the same features the system extracts and uses to judge the relevance of other images to the query image.

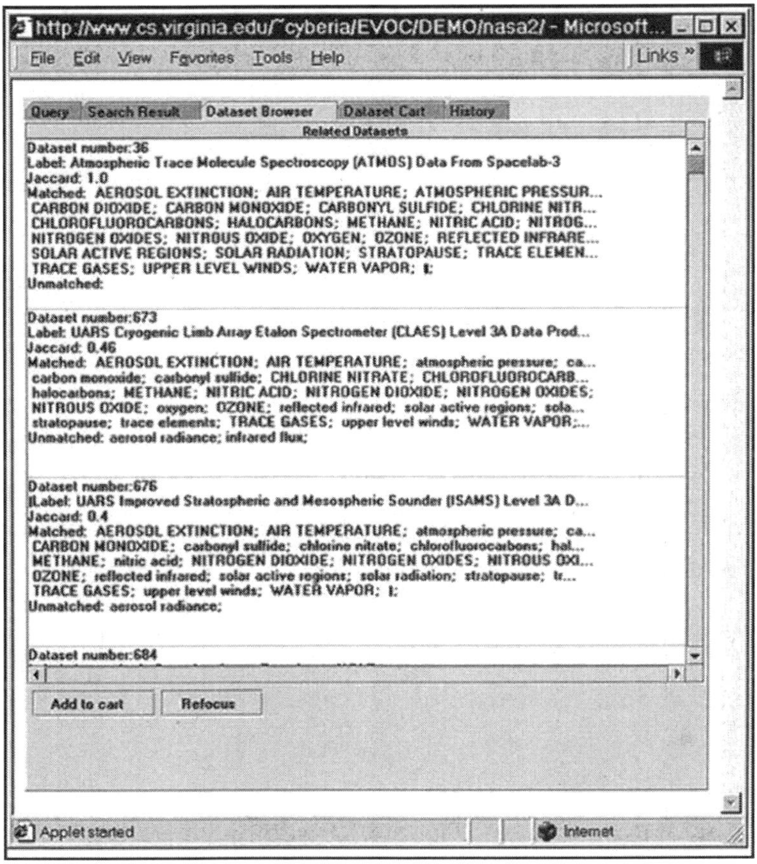

Fig. Relevant documents found in results from third consultation.

In French, Martin, Watson, and Jin, the standard type of CBIR system was extended by creating several additional representations of the images in the collection, thus creating multiple viewpoints (or channels) some or all of which can be used in the retrieval process.

We refer to this as multi-channel as opposed to single-channel CBIR. In the prototype multi-channel CBIR system, there are four viewpoints (channels) based on: the original images in 34 categories of the COREL image collection, their negatives, their greyscale images, and their negative greyscale images. Each of these was indexed using a basic CBIR feature-extraction technology using three colour and four texture features.

Using this multi-channel system materially improved retrieval performance over a single-channel system. Suppose we are searching for images of roses. Figure shows the top 40 results of consulting a basic CBIR technology using the original colour images (that is, the original colour viewpoint alone), with a white rose query image.

Only one rose is found. This query image does poorly as a query image in the standard colour channel, because colour information tends to overwhelm everything else.

The system of four channels is fully viewpoint parallel; the same query (transduced for the latter three viewpoints by taking the negative, black and white, and negative black and white of the query) is used to consult all four viewpoints.

One merge method for this system presents the top 10 results from each viewpoint in four parallel lists.

This less viewpoint transparent approach may be a more appropriate interface for image searching in such a system. Here we can see that the same image does rather better in the black and white viewpoints, where colour information cannot dominate.

Fig. Top 40 results of Consulting Original colour viewpoint with white Flower image query.

Observing this, the searcher may be better able to choose a query image suited to distinguishing between roses and non-roses. In this case, we choose the pink rose image that is ranked most similar by both of the black and white viewpoints. After this query progression, we consult all four viewpoints in parallel with the new query. Figure shows the results, and we can see that all the viewpoints perform much better on this query.

Figure shows the results of two alternative merge strategies, both of which combine the results of the four viewpoints based on similarity. Comparing these two rows with the first ten results of consulting only the original colour channel illustrates how much we can improve results for the same initial query, using viewpoint parallelism, query progression, and merging.

The framework of multiple viewpoint systems has helped identify other possible variations on and extensions to this CBIR system, such as adding another four channels based on another basic CBIR strategy, accepting multiple query images, including positive and negative feedback, automatic query progression, and various different merge methods, including some more complex approaches based on clustering.

Medical Articles

A three-viewpoint prototype system has been created for searching among the set of medical articles in the OHSUMED collection.

Descriptive text terms are used for one viewpoint, while a second is based on a limited set of MeSH (Medical Subject Heading) terms, zero to three of which are associated with each article.

A third viewpoint uses both text terms and MeSH headings. In this system, transition is based on article identity (each article is a viable query in all three viewpoints).

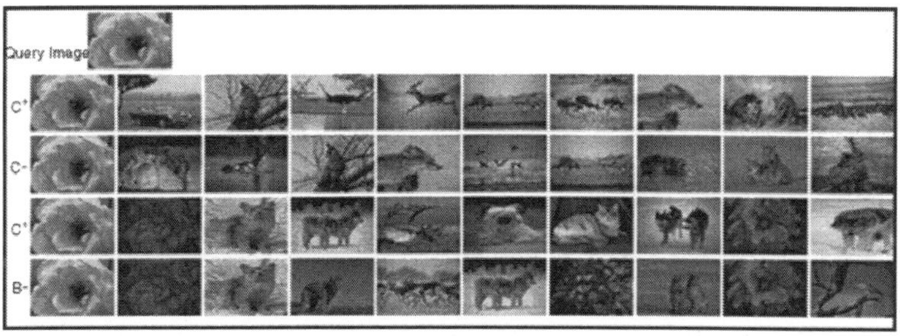

Fig. Top 10 results of Consulting each of the four viewpoints in the system in Parallel with the white Flower image Query

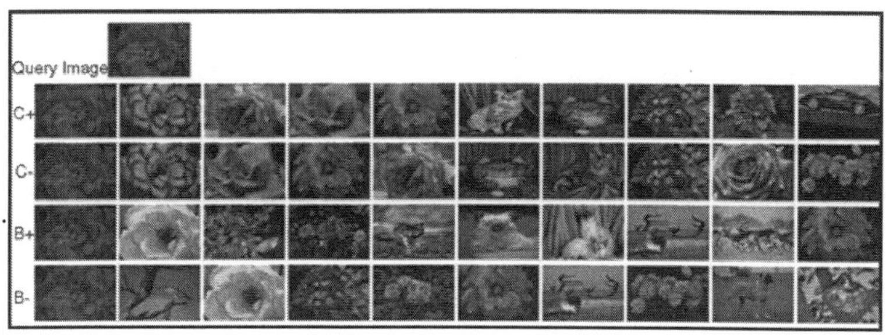

Fig. Top 10 Results of Consulting each of the four viewpoints in the system in Parallel with the Pink Flower image Query after Query Progression

One characteristic of this system that we have discovered in preliminary experiments is that these viewpoints differ considerably in result quality; results from the text term viewpoint and the viewpoint using both vocabularies have precision on average twice as high as results from the MeSH viewpoint. One interesting area for future work is a vocabulary for characterizing individual viewpoints, and describing how these characteristics affect how combinations of viewpoints work together.

This is an experimental system to which various search strategies and merge methods can be applied. Viewpoint parallelism is possible for various combinations of the three viewpoints, and several merging strategies, have been applied, including similarity-based and rank-based methods using various weights.

Several approaches to automatic query progression are being investigated in this system, varying how promising new queries are to be identified, how many of these there are to be, what viewpoints will be consulted with them, and how the results for them are to be combined with each other and previous results.

We can also model user-assisted query progression using our a priori knowledge of the relevant results for a query to filter the results of a viewpoint consultation. We choose the top ranked result (or results), which we know to be relevant (assuming there are any relevant elements in the result list) just as an intelligent searcher would be able to recognize a relevant result in the list.

DIGITAL LIBRARY SEARCHING

The Web sites of the ACM Digital Library (ACM DL) and IEEE Digital Library (IEEE DL) constitute a commonly used ad hoc multiple viewpoint system on the universe of Computer Science technical papers. Suppose a searcher submits the query "quad trees" to these sites, and finds that the ACM DL gives the largest set of relevant papers, while the IEEE DL gives relatively few.

A searcher experienced in using these sites in concert would not then assume the IEEE DL lacked useful information but would assume a vocabulary mismatch, and attempt to search for that content in an alternative way, for instance using an author of one of the papers in the ACM DL result list as a query to the IEEE DL and thereby discovering that the query is better phrased in IEEE parlance as "nearest neighbour methods."

In this case, the two viewpoints are first consulted (manually) in parallel; the consultation of the ACM DL viewpoint results both in document results and in keyword (author name) results suitable for use in query progression. A multiple viewpoint system designed with the ideas from our framework in mind first might unify these under a single interface to perform the parallel consultation automatically, and then might use a lens to extract from the initial results a list of author names from among which the searcher could choose, for user-aided query progression

Fig. Top 10 results of Merging Results from all four viewpoints Consulted with the pink flower image Query under two Different Merges.

A multiple viewpoint system consists of several viewpoints, representations of relations among data items that can be accessed through specific query languages, transition mappings that facilitate moving among viewpoints while maintaining a sense of context, and a merge method that arranges results from different viewpoints into a coherent whole. Multiple viewpoint algorithms determine how the elements of a multiple viewpoint system are used to transform an initial query into a final result.

Such an algorithm may involve various levels of user interaction. Multiple viewpoint systems are an approach to extending the utility of existing approaches to information retrieval by making available in a single system two or more representations of some domain of interest. We presented a framework and vocabulary suitable for discussing, characterizing, and helping to design such systems.

We also illustrated these ideas by means of several multiple viewpoint systems that had their designs driven by this framework. Effective information retrieval depends on a searcher being able to communicate to the system the nature of an information need, and thus information can be made inaccessible due to mismatches of vocabulary between a searcher and the retrieval system.

An important contribution of multiple viewpoint systems is their ability to expand the vocabulary of usable query terms for an information retrieval system. Further, we see multiple viewpoint system design as an interesting new area where heterogeneous methods of information organization and retrieval, as well as the approaches of different domains of study to the same body of information, can be used in concert without making fundamental changes to existing archives and tools.

DYNAMICALLY MAKING USE OF DISTRIBUTED DATA SOURCES

One major goal of grid computing is to establish highly flexible and robust environments to utilise distributed resources in an efficient and transparent way. Due to the highly dynamic nature of such environments where computational nodes may leave or join in, it is essential to bind service invocations to concrete service instances at run-time. This allows to flexibly reacting to changes in the environment. In a service-oriented world, application logic is encapsulated by means of services.

Standards like SOAP over HTTP can be used for the invocation of services, and WSDL for accessing information on the capabilities of services. When several instances of the same service exist in a grid environment, then it should be possible to dynamically make use of as many service instances as possible by parallelising a service call and by submitting requests in parallel to them. The goal of this parallelisation is twofold and depends on the characteristics of the services which are subject to parallelisation.

First, we aim to make use of as many services as possible to increase the quality of the result. This is particularly true for the access to data sources, encapsulated by dedicated services. Second, having multiple service instances accessible opens the possibility to speed up the processing of computationally intensive tasks. Whereas examples for the latter have been presented in detail in and large scale experiments with more than 2500 worker nodes have been demonstrated in using MW class library, this work focuses on the goal of enhancing the quality of the request when accessing data sources by means of services.

The contribution of this work is to introduce architecture of a service seeming to be an ordinary, callable service to the outside world, which is able to adopt its behaviour controllable by optional quality of service criteria, and the resources available on a grid. In short, such dynamic services use Meta information on the currently available service providers and their capabilities and partition the original request into a set of simpler requests of the same service types.

These requests are then submitted in parallel to as many service providers as reasonable, and their responses are finally integrated and returned as the result of the original request. In particular, this parallelisation shall be carried out without the need to modify existing functionality or interfaces, and transparently to the user and developer. Due to its master/slave nature, it is especially suitable for grid environments. To better illustrate the benefits of such an approach, the following scenario describes how these dynamic services can be used in healthcare applications.

A SAMPLE SCENARIO

GENOTYPE/PHENOTYPE CORRELATION

Donald, a patient, consults his family doctor telling him about pain in his chest, shortage of breath, and drowsiness. Besides these symptoms being an indicator for angina pectoris, Donald describes that starting a few hours ago, he additionally suffers from pain in his abdomen and changing paralysis of his right and left leg. Based on this description, the physician wants to ask for a second opinion and admits the patient to a hospital for further examination. The specialist who examines Donald in the hospital recognises some very specific clinical artifacts which raise his interest. Due to these symptoms, Donald has to undergo clinical as well as molecular genetic examinations, since this clinical fingerprint might be caused through a fibrillin-1 gene mutation. To find out more about Donald's potential genetic mutation, his clinical fingerprint is used as an input for a genotype/phenotype correlation. The quality and statement of such a correlation is highly influenced by the amount of data that can be processed. Collaboration among various healthcare institutions, where data is made available by genotype/phenotype correlation services, is therefore of great importance. Luckily, the clinical fingerprint of Donald was indeed listed in the data set of a partnering hospital, connected to the grid and dynamically included in the search, and correlates with the Marfan–Syndrome.

An expensive molecular biological examination in which this genetic defect is confirmed is conducted. Therefore, in addition to the acute vascular operation he has to undergo because of his clinical symptoms, his family can be invited for genetic screening to avoid similar costly, high risk operations in the future. Using the approach described in this work, the correlation service does not only consider the in-house service of a single hospital. Rather, it is a self adaptive, virtual service that dynamically and in parallel calls all available genotype/ phenotype correlation services in the system, thereby jointly accessing the data sources of several healthcare institutions.

As a benefit of the architecture proposed, the client application as well as the genotype/phenotype correlation functionality does not have to be updated or rewritten to participate in or benefit from such a self adaptive environment. Although the example is taken from eHealth digital libraries, the proposed architecture can of course be applied to other domains as well. Whenever it is appropriate to dynamically replace a single invocation of a service by multiple invocations, dynamic adaptation and parallelisation can be highly beneficial. The remainder of this extended abstract is organised as follows. We briefly describe the overall architecture and show the benefits of dynamic parallelisation for the application scenario. Finally, a conclusion and an outlook on future work are given.

OVERALL ARCHITECTURE

The goal of the architecture we propose is to improve the usability of a single service, as well as to facilitate faster and less error prone development for grid environments. This approach is based on the observation that, following the current proliferation of service-oriented architectures, the number of services and service providers in a grid will significantly increase. Especially services which are provider independent and are not bound to special resources can be distributed fast and widely in a grid environment or be deployed numerously on demand. Although the availability of many congruent services as well as the computational resources thereby offered seems to be within reach, adapting functionality for parallel execution is still necessary and tedious.

The task of partitioning request parameters and re-integrating results afterwards is highly application-specific and, from our perspective, cannot be solved in a generic way. Although we see the potential to identify classes of applications according to the mechanism they partition and re-integrate requests which allows to have pre-built splitter and merger services, an expert in the problem domain will be necessary to tailor them for the specific need or perform some additional, application domain specific work. We name a service, enriched with the capability to partition incoming requests and reintegrate partial results, a dynamic service.

Apart from that we introduce a Dynamiser component, which can be built generically and which is responsible for state management, failure handling, and service discovery. While the latter characteristic is independent concerning the twofold approach failure handling and state management differs. In case of a dynamic service aiming to leverage the result quality, the unexpected absence of a 'worker' service already in charge of a partial task does not hinder in producing a result. If partitioning the request of a computationally intensive task to gain better performance, the overall results rely on each sub task and the Dynamiser is responsible for compensating any failing 'worker' service.

The following logical units can be identified for dynamic services. The box in the center of the left side, labeled 'Payload Service', represents the actual service. It is responsible for providing application semantics, *e.g.*, a genotype/ phenotype correlation on a local database. This is usually a piece of business logic that has existed beforehand and is now supposed to be opened to the grid and enabled for parallel execution.

To achieve this goal, it is surrounded by another box, labeled 'Common Interface Wrapper', which encapsulates the 'Payload Service' and enhances it with a common interface.

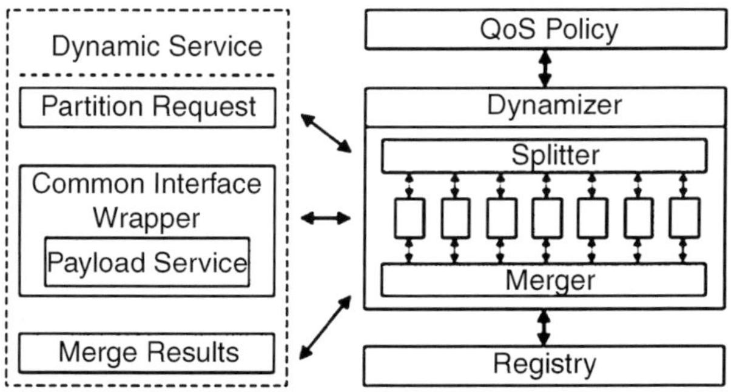

Fig. Overall Architecture

On top, 'Partition Request' encapsulates knowledge on how incoming parameters for the 'Payload Service' have to be partitioned, so that the original request can be decomposed into numerous new sub-requests. Each of these sub-requests can then be distributed on the grid and be processed by other instances of the originally targeted service.

The box at the bottom integrates results returned from the grid to provide the original service requester with a consolidated result. It can therefore be seen as the counter operation to the 'Partition Request' service.

The combination of these elements is referred to as 'Dynamic Service'. To find instances of the originally targeted service, a registry is used. This registry provides information on which services are available, how they can be accessed, and what their properties are. The 'Dynamiser', depicted on the right hand side, makes use of the services. It glues together the previously described services by making the parallel calls and coordinating incoming results. The 'Dynamiser' can interact with all services that adhere to a common interface, as ensured by the 'Common Interface Wrapper'.

It can be integrated in environments able to call and orchestrate services, or it can be packaged and deployed together with specific services. To make the best possible use of the 'Dynamiser', the user can send an optional description of the desired service quality along with the mandatory parameters needed to process the request. In this Quality of Service (QoS) policy, the user can, for example, describe whether the request should be optimised in terms of speed, in terms of bandwidth or if it should aim for best accuracy.

Since these specifications can be contradictory, adding preferences to rank the user's requirements is of importance. To better illustrate the mechanisms within the 'Dynamiser' regarding the user specified QoS policy, we consider the following example: the specialist from the previously introduced healthcare scenario specifies that he wants to use as many genotype/phenotype correlation information as possible and as affordable within a 300 Euro budget. The 'Dynamiser' finds 7 services with a total of 2 gigabytes of searchable data, each charging 60 Euros per query. Alternatively, there are 40 services available provided by smaller institutions, having just searchable amounts of data starting from 4 megabytes up to 30 megabytes and charging.50 per query. The algorithms on how to reconcile the user specifications, the details of the QoS description language and how to integrate this best with our existing implementation is currently investigated.

CONCLUSION

Like building collection and providing services, improving access to information should be the guiding criteria for libraries in the electronic era. Apart from hosting external information, they should also evolve local digitisation ventures to give more visibility to internal information. We have to design a new set of parameters to judge operational efficiency and performance effectiveness of libraries. Traditional libraries boasted that they attracted a lot of users to stay inside their premises for comparatively longer duration whereas a modern librarian will be more concerned about carrying information to users' desktops.

No library, no matter how rich its budget allocation and collection may be, is in a position to satisfy all the information needs of its users. As a person well versed in the intricacies of the emerging information market, the librarian should be frank enough to admit that the information needs of all users are not met by the library alone. Collaboration with other libraries through consortia or networks increases the amount of resources available to users. Most academic and research libraries spend a lot of public money for information needs of a small percentage of the population and optimising that spending for the benefit of more number of users is the need of the hour. Library professionals have a major role in the emerging print plus digital hybrid information environment that is looming large in many academic and research libraries.

This role can be properly identified and refined only through constructive interaction of administrative heads of institutions, library professionals and professional associations. There is no doubt that we are passing through a severe phase and this is the right time to have a close introspective and critical look at collections developed, services offered and professional skills required in the light of complex user needs, hazy use patterns and the ever-increasing spread of Internet, electronic databases and digital libraries.

4

Selection/Evaluation of Online Databases in Library

Whether or not to add online services to the library's collection or services usually is considered or evaluated extensively. Evaluation of online databases may occur at the time of initial selection of a database or service provider, when two or more databases are being compared for subject coverage or search efficiency and, less frequently, as part of a collection or service evaluation. Selection decisions are made by considering many of the same elements which enter into subsequent evaluations. The evaluation of whether or not to add an online service to the library centers around its use for subject searching but libraries also consider the database as additions to the collections. The substitution of online for a print portion of the collection has already been discussed.

STANDARDS FOR CREATING BIBLIOGRAPHIC DATABASES

The concept of "standard" in the field of library and information science is interpreted as codes of cataloguing rules, classification schemes, subject headings and various other documents contained recommendations for good library practice, all of which are subject to varying interpretation. But, for another professionals, standards are extremely precise technical specifications for communication between software and machines in an automated information-processing environment. For example, Operating Systems, TCP/IP etc. Standards are documented agreements containing technical specifications or other precise criteria to be used consistently as rules, guidelines, or definitions of characteristics, to ensure that materials, products, processes and services are fit for their purpose Field of bibliographic standards are not limited to the rules only but spread up to the authority files such as person names, corporate names, subject headings, classification schemes, series names, institution names, software and standardization form and format etc.

In beginning, during the initiation of automation to library professionals, there was not much focus on bibliographic standards and were creating databases in any formats. That affected to the automation of their libraries, which forced them to think over the issue. Now, gradually, the libraries and information centres are realizing the importance of bibliographic standards. Centres like Information and Library Network (INFLIBNET), Ahmedabad is playing important role in bringing all libraries together to work on a single platform of standards with linking under one huge national network *i.e.* UGC-Infonet. INFLIBNET Centre is an Inter-University Centre of University Grants Commission (UGC), working on Academic library system in India. In 1990, UGC launched it as a programme for five years on pilot basis. On June 1996, the programme was recognized as a full-fledged Centre. UGC-Infonet is a project of UGC being implemented by INFLIBNET Centre in collaboration with ERNET (Education and Research Network), New Delhi. It is an Intra-Network of Indian universities and colleges across the country based on the Open IP platform, employing state-of-the-art technologies like IP or TV, enabling online response to queries. The network facilitates Intranet and Internet access to its users on high data rates.

STANDARDS FOR BIBLIOGRAPHIC DATABASE

Well-known simple definition of database is a set of records and record is a set of fields, where, field is a combination of different pieces of information. Bibliographic database is a database of resources available at libraries in print format. With the revolution of information technology in the field of libraries, bibliographic catalogue has come up into the form of bibliographic database. For making compatible with these changes, there, many library institutions have come up with different standards and formats such as CCF, AUSMARC, CANMARC, UKMARC, USMARC, UNIMARC, MARC21, AACR2, ISBD, LCSH, MeSH etc. Some of the Internationally recognized standards and formats being used by many libraries of different countries for creating databases. As per the INFLIBNET's guidelines following standards are recommended for use:

Standardized Bibliographic Formats

During the inception of the Programme, The Task Group on "Union Catalogue, Data Capturing and Standardization" was constituted by UGC. The Task Group was assisted by a Sub-Committee on implementation of Common Communication Format (CCF) for data capturing and data exchange. Later on, the Sub-Committee formalized some fields based on CCF and named it as "Guidelines for Data Capturing: a user manual". During the initial stage of automation, Micro CDS/ISIS software (developed by Unesco) were suggested to use for creating bibliographic databases based on the format recommended by the Centre.

Simultaneously, other DBMS such as DBase, FoxPro, FoxBase etc. were also being used by different libraries for creating the databases. In addition, the Centre had also the library house keeping software called "ILMS – Integrated Library Management System" developed on COBOL language on Unix platform, and was distributed freely to the member libraries of the Centre. Later in February 2000, Centre developed another library house keeping software called "SOUL – Software for University Libraries" on Power Builder language on Windows platform by using the client-server architecture to keep in mind the shortcomings being faced in ILMS software. The software is developed based on the format formalized by Sub-Committee of the Task Force.

Later, early 2001, The Ministry of Human Resource Development (MHRD), Govt. of India visualizes building up a national database of library holdings in the country based on the MARC21 format. Further, after approval the committee directed INFLIBNET Centre to implement the MARC21 format in all libraries of the country. In this regards, the Centre formed the MARC21 Core Group during December 2001, which formalized the fields for implementing it with the SOUL library house keeping software. The main reason for preferring MARC21 over CCF and other formats was that most of the countries in the world use MARC and it is comprehensive having number of fields. Also there is constant development taking place in MARC21 and is updated regularly whereas CCF has become stagnant.

STANDARD FOR RENDERING INFORMATION/ BIBLIOGRAPHIC DESCRIPTIONS

AACR2R, ISBD and CCC are standards for bibliographic descriptions. But, INFLIBNET Centre suggests their participating libraries to follow the Anglo American Cataloging Rules-II (AACRII) Revised version for rendering bibliographic information.

STANDARDIZED SUBJECT HEADINGS

Different subject headings list are available, developed by different institutions such as LCSH, Sear's List of Subject Headings, MeSH, Thesaurus etc. But INFLIBNET suggests to its member library to use LCSH (for generalized subject headings) and Engineering Index, MeSH and thesaurus (for specialized Subject Headings).

STANDARD FOR CLASSIFICATION SCHEMES

There are various classification schemes have been developed by different organizations for classifying the books on different subjects. Functionally, most of the libraries are using the Dewey Decimal Classification (DDC) for assigning the Classification Number to the documents. But, under INFLIBNET umbrella, all the libraries are free to use any classification scheme for classifying the document, as it is very difficult for any library to reclassify the entire collection based on any new scheme. As per the library practice any classification scheme can be used as MARC21 has capability to adopt any kind of classification schemes.

ISO–2709 INFORMATION EXCHANGE FORMAT

This standard specifies the requirements for generalized interchange format that will accommodate data describing all forms of material. It describes a generalized structure designed specifically for exchange of data between processing systems and not necessarily for use as a processing format within systems. The format may be used for the interchange of records using various communication media. INFLIBNET Centre recommends to follow this Exchange Format for contributing records to the Centre. The exchange format has implemented too with the in-house developed software SOUL for exchanging records.

Physical Structure

General Structure of the Record:

Leader

Each record begins with a leader of fixed length of 24 character positions and is the first instance of the ISO 2709 format of a record. It contains:

- Record length (5 characters): The length of the record includes the leader, directory, data fields and record separator.
- Record Status Code (1 character): Always '0' for output files, ignored on input files.
- Implementation Codes (4 characters): These codes are defined for each specific implementation of the ISO 2709 format. Second character position represents Bibliographic level codes (*i.e.* s- serials, m- single volume monographs, c- multivolume monographs, a-component part) and rest of the character positioned not used. Here, Bibliographic level is defined here as per the INFLIBNET's use. For the MARC21 based records, it follows the description defined for bibliographic level in MARC21 bibliographic format.
- Indicator length (1 character): This is always '0', because here at INFLIBNET database indicator is not being used. But the value is '2', when we export records from SOUL to MARC21 in ISO 2709 format.
- Subfield identifier length (1 character): '2' The subfield identifier length. This shows the number of characters being used for the subfield identifier.
- Base address of data (5 characters): A decimal number indicating the number of control characters (length of leader plus directory and field separator) which precede the variable data fields. This number, when added to the starting address of the record, gives the address of the first character of the variable fields.

- For user systems (3 characters): These character positions are not used. Always '000' in output files.
- Length of "Length of Datafield" field (1 character): '4' the length of "Length of Datafield" in the directory. (Use of 4 characters permits datafields as long as 9,999 characters)
- Length of "Starting character" position (1 character): '5' the length is "Starting character position" in the directory.
- Rest (2 characters): These character positions are not used. Always sets on '00'.

Directory

A directory entry in this bibliographic record is made up of a tag, length-of-field, and field starting position. It is of variable length and consists of a series of fixed fields, referred to as "entries". One directory entry is associated with each datafield present in the record. Each directory entry is 12 characters in length and is divided into three parts:

- Tag: A three numeric ASCII character code identifying the datafield, which corresponds to the directory entry. In software, names of the fields are being used in alphabetical name, but during the export in ISO 2709 format and display on screen, it converts in three-numeric digit ASCII character code.
- Length of datafield: A four digit number showing how many characters are occupied by the datafield, including datafield separator but excluding the record separator code if the datafield is the last field in the record.
- Starting character position: A five-digit number giving the position of the first character of the datafield relative to the base address of data, *i.e.* the first character of the first of the datafields.

Datafields

A datafield consists of subfield and datafield separator:

- Subflield: A subfield consists of a subfield identifier followed by a data string, which is terminated by either another subfield identifier or a field separator. A subfield identifier consists of a subfield identifier flag *i.e.* cap (^) sign followed by one another character, that can be alphabet a to z (small or capital) and numeric 1 to 9, INFLIBNET Centre uses here small alphabets. For MARC21 based records "$" graphical sign is used as a subfield identifier.
- Datafield Separator: The datafield separator *i.e.* hash (#) sign constitutes the final character of every datafield. ASCII value 30 (character 1/14 of ISO 646) is being used as a field separator in MARC21 based data.

A datafield, which has a single subfield, will be organised as follows:

Record Terminator/ Separator

The record terminator is the final character of the record *i.e.* hash (#) sign. It follows the field separator of the final datafield of the record. ASCII 29 (character 1/13 of ISO 646) is being used as record separator in MARC21 based data.

OTHER STANDARDS RELATED TO BIBLIOGRAPHIC DATABASE

Z39.50 Retrieval protocol

Z39.50 refers to the International Standard, ISO 23950: "Information Retrieval (Z39.50): Application Service Definition and Protocol Specification", and to ANSI/NISO Z39.50. The standard specifies a client/serverbased protocol for searching and retrieving information from remote databases.

OAI (Open Archive Initiative)

The Open Archive Initiative (OAI) for metadata harvesting is a new protocol dedicated to solving problems of digital library interoperability by defining simple protocols, most recently for the exchange of metadata. Although, Z39.50 Information Retrieval Protocol is also one of the harvesting protocols. Some digital library systems are using for retrieving and searching the records for example Maxwell System. It is crucial to explain, discuss, and disambiguate the concepts and terminology used among OAI implementers to harvesting approach to interoperability. The harvesting protocol defined by the OAI is a request/ response protocol with 6 request types, *viz. Identity, ListMetadataFormats, ListSets, GetRecords ListRecord, and ListIdentifiers.* It has defined in such a way to support a common set of principles and a technical framework to achieve interoperability. Although, both the standards are not being used with the INFLIBNET database right now, but being explored to implement it in near future.

PURPOSE OF THE BIBLIOGRAPHIC STANDARDS

Mostly, purpose of using these standards for creating bibliographic databases or suggesting using it at libraries of India, has following reasons behind it:

- Pursuing Universal Bibliographic Control
- Exchange of information among union databases for the purpose of global resource sharing
- Cooperation at the local level, transferring data from one system to another

IMPORTANCE OF THE BIBLIOGRAPHIC STANDARDS

Following bibliographic standards for creating the databases produces following importance:

- It makes uniformity in records
- It provides better resource sharing between different resource centres
- It helps in exchanging of records and facilitates it without data loss
- It helps in creating national/ International bibliographic union database
- It helps to adopt any system and provides platform interoperability

USE OF BIBLIOGRAPHIC DATABASES IN COLLECTION EVALUATION

There are two areas where online bibliographic databases have played a role in collection evaluation. These are in comparison of collections in coordinated collection development and in evaluation of periodical collections.

Bibliographic Utilities in Coordinated Collection Development

The ALA "Guide to Coordinated and Cooperative Collection Development,, states that these functions presume easy bibliographic access not only to cataloged items, but also to automated order and in-process files when available. Online access is easy, especially when compared to no access, use of many microfiche or book catalogs, or making guesses based on known collection development policies.

It is well known that online catalogs have revolutionised resource sharing. They are used by selectors considering retrospective purchases to determine whether a title of suspected little future use is held by an institution with which one has a cooperative arrangement or from which one can borrow readily. But moving from sharing of existing collections to a coordination of future collecting is a quantum leap. Pat Battin ably expressed the situation when she stated: "When one's resources are not equal to the demand, dependencies replace resources in the sharing equation."

Before resources can be coordinated, existing strengths and collecting policies must be analysed. An essential component of this process, as Reed-Scott states, is agreement on the methodology or methodologies for evaluating their collections. A major product of Research Libraries Group's Cooperative Collection Management Development prog-ramme is its RLG Collection Development Manual, which describes how member libraries should report existing collection strength and current collecting intensity.

Member libraries have completed the conspectus in many subject areas and have accepted collection responsibility for the group in defined subject areas based on analysis of the results. The conspectus results are now online on RLIN. Why online? The information is easier to search this way and there is access by subject words and phrases, institutions, Library of Congress classification number, primary collecting responsibility, and collection level.

The multiple access characteristic and currency of information facilitate its use for comparing and analysing collections. Gwinn and Mosher describe the development of the conspectus and its use in regional and specialised national planning. The conspectus is a powerful collection evaluation tool and Association of Research Libraries has evaluated the adoption of the RLG Conspectus On-Line for use by a larger, less cohesive group of research libraries.

The Association of Research Libraries has recommended that it be adopted with modifications to enable national cooperation in collection development to become an ongoing reality. If this happens, collection evaluation results will be online on a grand scale. Although collection strengths cannot be compared online, OCLC participants can conduct analyses of their tapes between any two or more institutions. Interpretation of the results of overlap studies is not clear-cut and they do not seem to have been widely applied in coordinated collection development.

Serials Evaluation

In 1978 Barbara Rice surveyed the use of bibliographic databases in collection development activities and found that they were being used in the selection process for verification, but little was being made of them in collection evaluation. While that paper was being written, BRS and DIALOG both announced the availability of a collection development service which lists the total number of times journals are cited in the subscriber's searches for a six-month or one-year period. Lancaster/however, echoes Line's criticism of the use of citation counts to evaluate periodical holdings, and states that, "no measure of journal use other than one derived from a local-use study is of any significant, practical value to libraries."

On the other hand, use studies are viewed with considerable suspicion by many and the controversy has by no means been resolved.

Recently, ALA published its "Guide to Collection Evaluation through Use and User Studies," and citation studies are listed as one possible type of user study. The guidelines conclude with a warning that no technique alone is sufficient for evaluation and that anyone type has distinct advantages and disadvantages.

All use studies are cumbersome; and online citation methods, especially the collection development services, offer a quick way to compile a list of titles which patrons may well have requested from the library.

Since, Bourne and Robinson's early article describing the use of references from online selective-dissemination services to test document delivery, there have been a number of articles describing the use of citation counts from online bibliographic databases to identify titles for addition to the collection and for collection evaluation.

Hafner, Rice/Seba and Forest, Danilowicz and Szarski, and Trubkin all used lists which they generated from retrospective search or selective dissemination services. Garfield maintains the validity of this technique and has used it to produce his *Journal Citation Reports* for both *Science Citation Index* and *Social Sciences Citation Index.*

Sprules pointed out that the technique may be valid for a special, discipline-oriented library, but that it did not work for a large multidisciplinary collection. Part of the problem with all use studies is that each type measures a different use, and opponents and proponents are at odds because we really have not defined what 'use' is.

When Rice compared lists of chemistry titles generated by BRS's collection development service with those generated by *Journal Citation Reports,* an in-house use study, faculty choice, and the "List of 1000 Journals Most Frequently Cited in Chemical Abstracts," she concluded that no list can match the unique purposes of anyone collection. The BRS collection development service seemed most useful for identifying titles which should be added to the collection. However, the BRS and DIALOG services were not popular and are no longer available. Collection development staff and serials librarians obviously did not regard them as valid selection tools.

VENDOR SELECTION

Many directories, abstract/index services, and business or financial files are made available through three major vendors, BRS, DIALOG and SDC. A library may select one or more of these services, and, in so doing, it must acquire hundreds of supporting reference tools. In fact, in selecting a vendor package, many files are often added to the collections which would not have been if considered on a file-far-file basis. In addition, specific 'files are available from government agencies or professional organisations. The primary consideration in most selection or evaluation decisions is subject. For a monograph or serial the selector asks whether the title is in a subject collected by the library, and the type of treatment of that subject-*i.e.,* basic or research.

The selector of a database vendor has a more complex problem, because, as Nichol points out, each vendor has some unique and some duplicate databases. However, an overriding concern is still how well the blend of databases offered match the library's collection development policy. Williams, Nichol, Lancaster, and Stern summarise the other evaluative criteria used. Cost and means of searching are the primary considerations.

This results in the following questions being applied to the potential vendor's products:

- How simple or complex is the system to use?
  - How much training is needed?
  - Is training readily available?
  - Can users search themselves or must librarians perform the searches?
- What are the comparative costs for:

  - Online time?
  - Communications?
  - Printing?
  - Royalties?
- What restrictions on access exist?
  - Must the library subscribe to some print equivalents?
  - Can it charge for the products?
  - Is use restricted to searches from one portion of the searchers' organisation only?
- How does treatment of important individual databases compare?

These same criteria apply no matter whether one is considering choice of vendors, if broad coverage is to be obtained, or whether or not to obtain a given database direct from a producer when only one or two subjects are being considered. No one consideration dominates and different libraries make different choices based on their clients' subject needs, library staff skills and interest, budget and organisational structure. The criteria for comparing treatment of a subject area or the same database by different vendors follows.

Selection/Evaluation of Individual Databases

There is ample literature which can help make the choice between individual databases. Most of this has been written from the point of view of the searcher, who is evaluating how well similar databases meet specific user needs. These reports can also be valuable in vendor selection when specific subject areas are more important than others, or when a decision of whether to obtain coverage from a vendor or direct from the producer is being made.

First, there are the directories which were listed earlier in the section on 'Bibliographic Databases.' These titles typically give subject coverage, date coverage, frequency of updating, availability of tapes, producer, and vendor. Next, there are review articles in the trade literature such as *RQ, Database, Online,* and *Online Review.* And, finally, many journal articles have appeared comparing specific databases or subject coverage by two or more databases, or vendor coverage of the same database.

The following list is by no means comprehensive, but is indicative of the scope of published evaluations. Notes are added where the scope is not clear from the title. Methods of evaluation in these articles varied. The 'Georefi Geoarchive' article evaluated recall and precision for twelve subject searches and also compared timeliness and document type coverage.

The 'ERIC and LISA,, article compared precision and recall also. The authors, who were comparing results with known items from manual searches, were surprised at the low recall percentages for the online searches. The 'IRL/BIOSIS' article compared journal coverage overlap, indexing practices and currency, but not recall and precision. Those articles which covered one or more databases in a subject area used the following evaluative criteria: subject coverage, file size, document type, date coverage, quality, and depth of indexing, proportion of unique results obtained, proportion overlap, currency, and cost for different vendors.

Donati used a different approach in the decision analysis article, selecting business databases in relation to crucial questions. The first decision point is whether or not information on a principle, practice or problem is involved, or whether information about a specific product or industry is needed. Further, key questions within each category are then analysed in relation to ABI, F & S Index, PROMPT, and other business databases.

It is apparent from reading these articles that there is no standard set of evaluative criteria which have been developed for evaluation of bibliographic databases. They, like the spelling of the words *database* and *online,* vary. What weight is given to each factor? How does a library reach a decision as to which vendor to select or which databases to search when the problem is so complex? Evaluation of specific systems overlaps with comparison of individual databases within each system. The decision process itself is not reported in the literature.

Finding out what happens in practice would involve analysis of how libraries who have recently decided to provide online search services made the following decisions:

- Should we provide online services?
- Which databases should be provided?
- From whom should we obtain the database(s)? The criteria for vendor selection would then apply.

In actuality these decisions may not proceed in the order and each one may be made by a different group within the library's administrative structure. Some libraries select a vendor with primary consideration being given to subject coverage or comparison treatment of individual databases, whereas in other libraries considerations of cost and staffing impact may prevail.

Is there a preponderance of anyone consideration over another? What factors cause different libraries to weight criteria differently? Factors which are certainly important are what group(s) is making the decision, where the money will be coming from, what library unit will be administratively responsible for service, prior experience of staff with databases, and the uses which will be made of the system.

Articles in the premier issue of the journal *Science* and *Technology Librariei* featured articles on planning to initiate online search services and described the issues which the authors' institutions addressed in the planning process. The articles did not, however, describe how the different factors were weighed in the decision process. At this point, it should be emphasised again that for the most part these decisions are not made as collection development decisions but primarily as service decisions.

Further, declines in library budgets may force libraries to evaluate whether such service should be continued, just as we now evaluate whether to cut monographs or serials, and, if serials—which ones. Databases have been treated as separate entities and are usually budgeted separately, but with their introduction to the collections, some libraries may come to evaluate them in relation to the acquisitions budget and the resource sharing budget.

At present, though, few libraries would probably extend the concept as far as did *Online Libraries and Microcomputers* when it suggested that: "With the proliferation of full-text databases and information sources which are only available online, it makes a great deal of common sense to fund equipment from the acquisitions budget." In this case the equipment being referred to are the computer terminals, modems and printers required to use online tools.

It would not be very different from the situation where a microform dealer offers a reader or reader-printer with large microform purchases. The money in this situation doubtless comes from the acquisitions rather than the equipment budget.

At present, database acquisition and maintenance are not usually part of an acquisitions budget, although purchase of print reference tools is. Fees for bibliographic utility use primarily come from the cataloging budget, although the utility may be used for resource sharing. In reality, many libraries have budgets with rigid categories of salary, acquisitions and supplies/equipment. Practically, it is difficult to shift the budget line from which something is taken once precedent has been established.

BENEFITS OF WEB-ENABLED DATABASES

Web-enabled databases have certain advantages over other means of sharing/publishing information over internet. These advantages are common to bibliographic databases also where libraries can put their OPACs and other databases on web. According to L.J.Haravu; Kristin Aantelman and; Chong Ho Yu , the benefits of web-enabled databases are as follows:

- Global/wide ac cess to data with a sin gle user in ter face
- Format in dependent ac cess of data (text, graph ics, au dio, video, etc.)
- Up-to-minute up dated ac cess of data in real time
- Dynamic updation of data from many locations
- Cost-effective way of data sharing
- Instant feedback from users
- Seamless links from resource to resource
- Unlimited download/printing
- Environmental friendly.

Besides, Ortiz-Repiso and Norm Medeiros have written excellent papers on differences between traditional v/s innovative means (web OPACs) of library catalogs, while B. Ramesh Babu, *et al* have presented an overview of web OPACS with their advantages in libraries.

DATABASE TOOLS

In the early days of database development, it was the flat-file system to store data in a single file by using field separators and record separators. Later, such flat-file systems were facilitated by an index in which a single index file stored keywords and pointers to the records that were stored in main file. This made retrieval more efficient, still flat-file systems were seriously inefficient. It showed data-redundancy, poor data control, and did not supported complex data types (audio, video, graphics, etc.). After 1960s, two database models were developed in quick succession to solve the limitations of flat-file systems. These database models were Hierarchical Database Model and Network Database Model. The Hierarchical Database composes of a root segment, parent segments and child segments. This model depicts a set of one-to-many relationships between a parent and its children. However, this model has number of limitations. It does not include ad hoc querying capability and, a multi-parent relationship is difficult to implement, as in a many-to-many relationship.

The Network Database Model attempted to deal with many of the hierarchical model's limitations. The network database structure easily accommodates the multiple child, although, its structural complexities often limit its effectiveness and efficiency. Both of these database models are obsolete now mainly because of their incompatibility with web environment and have been replaced by RDBMS. RDBMS is the current database implementation standard being used for publishing information on the web. It includes the following features which make it suitable for web environment:

- Provide extremely useful tools for database administration;
- Adhere to powerful query language SQL (structured query language) developed by Microsoft Corporation;
- Compliant with ODBC/JDBC and other database interface tools;
- Work in client/server mode;
- Offer distributed database and distributed processing options; and
- Have referential integrity controls to ensure data consistency and, thus, suitable for web environment.

It is easier to design applications in RDBMS due to the following features:

- Requires less programming skill
- Availability of third party tools, and
- Inbuilt web interface.

These all features of RDBMS have made them ideal for library applications to setup bibliographic database solutions and publishing them over the web. In the early days of library systems development, vendors have designed library applications software by using pre-relational database technology. Still some library systems suppliers are continuing to maintain and develop such products.

These proprietary library applications software have their own advantages and disadvantages. However, in the library management systems marketplace, there is a growing trend towards the use of RDBMS. Some of the common RDBMS which can be used to design in-house databases in libraries are *MS Access, SQL Server, Oracle, Informix, Sybase, File Maker Pro, SAS,* etc. However, the selection of suitable RDBMS for library applications depends on the particular library requirements, kind of applications (bibliographic/full-text/ numeric), the application level (database level/data warehouse level), magnitude of data (number of records/length of fields), nature of data analysis (basic statistics, *i.e.*, sum, average, mean/advance statistics) and, comprehensiveness and inter-operability.

Other points to be considered while selecting database tools for library applications are easiness, user-friendliness, flexibility and low cost. In most of the cases in libraries where bibliographic databases are dealt with, commonly available consumer database products such as *MS Access*, and *File Maker Pro* are sufficient. These products can support up to 1GB of data and provide cheaper solutions. However, these database tools are suitable for small databases and not useful for large databases, hence provide limitations in web environment.

There are specific database solutions for large databases available from *MS SQL Server, DB2, Oracle, Informix, Sybase,* etc. These database tools support up to several terra byte of data; permit thousands of simultaneous users; work in client/server mode; show natural affinity towards web environment and, thus, suitable for large bibliographic, web-enabled databases in libraries. However, to design full-text databases in libraries where large files are to be stored and retrieved, these tools do not offer good solutions as most of these tools support 200-255-400 characters field length. Although, many of these tools allow unlimited entries in memo field, the data inside a memo field are not searchable and thus, offer limited utility.

In this respect, *MS SQL Server* has extended the searchable field length up to 8063 characters and thus, provide solutions for moderate full-text databases. As a common trend, a number of libraries have been using open source software available either free or on nominal prices. These database management systems include the most common *mySQL, mSQL* and, recently updated *PostgreSQL*. These database tools are easy to work and run on various platforms such as UNIX, Lynux, NT, etc. Besides, there are some library specific text retrieval database tools for management of full-text large files, generally known as ‘Free Form Databases’, provide powerful search engine. Although, in some ways they are at the opposite end of the RDBMS, little database structure imposed on the designer and, thus, provide an easy and readymade database structure.

However, they provide some limitations in achieving integration in the modules other than searching such as cataloguing, classification, management module, etc. These software are *BRS/Search, Basis Plus, Status,* etc.

WEB TECHNOLOGY

World Wide Web or WWW or web, sometimes wrongly mentioned as synonymous to internet, is a sub-set of it and is a most promising mode of publishing/sharing of data/information. Now, the web has emerged as the dominant protocol over internet due to its special features like easy interfacing of diverse platforms/technologies; provision to incorporate text, graphics, audio and video, etc.; permitting to access data/information in a non-linear way and; jumping from one document/resource to another through hyperlinks.

The superiority of www over other modes of online sharing *viz.* e-mail, FTP, Telnet, Gopher, etc., has been well explained by Paul Scully. In fact, web has provided a single user interface to facilitate the user interaction with the databases or systems resources. The web uses unique URL (universal resource locator) address which facilitates the access of information seamlessly across the diverse platforms in a client-server mode. The actual data represented in a structured way reside in a powerful computers called server, while the latter is equipped with server tools/software to populate the information over web.

The client/user equipped with web browser such as Microsoft Internet Explorer (MSIE) and Netscape Navigator, etc., which interact with the server through common communications protocol TCP/IP over high speed network/ internet. In fact, the client/user sends its query to the server while the latter processes the request and gets the response/results from the database and sends it back to the client/user over the web.

COMPONENTS OF WEB-BASED SYSTEMS

Web Browser

It is a software that helps users to interact with the server for sending queries and getting results over the web. MSIE and Netscape are the most popular web browsers, both of these are available free.

Web Server

Web server is the software that helps in sharing the system resources/ files over the internet through web browsers. The latter communicate with a web server via the standard Hyper-Text Transfer Protocol (HTTP). In fact, web servers receive queries from the client, process it, get data from databases and send it back to the client over web. The popular web servers are Apache, Microsoft IIS, iPlanet from Sun-Netscape alliance, and newly developed *Zeus* from Zeus Technology Ltd. Although web servers are increasingly found as components within full-featured server operating systems, there are some basic selection points that should be highlighted. These points are scalability and performance; high availability and reliability; interoperability and open standards; system administration and; security. In fact, there are not much choice in the web server segments as many of them come along with database tools, show natural affinity with the database tools from same vendor, and some other work better with certain platform/operating systems. According to the widely followed Netcraft web survey, approximately 60 per cent of web servers run Apache, with Microsoft's IIS and the Netscape/iPlanet web server as its major competitors. However, Gartner studies have given Netscape/iPlanet a larger share of public web sites, followed by Apache and Microsoft/IIS. Apache is being used for the public sites of companies such as Merck, American Express, Texaco, Chrysler, and others.

However, it is easier to find both Microsoft/IIS and Netscape/iPlanet as the servers for large corporate public web sites when using the lookup facility offered by Netcraft. Also, for intranets, most counts credit Microsoft/IIS and Netscape/iPlanet as the leaders, followed by Apache, IBM's Lotus Domino Go server, and others. Among hot e-commerce sites, E*Trade runs the Netscape/iPlanet server, eBay runs Windows/IIS, and Amazon runs Apache (the Apache-based Stronghold Secure Server), according to the Netcraft web survey .

WEB AUTHORING TOOLS

Basic web server software does nothing except it sends HTML data in response to a browser request. However, certain other web-authoring and scripting tools are required to extend the functionality of web server to extract the data from databases. These web-authoring tools (*HTML* and its derivatives; and other Markup languages, etc.) and scripting tools (*Perl, C++, Java Script, JScript, VBScript,* etc.) are required to write web pages and scripts to interact with back-end databases. In early days of web-based applications, *CGI* (common gateway interface) programmes were used extensively to extend the server functionality by allowing web users to interact with the web server to request specific data from the databases. Although, writing *CGI* programme is difficult and requires programming skill, however, it works with high reliability.

Now a days, a number visual editors are available to generate the web pages and write scripts automatically. The common editors are *Microsoft Front Page, Visual Interdev, Netscape Composer, Web Builder,* etc. Besides, other technologies have been introduced to communicate with the back-end databases. These technologies are Microsoft *Active Server Pages (ASP*) and *Java Server Pages (JSP)* from Sun Micro Systems. Both the technologies have combined the HTML codes with the scripts in a single page and thus, making it easier to interact with back-end databases. During last few years, object-oriented and component based solutions were added to further make it easier to interact with the back-end databases. These solutions include:

- Microsoft COM/DCOM,
- ActiveX Data Objects (ADO);
- OMA and CORBA (Common Objects Request Broker Architecture) from Object Management Group;

- Sun's EJB (Enterprise Java Beans),
- Java Applets (for client) and
- Java Servlets (for server), etc.

Besides, some database connectivity tools such as ODBC and JDBC have also emerged as in-built features of operating systems, etc.

FREE WIZARDS AND THIRD PARTY TOOLS

Writing HTML codes and scripts for database interaction is the most difficult part, requires programming skill, systems logic and manipulation planning, especially for non-computer professionals. However, a number of free wizards and third party tools are available on internet which can generate hundred of lines of codes automatically with a single click, thus, making it easier for non-skilled users to set up web-enabled database solutions in libraries. Some of the free wizards are Rule Zero, Power ASP, Active Server Pages Tools and Components, etc. Besides, *Microsoft FrontPage* also provides database wizard to generate *ASP* pages/*VBScripts* automatically to interact with back-end databases, while *Visual InterDev* provides a visual interface to develop a web-enabled web site with minimum efforts.

FULL-TEXT DATABASES

Bibliographic databases were initially described as falling into three major types: bibliographic utilities, online equivalents of print abstract-index services and full-text databases. Full-text databases have been on the scene since, 1977, and in the last two years access to them has begun to change dramatically. The major and obvious difference between full-text and other bibliographic databases is that the full document is available for search and for retrieval. Let's first consider the effect on search strategy.

In the other bibliographic databases, documents are described by information extracted from the document and information added by a cataloger or indexer such as subject headings, index terms or an abstract.

The searcher retrieves a reference to the document by searching any combination of the extracted information. In full-text searching, a user can search any term in the document in natural language. There is no need to translate hi s query into controlled vocabulary terms, which usually forces a more general search. On the other hand, the user must know all possible synonyms or ways of expressing the subject for which he searches and must deal with more false drops resulting from the fact that most terms have more than one meaning or context in which they may occur.

Perez summarises the advantages and disadvantages of controlled vocabulary and free text searching in newspapers and other general publications. Newspapers are examples of a type of publication which are available in two different ways online-either as files which are the equivalent of abstract/index files or in full text. *The New York Times* is an example of this. New York Times Information Bank (NYTIB) became available online in 1973.

It consisted of bibliographic citations and abstracts for *The New York Times* and other major newspapers. Searching was by descriptor terms, and, in this form it found quick acceptance in libraries within traditional reference—much more quickly than the other bibliographic databases. In 1975, just two years after the first commercially available NYTIB installation began operating, Bachelder reported that 50 per cent of NYTIB terminals in public, college or university libraries were at the reference desk.

Why libraries were so quick to place this database in the reference collection is not clear to this writer, although Bachelder maintains that the reason is "obvious: the Information Bank is an excellent reference tool.,, The problems associated with making effective use of the NYTIB in reference were ably described by Rieche.

In 1980, search capability was enhanced by providing free-text access to the abstracts, and in July 1981 the *New York Times Online* was introduced, offering full-text access to the paper from 1 June 1980. In April 1983 *The New York Times* stopped offering the NYTIB, but made it available through Mead Data Corporation. Mead incorporated the Information Bank and the *New York Times Online* into its NEXIS service which, since, 1979, had offered the *Washington Post,* AP, UPI, and PR wire services online in full text. Other full-text systems for online newspaper searching are INFOGLOBE and VU/TEXT. In addition, many newspapers are available in the index form or index plus free-text searching of summaries. All of these are thoroughly described by Nina Ross. Stephen Smith reviewed the changes which had occurred in online news retrieval in 1983.

Many of the newspaper files exist in combination with other files which contain information that users need on a very timely basis, primarily business, financial or legal information. Mead Data Corporation, which produces NEXIS, is also the producer of LEXIS, one of the major full-text legal databases which are commercially available.

The other, WESTLA W, is a product of West Publishing Company. The two have been competing for users of Computer Assisted Legal Research Systems (CALR) since, their introduction in the early 1970s. Larson and Williams review the literature on the evaluation of LEXIS, WESTLA W, and the other CALR systems, JURIS, AUTO-CITE and FLITE. They identify the following interrelated evaluation criteria: time saved, cost effectiveness, efficiency, quality of results, manual *v.* computer effectiveness, user friendliness and operation by end-users compared to trained specialists.

The new evaluative criterion appearing here-not found in those listed when evaluating vendors of bibliographic databases or comparing databases-is end-user searching compared to trained specialist operation.

The legal systems were developed by or in close cooperation with lawyers and bar associations to search the text of cases or to trace the history of cases and certain compilations of law, such as the *United States Code.* Their first widespread use was in law schools, during the time period 1977-80 as reported by Neth, Mersky and Christensen, and Munro *et al.* Neth reports that the terminal at Case Western was installed in the law school and used by students and faculty members. Mersky and Christensen, describing experience in Texas law schools, imply that the terminals are in libraries when they show that acquisition of LEXIS or WESTLA W depends on the size of the library budget; and they confirm this by reporting that, in most instances, training is coordinated through the law school library or in others by a full-time member of the teaching faculty. In any event, the persons being trained are students, and one would predict that CALR should soon be in great use in law firms.

Myers in 1978 surveyed the impact of LEXIS on large law libraries. Of the respondents, 86 per cent had a terminal, and for most subscribers the terminal was in the library or an adjacent office. Many of the librarians had had LEXIS training. However, most of them were not doing many searches, the majority reporting zero to four per week. Unfortunately, the number of searches done by lawyers was not reported. More recent studies could not be found, but, on the basis of that report, it is safe to say that legal databases do not yet seem to have become as much a part of law library collections as have bibliographic databases.

Will this continue in the future? In 1980, Greguras *et al.* described the changing information needs of the legal profession. Probably in response to expanded needs for information beyond the purely legal, Mead and West are now brokering access to DIALOG, BRS, SDC, Legi-Tech and a wide variety of specialised databases to LEXIS and WESTLA W subscribers. Will lawyers learn the idiosyncracies of DIALOG, BRS or SDC databases, or, needing assistance with these, will the lawyers see that librarians are competent searchers and leave the searching of bibliographic as well as full-text legal databases to librarians? Although there is little evidence that full-text legal databases have found their way into library collections, other databases have.

Just as the bibliographic and full-text legal databases came of age in the 1970s, the 'News and Trends' section of *Online Libraries and* M *icrocomputers* predicted that the 1980s may be the age of the online full-text books, periodicals, directories, texts and encyclopaedias. Perusal of the BRS and DIALOG database catalogs shows a variety of full-text files.

Notes are added to the following titles if the database is not the online equivalent of the same print title:

- American Chemical Society Primary Journal Database (BRS). Full text of 18 primary ACS journals.
- Kirk-Othmer Encyclopaedia of Chemical Technology (BRS).

- American Men and Women of Science (BRS, DIALOG).
- Mental Measurements Yearbook (BRS).
- CHEMLA W (DIALOG). Full text of U.S. Federal regulations, as published in the *U.S. Code* and updated in the *Federal Register,* for manufacture, use, storage, transportation, and disposal of chemical substances.
- CHRONOLOG NEWSLETTER (DIALOG).
- Critical Care Medicine Library (BRS). Full text of twenty-five prominent medical textbooks in emergency and critical care medicine.

At present, use is expensive, but future development of optical disk technology may change this. The age of the electronic journal, predicted for some years is still not with us, although it is certainly closer. More and more full-text databases are available. An advertisement in the April 1984 *American Libraries* announced that full text of many of the articles in *Magazine Index* and *Trade and Industry Index* would soon be available online. As more directories and journals become available online, libraries will be questioning whether or not to subscribe to one or both and the print *v.* online migration may become more extensive than earlier reported. But in this case the choice is not print or online for a secondary service such as an abstract/index tool, but print or online for the full entity, *i.e., American Men and Women of Science,* or *The New York Times,* or a court opinion. Access is usually faster and greater, but costs are higher.

NUMERIC DATABASES

A numeric database is a computer-readable collection of data which are predominantly numeric in nature: Numeric databases were developed before bibliographic databases and have been described by Luedke, *et al.* Initially access to these data was through the information analysis centers, professional organisations, or government bodies that produced them. More recently, the development of software packages for access and further analysis have made feasible the use of numeric databases by other than the producers.

Fried *et al.* describe an online numeric database as a system-a combination of numeric database and search system which retrieves data and presents it online to the user. Fried was the first in what was to be a series of online columns on numeric databases. Only two such columns appeared. Economic and financial data are the most accessible commercially. This is probably because there is a fairly large audience for this type of information and thus commercial vendors have a market for it.

Major vendors are Data Resources Inc., Wharton Econometric Forecasting Associates, Chase Econometric Associates, and A.P. Sharp, Inc. Information is available either online through a time-sharing system or via direct access to the producer's computers. Although some special libraries doubtless access these systems, there is little use reported.

A 1977 survey by Wisdom and Houghton in Great Britain showed that the files were being used primarily by financial analysts, economists or managers. Only a handful of librarians were using data files other than Predicasts. In 1976, Predicasts and Lockheed began the first combined online bibliographic and numeric data retrieval and analysis system, Predicasts Terminal System (PTS). In addition to the Predicasts literature, the system gave access to economic, social and industrial numeric data. It was this venture that doubtless introduced many libraries to numeric databases for the first time.

A 1983 DIALOG catalog listed twelve numeric databases, all in the area of business and economics. The first listing of online non-bibliographic databases in *Online Review* in 1977 contained 127 entries, and in six months that number had increased to 246. Online non bibliographic databases do not seem to have found their way into libraries to any large extent, with the exception of those available through DIALOG. The major reporting of library use or involvement is in the area of social science data, involving tapes, rather than online use. The Winter 1982 issue of *Library Trends* was titled "Data Libraries for the Social Sciences.,, Rowe described the need for incorporation of knowledge about machine-readable data files (MRDF) into the reference process but stated that MRDF are normally housed at data libraries in academic departments, research institutes or computer centres.

She went on to say that a few libraries have incorporated MRDF into their collections and a few others have acquired codebooks or documentation, but not the tapes. Most libraries, she continued, have done nothing. Those libraries which have are described elsewhere in the *Library Trends* issue and by Ferguson in a *Drexel Library Quarterly* issue devoted to "Machine-Readable Social Science Data.', Jones described complete integration into collection and services and Ruus described a data library operated jointly by the library and computing centre. The difficulties attendant in housing the tapes and documentation separately from the computer may be overcome if these files become available online. The Summer-Fall 1982 issue of the *Drexel Library Quarterly* was devoted to numeric databases.

Bartkus described the use of scientific numeric databases in reference and information services at duPont. There, scientific numeric databases have been selected and used by either the engineering or information services department, whereas access to commercial and business databases has been coordinated through the information services department. Bartkus predicted that numeric databases will tend to be searched by the individual, rather than an intermediary, because other databases will be available to the individual to manipulate the data extracted, and because the individual uses it directly in his work.

Access to the databases has been centered in the organisation of the searcher-user, rather than the library. Bartkus went on to outline several possible roles for the library in the acquisition and use of numeric databases; a clearinghouse coordination or specialist services function. Wherever they are selected and evaluated, the criteria described by Ewbank may be applied.

The evaluation process for numeric databases has multiple steps, as does selection of a bibliographic database, since, both the database and the system used to access it must be evaluated. The evaluation revolves primarily around the content of the database, the system used to access it, and factors relating to management of the database.

Factors to consider relating to content evaluation are scope completeness, source coverage, the process by which data are selected and evaluated, redundancy, references, consistency amongst units measured. Factors to consider in relation to database management relate to production and maintenance of the file. Is there adequate technical and institutional support? periodic update and revision? adequate documentation? A key element of evaluation which must be performed in the case of numeric data is that of the access system.

As Wisdom and Houghton point out the searcher of a bibliographic database is looking to see whether or not information on a subject exists, whereas the searcher of the numeric database knows what is available and searches to find it. He/she needs a good access system and ways to extract and further manipulate the data.

Ewbank recommends evaluation of system documentation, indexing system, availability, report formats, and protection from user changes. Although his criteria were developed primarily for scientific data, Autrey applies identical criteria for social science numeric databases and then goes on to raise several issues specific to social science files, namely, user training, privacy and confidentiality of computer records of organisations' internal data and those from personal questionnaires and interviews.

Scientists are usually conversant with computers and have used them in their work for a generation now, whereas social scientists have only come to use them more recently. More training or more user friendly systems are presently necessary in order for social scientists to use numeric databases online. In a 1983 review of 'Online Searching in the Reference Room' Bonta specified three different areas of expertise involved in searching online databases: knowledge of the database being searched, knowledge of the search system, and knowledge of the subject itself. Greater knowledge of the subject matter has been suggested to be more crucial for searching numeric databases, and perhaps for that reason they have not found their way into libraries.

However, even in those institutions where persons with advanced degrees are employed as searchers, the user's need to incorporate the information obtained directly into a work product or to manipulate the data further make intermediary searching a hindrance rather than a help. Rumble has summarised the basic reasons why only a fraction of the existing numeric databases in science are actually available online. These are the high cost of data entry, difficulties in database building, lack of obvious economic benefits, a small number of well-articulated demands, and lack of encouragement from major online vendors.

END-USER SEARCHING

Just as end users search numeric and full-text databases, especially legal and newspaper files, the time for end users to search bibliographic databases may have arrived. BRS introduced its AFTER DARK service in January 1983 and DIALOG its KNOWLEDGE INDEX service in November 1982. Special evening rates and simplified search strategies are offered to encourage individual users, many of whom have all that is necessary to access these files.

A search software package using one language to search the different major vendors-SCI-MATE-has also recently been developed in combination with a data management package by Institute for Scientific Information. In February of 1984, Menlo Corporation announced a software package for use with DIALOG databases which is menu driven and guides users through searches and database selection. The software is available with several microcomputers. Other end-user software packages are available. Will patrons prefer to do the searches themselves or will they still turn to librarians as intermediaries?

The conditions seem similar to those which have caused users of numeric databases to do the searches themselves, *i.e.,* knowledge of subject content, an easy access system and a tool for further manipulation of the information. Some libraries have already subscribed to BRS AFTER DARK for patron use.

KNOWLEDGE INDEX offers document delivery in connection with the service, an attractive feature for the user who would like to avoid the frustrations of dealing with a library and would prefer to have the document delivered to his home or office.

On the full-text systems, of course, the document can be printed online, in some cases in advance of when the information is available in print. Some independent dealers are beginning to offer selective database coverage, either through one of the major vendors or independently.

For example, EXEC INFO service offers a combination of full text-*Harvard Business Review* and *Academic American Encyclopaedia-and* bibliographic abstract-index-Management Contents and ABII Inform-through BRS for a flat monthly rate. VU/TEXT offers a wide package including full-text news-papers, the Pennsylvania Legislative Database, PTS Prompt, ABI/Inform, and current stock market quotes.

These developments are summarised by Smith. Although Stabler argued at the 1984 National Online Meeting that librarians will continue as intermediaries for the bibliographic databases, her arguments are based on 1983 technology where only a limited number of files are available through the simplified search routines of BRS/AFTER DARK or KNOWLEDGE INDEX systems and the fact that, since, the access system has been simplified to encourage end users, search results are not as comprehensive or specific as those performed by librarians. This could change, depending on the success of these new services, users' direct access to more full-text files, and development of simplified search software.

INTEGRATING XML DATA SOURCES USING RDF/S SCHEMAS

Digital libraries are collections of resource descriptions that actually describe the catalogue data. In general, these metadata are stored in diverse sources distributed on the Web. One of the main challenges for the digital library community is the integration of such metadata sources in order to provide users with a common vocabulary for searching and browsing them. The Semantic Web offers relevant approaches and standards that can handle these problems.

More precisely, RDF can be used as a common framework for expressing the information by providing a semantically rich representation language for metadata. In this context, a SW integration middleware should be employed for the integration of the heterogeneous and distributed sources. In particular, we propose a SWIM that provides a useful, comprehensive and high-level access to library metadata that reside in relational databases (RDB) or XML sources, by offering a virtual, mediated RDF/S schema. There are many issues involved in the functionality of a SWIM. In particular, a SWIM should facilitate users to formulate queries against the mediated RDF/S schema using declarative languages, as well as, support further abstraction levels using declarative view definition languages. In a nutshell, SWIM should offer the following services:

- Establish mapping rules between XML and RDF and between RDB and RDF,
- Verify the conformance of these mappings w.r.t the semantics of the employed schemas,
- Reformulate RDF/S queries against RDB or XML sources, and
- Combine these queries with RVL views.

In order to address effectively and efficiently the requirements, we should choose a uniform and expressive logic framework to define SWIM integration services. This framework should exploit background theory on conjunctive queries and query containment and minimisation.

An architecture based on mediators is highly beneficial for deploying a SWIM. There exist two main approaches for integrating data sources using mediator- based architectures: Global-as-View (GAV) and Local-as-View (LAV). The former provides descriptions of the global schema in terms of the views of local sources and relies on simple query reformulation techniques. The latter considers local sources as materialised views specified in terms of the global schema.

LAV supports easily the evolution of the data integration system by just adding or removing the descriptions of local sources. In our work we advocate a hybrid approach called GLAV, which combines the previous advantages and exceeds the expressive power of both GAV and LAV.

A MOTIVATING EXAMPLE

Let's assume an XML source whose content is described by a DTD or an XML Schema. XML data from this source contain information about Museums, exhibiting some artifacts for which we want to know their creator. Data stored in such sources can be queried using an XML query language like XPath, or XQuery. Now suppose that we add on top of this repository an RDF/S schema from the cultural domain.

This mediated RDF/S schema can be queried using RQL and it can be used for defining personalised views with the help of RVL. However, since there are no actual RDF data, we need to reformulate the RQL queries expressed against this virtual RDF/S schema into queries appropriate for our XML source. For example, the following RQL query:

```
SELECT X
FROM {X}exhibits{Y}, {Y}denom{Z}
WHERE Z = "Louvre"

will be reformulated to the following XQuery query:
```

Fig. Republishing XML as RDF

This reformulation involves several challenging issues. First of all, the schemas employed by our XML sources and the RDF/S mediator are different. Their discrepancies, usually called heterogeneity conflicts, can be classified under three axes: syntactic, structural and semantic. As we can see in our example, we need to view the XML data through the RDF data model, to resolve categorisation conflicts, given that in RDF/S there is a class hierarchy while in XML there isn't, as well as address naming mismatches; for instance the 'name' of a Museum in XML is called 'denomination' in RDF/S.

In order to reconciliate the heterogeneous representations of our data we need to define appropriate mapping rules. Choosing an expressive but tractable logical framework to map data from XML to RDF/S is crucial for the success of a SWIM. These mappings are used for reformulating queries issued against the virtual RDF/S schema into queries acceptable by our XML sources. However, more complex mappings render query re- formulation harder. Query reformulation becomes more complex if we take into consideration the presence of constraints capturing the semantics of both the RDF/S and XML data models, as well as, application-specific constraints coming from the schema of XML sources. So, there is a need for a sound and complete reformulation algorithm. Since reformulated queries are evaluated to remote sources and mediator queries resulting from automated manipulation/generation may entail redundancies, their optimisation is crucial. In particular, optimisation tries to eliminate redundant queries and to simplify queries by removing redundant predicates.

CONTRIBUTIONS

In this context, we propose a middleware called ICS-FORTH SWIM supporting the following functionalities:

A Formal Framework for Mapping Specification

Choosing a logical framework for defining the mappings is of great importance. Our idea was to represent both RDF and XML data models as first-order logic predicates and capture their semantics through appropriate constraints. In this way we reduce RDF to XML query reformulation problem to the relational equivalent one, and thus, we can reuse existing techniques for relational query containment and minimisation. More precisely, we rely on Linear Datalog for establishing the mappings and translating the RQL/RVL queries and views issued against the virtual RDF/S schema.

The head of the Datalog rules consists of a conjunction of view clauses employed by the RDF/S view definition language RVL, and the body consists of XPath atoms that facilitate querying tree-structured XML sources. The former is used in order to point out the instantiation of RDF/S schemas with appropriate resources residing in our XML data sources. Employing some non-interpreted built-in predicates for handling more intricate cases enhances the expressiveness of the mappings. As far as these mappings are concerned, they are interpreted in a constraint - oriented way implementing the GLAV approach of our middleware. We can map a view over the global RDF/S to a view over local XML sources, and each of these mappings is captured with the help of constraints. Constraints describe both the RDF/S schema in terms of the XML sources and the XML sources in terms of the global RDF/S schema.

Query Reformulation and Optimisation

Another powerful functionality of the SWIM is its ability to reformulate queries. RQL queries, expressed in terms of the RDF/S virtual schema, result in minimized queries expressed in terms of the XML sources by gradually applying a number of chasing/backchasing, steps. The use of this algorithm is proven to be sound and complete for disjunctions of conjunctive queries in the presence of disjunctive embedded dependencies. This is guaranteed by the use of the Chase/Backchase algorithm given this type of input.

A query is chased with the help of the constraints that have been defined to express the semantics of the XML and RDF data models and in addition, with constraints coming from the XML data sources *i.e.*, specification of keys and foreign keys, as well as, of domain constraints. The result of chasing is back chased for producing a minimal reformulation. These minimized queries are simplified and the redundant ones are eliminated. In this way we guarantee that we query the XML sources with the minimum possible queries. Finally, the minimized reformulated queries are translated into XPath and/or XQuery.

ONLINE CATALOGUE USER EDUCATION

The central question that directed this study, "What might be the components of a model programme to instruct users of an online catalogue?" challenges a commonly held view within the field of librarianship and information science. This view is that an effective "user friendly" inter-active computer system-such as an online catalogue-should not require instruction at all. While such a view is not universally held, it is common especially among system developers and others who are steeped in the use of computers in libraries and elsewhere.

A frequently articulated design specification for end user oriented systems is that all system use instruction should be provided as part of its interface-through such things as introductory help screens, user prompts, and labeling conventions-and should be all that even the most naive user needs to know to be able to effectively use that system.

A corollary of this view is that efforts to develop an instructional programme for the online catalogue suggest that the catalogue is not fulfilling its purpose and that its design is flawed. With this logic, any effort to provide instruction in online catalogue use by public services staffs might be viewed as wasted effort at the least, and provide implicit criticism of the designers as well.

Though the project from its inception questioned this view of the incompatibility of "user friendly" online systems and instruction pro-grams, it did not simply embrace the contrary view that formalized instruction must be given to all online catalogue users. Interactive systems for the general public are simply too new and untested for us to assume either of these positions without a period of considerable experimentation and practical examination of what works and what doesn't work for our users.

A certain amount of curiosity, fascination, or mystique naturally accompanies technological evolution. At this early stage of online catalogue implementation, learning from the practical experiences of others, as well as from more formal research findings, is essential if we are to move beyond these phases in our programme development. Baker and Nielsen review much of the early literature on the debate about the value of online catalogue user education, pointing out particularly the sampling bias in the widely cited CLR *Online Public Access Catalogue* (OPAC) studies, a bias which caused users who experienced difficulties in using online catalogues to be underrepresented in the findings.

We became interested in creating a model programme for educating online catalogue users for a variety of reasons:

- There was (and is) wide recognition that the perfect online catalogue simply does not (yet) exist.

- There was (and is) a perception by many librarians that the online user interface may not accommodate all user needs at present and may never do so.
- "User friendly" systems are not indeed friendly to all, judging from the experiences of many reference librarians who have worked with users trying to master such systems.
- The pace of change in interface improvements can seem painfully slow once any online catalogue system "works" in the sense that it meets managerial (not necessarily user) criteria for "satisfying."
- A general training programme that conveyed infor-mation retrieval concepts might aid users as they moved on to other automated systems both within and beyond the library setting.
- The numerous online catalogue instructional prog-rammes that had been initiated in various settings-particularly in academic libraries-suggested that making an effort for consistency in instructional planning was worthwhile and beneficial.

LEARNING OBJECTIVES

In order for a model online catalogue user education programme to be applicable to a variety of institutions and for the programme to be formally evaluated, it was critical to the Northwestern project that programme learning objectives be stated and generalized beyond those associated with a particular system. The first step in the execution of this research project involved formalizing a set of such objectives which would serve as the basis for teaching the use of an online catalogue. Much of the conceptual work related to this aspect of the project is described by Baker.

In planning the framework of instructional objectives, there was extensive discussion with librarians at each of the participating libraries. These discussions centered on identifying a set of ideal objectives (or goals of instruction) without linking them to features of specific systems or tying them to specific methods of instruction. With the goal of developing a generic instruction programme with generalizable objectives, it was essential to look at online catalogue instruction as it could be applied across many systems. By focusing on such general expectations of online catalogue users, we felt that skills might be more easily transferred across systems.

WHAT TO TEACH: CONCEPTS OR PROCEDURES

In determining an appropriate direction for our online catalogue teaching, two concerns were raised. The first involved what technical aspects of the system's structure should be presented to users; the second questioned the manner in which such aspects should be included in the learning activity. With one of our project objectives being to work towards developing transferability of skills learned about one automated system to skills needed for another, an emphasis on teaching concepts and structure, rather than procedures, was endorsed. In addition to increasing the likelihood for transferability of skills, teaching system structure is useful for conceptualizing the workings of a system. When the way a system works is not transparent to the user, there is little opportunity for self-diagnosis of errors or decision-making for search strategy development.

This instructional approach has been supported by other research in the ways humans interact with computers. Works by Christine Borg-man, Ramsey and Grimes, and others discuss the importance of conceptual models in teaching interactive systems and the resulting mental model the user has available for error diagnosis and problem solving. Such conceptual models are often built around metaphors and often illustrate techniques designed to communicate an overall context for system behaviour to the learner.

Learning occurs whether it is structured in a systematic programme or whether it is coincidental. Coincidental learning of a system through the use of prompts and help screens may actually prove to be an effective means for learning procedures. Focusing an instructional programme around conceptual models does not by any means diminish the necessity for a user to have a functional understanding geared towards learning system-specific searching techniques. These techniques may actually be more easily acquired from instruction embedded in the system once the conceptual model has been learned.

One of the most important functions of the user interface for online catalogues has been to provide this task-oriented training. With so many automated systems being used in libraries around the country, transferring skills learned about one sys-tem to another may prove quite difficult. Designing instruction around a conceptual *v.* procedural framework may provide ultimate transfer-ability of learning in the use of online catalogues.

EVALUATING THE MODEL

Because the objectives developed for online catalogue instruction involved acquisition of both cognitive and behavioural learning, it was important to develop an evaluation strategy that addressed objective achievement of a group of representative users at solving both cognitive and behavioural problems. Both pencil-and-paper responses and observation of "hands-on" online catalogue activity were deemed critical to assess the project.

Another issue important to the study was that of cumulative learning. Because the library patron often learns the use of research tools in stages (such as by trial use followed by assistance from a librarian), cumulative learning, or learning that builds on previous learning, frequently occurs.

In the case of learning to use a library catalogue, cumulative learning is especially salient: many users are exposed to repeated instruction in the use of the catalogue in elementary school; many users rely on experience as the most available teacher of library use skills. Bibliographic instruction librarians are aware of the problems inherent in this situation, for they often must help students "unlearn" previously incorrect information concerning the card catalogue.This concern with the effects of cumulative learning led to the development of an experimental design which allowed us to examine and evaluate the effects of two types of bibliographic instruction methods-both individually and combined-taking into account the order of their presentation. The research design protocol called for the creation of two experimental groups (each of which took two tests and participated in two instructional sessions) as well as the use of a control group which only took two tests but received no instruction.

The instructional treatments included a classroom-like presentation on the online catalogue (what Northwestern has dubbed a "LUIS Workshop"), and the reading of a printed brochure designed to convey instructional content. As the tests themselves required participants to use the online catalogue to answer some of the questions, all three groups were exposed to the catalogue and its introductory (tutorial) and "help" screens. The two tests were composed of questions designed to test the same knowledge.

The control group took the first test followed by a "placebo" presentation (a short non-instructional film) and then the second test. The first experimental group, which as suggested, call Group "A," received the classroom instructional session followed by the first test and then read the instructional brochure and took the second test. The second experimental group, which as suggested, call Group "B," read the brochure and took the first test and then received the instructional session and the second test.

SAMPLE SELECTION

A random sample subject population of ninety freshmen students was selected for participation in the study using a sampling technique that insured equal representation by sex and representation by academic major corresponding as much as possible to national norms derived from American Council on Education data.'

Only freshmen who had previously participated in LUIS workshops were excluded from participation. As an incentive for the subjects to commit to participation when they were contacted by telephone, each student was offered a free ticket to a commercial movie theater upon completion of the experiment.'

DATA COLLECTION

The principal means of data collection for the study were a battery of two written tests prepared for the study and transaction data collected by the NOTIS computer as subjects interacted directly with LUIS. The first test consisted of fourteen questions related to background characteristics of the students, forty-five questions tapping knowledge of LUIS-including some which required use of the terminal-and eight attitudinal questions asking how the students liked various features of the catalogue.

Eight catalogue search "practice questions" for which students had to use the terminals were also included. The second test included the same type of questions as the first except for the fourteen initial questions tapping demographic variables. Pretesting of the two tests with twenty randomly selected Northwestern students verified that the tests, though different, were measuring acquisition of the same learning.

Monitoring online catalogue transactions as a means of collecting data was accomplished through utilization of NOTIS software developed initially in connection with the CLR-sponsored OPAC studies of 1980-82 in which Northwestern was a Research Libraries Group participant. The room in which the experiment was conducted was equipped with sixteen online catalogue terminals, each having adjacent to it a copy of the *Library* of *Congress Subject Headings.*

Subjects were instructed to write on their test booklets the identification number of the terminal at which they were searching for the test but were not told that their transactions were being recorded. This protocol device provided a means of unobtrusive measurement of online catalogue use in which transaction data could be associated with user characteristics recorded on the test booklets.

This strategy is especially notable as a monitoring technique as it allows exemption from institutional and federal guide-lines for research on human subjects-due to the educational testing nature of the experiment-and yet is less obtrusive than other monitoring experimental designs in that subjects are led to assume that pencil-and-paper is the sole method of data collection.

ANALYSIS

Following the completion of the data gathering, the 178filled-out tests were first paired by student identification number and subsequently coded for machine processing. Eighty-seven usable pairs of tests were so coded and input for processing using the Statistical Package for the Social Sciences (SPSS). Tabulated responses were scored using a key of correct test items, and raw percentage correct scores were computed.

Analysis was also accomplished in regard to a number of study questions by grouping the raw percentage scores into "high", "middle", and "low" performance groups. This grouping enabled as well the analysis of student performance considered in terms of degree of achievement of five important learning objectives established in conjunction with the model programme developed at Northwestern. A fuller description of the methods used to reduce the data, as well as detailed findings on the effect of demographic variables on perfor-mance, are provided in the authors' final report to the Council on Library Resources on the project."

An indicator of overall test performance for each of the three test groups is the average (mean) test score, again expressed as a percentage of questions answered correctly. Table provides a clear picture of group performance showing the score for each group on both test one and test two. On both tests the performance of the control group was the lowest. Group "A", which received the lecture instruction prior to test one, performed best on test one overall, and their score on test two surprisingly dropped.

Group "B", which read the brochure prior to test one, performed less well on the first test, but, following their receiving the live instruction, performed nearly as well on test two as group two had on test one. Analysis of variance tests with the test one and test two data for the mean score by group revealed that the within-group variation on both scores was less than the variation between groups indicating that the different means for each group are statistically significant.

Table. Average Test Score by Group

	Test 1	Test 2
Control Group	54.66	53.21
Group "A"	77.5	63.3
Group "B"	61.66	76.94
ANOVA Significance <.001		

These average scores represent overall test performance in only a general way and are presented in this manner as a way to look at the cumulative learning issue that was of interest in the study. Because of the length of the instruction period and the opportunity subjects were given to interact with the instructor, the superior performance of group "A" on test one was expected. Why the "A" group's performance dropped on the second test-following their exposure to the brochure-cannot be adequately explained by the analysis presented here, but we may hypothesize that test fatigue may have been an important factor.

Recalling that the "A" group's taking of the second test was nearly ninety minutes into the period set aside for the experiment, and that the intervening period between tests for this group was much shorter than for group "B," it seems highly likely that group "A" was simply tired of responding to questions on the second test. Group "B," while spending as long on the experiment overall as the "A" group, did have a consider-ably longer intervening period between the two tests.

In the matter of evaluating the achievement of specific learning objectives we were less successful. Although we established a means to analyse the result of the evaluative test in a way that treated the achievement of each objective separately, we must acknowledge that a conceptual dilemma exists. As certain objectives dealt more concretely with the learning of definitions and concepts that were easily tested for, while other objectives-concerned as they were with the execution of procedures-were inherently more difficult to test for, we cannot make clear conclusions regarding different levels of attainment on the test.

Different attainment levels may reflect more about the tests themselves than about actual superior performance in online catalogue searching. Because our knowledge of online catalogue users is still so incomplete, instructional evaluation is made difficult especially in respect to validation of the appropriateness of certain cognitive learning tasks for successful performance in searching. There is some danger in evaluation studies of this sort to direct instruction to successful completion of the test rather than to the achievement of skills that the test has been designed to measure.

With these considerations in mind, an analysis of the data showed that the group that had the workshop first scored significantly higher on procedures such as using equipment than the group that had the brochure. One of the most interesting facts is that the control group scored higher than both of these test groups on procedural knowledge. But in interpreting and structuring searches the workshop group did significantly better.

It was followed by the brochure group and then the control group. In terms of concepts, the control group fell far behind the other two test groups with the workshop group in the lead. Among our findings on the analysis of the transaction logging was that subjects who had a workshop presentation made fewer errors than those whose first instructional exposure was to the printed brochure.

What do these findings allow us to say about the cumulative effects of two learning experiences with online catalogue instruction? Because there is no clear pattern in improvement on all the objectives for any of the three groups it is difficult to say. The order of presentation of the two learning experiences-the brochure and the lecture-did not appear to affect group performance on all five learning objectives in the same way; for some objectives a score increase between test one and test two might have been the result of the lecture having been given first, for other objectives it might have been the brochure being presented first. Further work is in order to refine the analysis and sort out what factors may lead to improved test scores.

DATA USED IN LIBRARY SYSTEMS

While the Library places an understandable emphasis on cataloguing and other standards for the description of library materials, there are a number of underlying standards which are also of major importance in ensuring the interchange of library data.

Character Sets

The data which describes library materials or electronic information resources is, in the final analysis, composed of characters which belong to the world's scripts. There are a number of standards which govern these character sets, including the international standard ISO 10646 which is functionally identical to the UNICODE standard, and code sets for East Asian languages such as the US standard Z39.64 (East Asian Character Code for Bibliographic Use).

The Library has a low level of participation in the development of these standards. It monitors developments through its participation in Standards Australia Committee IT/19. It also monitors the use of East Asian character codes in products used by its National CJK Service.

Responsibility for this area rests with the Information Technology Division.

Data Elements

The International Organization for Standardization (ISO), through its Technical Committee 46, Subcommittee 4, has developed a range of library automation standards. One of the working groups of Subcommittee 4 (Working Group 7) has developed a family of data element standards (ISO 8459) which can be used as a data dictionary to support the automation of library technical services.

Data element standards have been defined for Interloan, Acquisitions, Information retrieval, Circulation, and Cataloguing and metadata. Further work will concentrate on a consolidation of all the parts into a unified data dictionary standard.

As discussed below, the Library has recently developed a draft data dictionary, based on the international standard ISO 2146 (Directories of libraries, archives, information and documentation centres, and their data bases), to support the future development of its directory services. The Library is leading a review of ISO 2146, which commenced in May 2000, under the auspices of Working Group 7.

The Library has also been active in the identification of data elements for preservation purposes. These activities are discussed in the section on Preservation Standards.

The Library also notes the existence of a framework standard, ISO 11179 (Specification and standardization of data elements) which it will observe, along with ISO 8459, in the construction of data dictionaries to support its own automated services.

Responsibility for this area is shared as follows:

- Resource Sharing Division: monitoring of the ISO 8459 family of standards;
- Collections Management Division: maintenance of the preservation metadata element set;
- Information Technology Division: monitoring of the ISO 11179 standard.

Item Identifiers

A key type of data element is a unique number which identifies a book, serial, journal article, electronic resource, or other type of information resource. Most of the standards applicable to this area have been developed within Subcommittee 9 of ISO Technical Committee 46. Examples include ISBN, ISSN, ISMN, Serial Item Contribution Identifier (SICI), Book Item and Component Identifier (BICI), and Digital Object Identifier (DOI).

The Library has historically had a strong interest in item identifiers, and it has endeavoured to ensure that processes are in place for the routine assignment of several of the above identifier types to Australian information resources. The Library has relinquished the Australian ISBN agency role, but remains the national centre for ISSN and ISMN.

In the United States, a national standard has been developed for the identification of journal articles and other individual serial contributions. This standard is known as the Serial Item Contribution Identifier, or SICI. A similar standard for non-serial items, the Book Item and Component Identifier (BICI) has been released as a Draft Standard for trial use.

The Library will continue to monitor the development of the SICI and BICI standards, and it will work through Standards Australia and ISO committees to seek their endorsement as international standards. The Library will encourage their implementation in Australian citation databases and related services.

The Library has a strong interest in current developments aimed at providing authoritative and persistent identification of digital information resources. In April 2000 the Library engaged a consultant to examine and report on existing standards and processes for persistent identifiers, and a report of the consultant was released in June 2001. The Library has implemented the recommendations of this report and is now allocating persistent identifiers to the digital objects in its care, according to the guidelines in Appendix 1 of the report. It is managing persistence of its resources through a combination of managed URLs and a resolver system based on directing query strings to our application delivery mechanisms for digital materials detailed in Appendix 2 of the report.

In collaboration with the CASL Digital Issues Working Group and the State Library of Tasmania, the Library is looking at the feasibility of an Australian Digital Resource Identifier (ADRI) and a national agency for its implementation and allocation.

In 2001 the Library released a statement on Managing Web Resources for Persistent Access.

The Library is also an active member of an international working group (the Persistent Identifiers Task Force) which was formed to develop standards and guidelines for national libraries in the use of persistent identifiers. This Group has met twice, in April 1999 and March 2000.

The Library has agreed to participate in a pilot project with the ISSN International Centre to explore the concept of an Electronic Archive Registry and its possible role as part of a resolution system.

Responsibility for this area is shared as follows:

- Collections Management Division, Technical Services Branch: oversight of the ISBN, ISSN, SICI and BICI standards, monitoring of persistent identifier standards, evaluation of test beds;
- Information Technology Division: monitoring of technical aspects of persistent identifier standards, technical support for test beds;
- Resource Sharing Division: delivery of the Library's PURL service.

Full Text Markup

Text markup is of critical importance in the provision of online access to documents. This process involves the insertion of markers which clearly delineate the logical components of a document, such as the author information, title information, abstract, executive summary, chapter headings, and bibliographic references. Markup facilitates the browsing of documents through the Web. It also facilitates search access and the extraction of metadata. The wide scale adoption of standard markup schemes by publishers could greatly facilitate the efficient construction of digital libraries.

The framework standard for document markup is known as the Standard Generalised Markup Language or SGML. Within this framework, there is a multitude of specific standards for the markup of particular types of documents, such as books, journal articles, law reports, theses, or manuscript finding aids. Each of these standards is known as a Document Type Definition.

Examples of the application of SGML are the HyperText Markup Language (HTML, the original basis for browsing documents on the World Wide Web), the Extensible Markup Language (XML, designed as an improvement on the HTML standard in the separation of content from presentation), the Text Encoding Initiative (TEI) and the Encoded Archival Description (EAD).

The Library will give increased attention to these standards, because of their importance in the management of digital information resources. The Library is trialling the use of XML and EAD (mentioned above under Special Collection Descriptions) for its collection guides, manuscript finding aids and other appropriate web publications.

Responsibility for this area rests with the Information Technology Division.

System Interconnection

The development of library networks over the next decade will be based on the interconnection of distributed library systems, and the use of client/server technology. The implementation of certain key technical standards will allow particular applications such as searching and interlibrary loan to be managed cooperatively between two computer systems.. The three key standards are Z39.50, the international Interlibrary Loan Protocol, and the Open Archives Initiative Metadata Harvesting Protocol.

Z39.50 (ISO 23950)

The Z39.50 standard specifies the structures and rules which allow a client machine (such as a personal computer or workstation) to search a database on a server machine (such as a library catalogue) and retrieve records that are identified as a result of such a search. The rather arcane designation for this standard derives from the fact that it was the 50th standard developed by a committee known as "Z39", the committee of the American National Standards Institute that has the responsibility for library automation standards. While technically a US national standard (Version 3 of which was adopted in 1995), Z39.50 has also been copied or "cloned" as an international standard, known as ISO 23950. The standard has been of major importance in supporting access to distributed library databases and catalogues. The Library of Congress undertakes the role of maintenance agency for the standard. Through its participation in Standards Australia Committee IT/19 and related bodies, the Library has been active in monitoring the development of the Z39.50 standard and in ensuring that it became an official Australian standard. The Library continues to participate as resources permit in meetings of the Z39.50 Implementors Group, an international body which works by consensus to approve the development of the standard.

From 1998 the Library participated in a group, convened by the National Library of Canada, which developed what is now known as the Bath Profile. This Z39.50 profile was drafted in August 1999 at a meeting held in Bath, UK. The profile builds on the work of earlier profiling projects and defines a range of author, title, subject, keyword, date of publication and standard identifier searches which should be supported, the exact combination of attributes required to specify each search type and the expected behaviours. The profile addresses the range of functionality which users expect to be supported by library catalogues. In addition the profile defines levels of conformance for cross-domain searching.

The Library has implemented the Z39.50 standard in its key bibliographic services: Kinetica; the National CJK Service and its catalogue. The Library also maintains a national directory of Z39.50 targets.

Libraries will add holdings and original cataloguing data to the national union catalogue, through Kinetica, as part of the process of obtaining records for their local systems. The Library recognises that, while union catalogues are of great benefit to library communities, more flexibility is required in the process of updating them. For this reason, the Library has taken a strong role in supporting the concept of the Union Catalogue Profile. This Profile is intended for use with the Z39.50 standard to allow a cataloguer to update a database in a distributed environment, effectively supporting the simultaneous update of local and union catalogue systems. The National Library, in collaboration with others, has discussed this profile with the Z39.50 Implementors Group, and it hosts the Profile on its web site.

Work on the Z39.50 standard is a priority activity for the Library, because of the importance of the standard to the development of the open, distributed library network. The Library will continue its high level of involvement in the monitoring of the standard, in contribution to the maintenance of the Union Catalogue Profile and the Bath profile, in support for the standard in the Library's own systems, and in collaborative projects which are based on the standard.

Responsibility for this area is shared as follows:

- Resource Sharing Division: implementation of the standards.
- Information Technology Division: input into the development of the standards.

Interlibrary Loan Protocol and Related Standards

The Interlibrary Loan Protocol is designed to support the interconnection of separate computer systems which are managing the interlibrary loan process. It supports the control and management of ILL transactions for both lending and borrowing activities. The Library has not taken an active role in the development of the Protocol. However, it has cooperated closely with the Australian Vice Chancellors Committee through the JEDDS and LIDDAS projects, which are based on the Protocol. The AVCC, through its project manager for JEDDS and LIDDAS, represented Australia at recent international meetings of the ILL Protocol Implementors Group. The Library's Kinetica Service is using the Fretwell Downing VDX software, which supports the Protocol.

Related to the Interlibrary Loan Protocol are standards which support electronic document delivery services, such as the "header information" standard developed by the Group on Electronic Document Interchange (GEDI), and the Multitype Internet Mail Extensions (MIME) standards which support transmission of a document image over electronic mail. These are important areas of activity for the National Library, because these standards will underpin the development of a national and global distributed interlibrary loan network. The Library will continue to monitor the development of these standards, partly in cooperation with others through the LIDDAS Steering Committee.

Responsibility for this area rests with the Resource Sharing Division.

Open Archives Initiative (OAI) Metadata Harvesting Protocol

The National Library has embarked on an exploration of the use of the Metadata Harvesting Protocol in its proof-of-concept to support resource discovery of digital Australiana. Metadata will be gathered from a wide range of information managers according to the OAI protocol and the proof-of-concept will also become a target for similar initiative being conducted by the University of Michigan's OAIster project. The National Library has also become a signatory to the Budapest Open Archive Initiative which 'aims to accelerate progress in the international effort to make research articles in all academic fields freely available on the Internet.'.

Responsibility for this area rests with the Coordination Support Branch.

Directory Services

Directory services provide a critical underpinning to the library and information infrastructure, allowing the discovery of relevant information suppliers, and providing access to information about the methods and conditions of supply. The Library has created and published a number of directories of Australian library collections and services. It has developed the Australian Libraries Gateway and the Directory of Australia's Oral History Collections to provide a single web interface to these directory services. The Library has recently developed a draft data dictionary, based on the international standard ISO 2146 (Directories of libraries, archives, information and documentation centres, and their data bases), to support the future development of these services. As this standard is now over 10 years old, the Library is leading a review of the standard through Committee IT/19.

Directory services play a significant role in supporting interlibrary loan services. The Library has developed the Australian Interlibrary Resource Sharing Directory, which includes a national register of library symbols. The Library is also participating in ISO Technical Committee 46, Subcommittee 4, Working Group 8, which is developing a standard for an internationally accepted system of library codes or symbols. A recent paper sets out relevant standards initiatives and projects related to directory services to be undertaken by the Library and by Committee IT/19.

The Library is conscious that directories will increasingly be based on distributed services, rather than on centralised directory databases. For this reason, international directory service standards such as X.500 are likely to become more important in the cooperative development of library directories. X.500 is actually a series of ISO standards which define a global directory service that is independent of any computing application or network platform. An X.500 service will utilise a collection of directory servers, each holding a portion of a global directory information base. Because the X.500 standard is quite complex, the Internet community has defined a standard called the Lightweight Directory Access Protocol, which conforms to the X.500 model and is becoming widely used.

The Library will aim to develop its technical expertise in these directory protocols, and it will consider how to apply these standards to the future development of the Australian Libraries Gateway and the national interlibrary loan network. The Library is cooperating with Macquarie University in relation to the international project known as PRIDE (People and Resources in a Distributed Environment) which will develop services based on the X.500 standard. In particular, the Library is working with Macquarie University to develop a draft directory schema.

The Library is also trialling the Open Directory software (which supports X.500) with the aim of migrating the Interlibrary Resource Sharing Directory to this platform in the medium term.

Responsibility for this area is shared as follows:

- Information Technology Division: monitoring of the X.500 standard, participation in the development of a draft directory schema, monitoring of data dictionary standards, leadership of the review of ISO 2146, implementation of the Open Directory software;
- Resource Sharing Division: support for the Australian Libraries Gateway, participation in the PRIDE Project, monitoring of standard library codes.

Preservation Standards

Preservation of Physical Collections

Despite the growth in digital collections, the Library will continue to be responsible for its very large, important and growing non-digital collections. Preserving these collections draws on a range of best practice approaches. The Library takes an active role in monitoring and contributing to developments, especially in the areas of conservation treatment, storage environments and strategies for dealing with intrinsically unstable information carriers such as cellulose acetate photographic materials and acidic newspapers.

The Library played an especially active part in the development of an Australian standard for "permanent" paper, through Standards Australia Committee MS/48 (AS 4003-1996)-see Australian National Permanent Paper Campaign for further details. The Library will continue to support the use of such standards by publishers, as a way of reducing the potential costs of preserving future additions to the Library's book collections. Responsibility for this area rests with the Collection Management Division: Preservation Services Branch.

Reformatting Standards

The Library accepts reformatting or copying as a legitimate tool in support of its preservation programmes. Identifying and using appropriate standards is a key foundation of the Library's approach to reformatting, whether using analogue or digital technologies.

Preservation Microfilming

In the area of preservation microfilming, the Library has gained extensive experience and played a leadership role in standards development in Australia. It was the main instigator in re-shaping the Standards Australia Committee MS/4 to focus on preservation issues, and actively contributed to the development of draft preservation microfilming standards through that Committee. In addition, the Library published in 1998 Guidelines for preservation microfilming in Australia and New Zealand to assist in the adoption of best practices.

More recently, the Library is collaborating with the State Library of South Australia to develop training materials in preservation microfilming, suitable for use in the South East Asia and Pacific regions (in which the Library has special responsibilities as a Regional Centre of the IFLA Preservation and Conservation Programme). Improved knowledge of and compliance with standards and best practices for preservation microfilming have been identified as important goals for these regions.

Digital Reformatting

While microfilm has been a very useful preservation reformatting methodology, digital imaging technology has opened up the possibility of greatly enhanced access to the content of collection materials.

The Library makes digital copies of physical collection items in order to enhance access and to support preservation programmes. Standards play an important part in ensuring widespread accessibility, and in defining formats and methods capable of surviving a number of technology changes. The Library is also seeking best practices that will minimise the risk to material being digitally copied.

Currently, a standards approach to digital imaging applies mainly to image file formats. The Library takes account of a range of graphic interchange standards including TIFF (Tagged Image File Format), JPEG (Joint Photographic Experts Group), and GIF (Graphic Interchange Format) standards. The Library has also used some proprietary standards such as Kodak PhotoCD for processing and storage of images, Adobe PDF (Portable Document Format) for delivery of multi-page documents, DigiMarc watermarking to protect the intellectual property of creators and distributors of digital images, and Lizard Technologies MrSid wavelet compression tools to make large images such as maps deliverable over networks. Recently, the Library has trialled the use of Ebind, a method of binding digital images together using an SGML document type definition. Ebind supports management and display of digital copies needing to reflect the hierarchical and sequential structure of documents such as books.

The Library seeks to use open, non-proprietary standards wherever they can deliver the functionality the Library requires.

Other elements of digitisation programmes such as selection and preparation of materials, digital capture, and management of digital collections, are currently less standardised, although many forums are attempting to prepare best practice guidelines in these areas.

The Library has been an active member of the Corporate Management Forum Information Technology Working Group Digitisation Subgroup, which produced some basic guidelines for national institutions in Australia.

The Library also participates in the RLG PRESERV programme, which has prepared a number of digital imaging guidance documents, and the NISO Committee AU on Technical Metadata for Digital Still Images.

The Library has developed its own Digitisation Policy, which sets out many of its own intentions, and is engaged in a major digitisation programme which will build on experience gained in a number of its own previous projects, as well as that of others such as the Library of Congress' American Memory and the Making of America project. Over the course of its initial integrated digitisation programme in 2001-2002, the Library expects to clarify and report on the standards it finds most useful in all areas of digital imaging, and to clarify its intentions regarding the roles of digital imaging and preservation microfilming.

Responsibility for these areas rests with:

- Collection Management Division: Preservation Services Branch
- Corporate Services Division: Coordination Support Branch, and IT Division.

Preservation of Digital Collections

The Library is involved in developing digital archiving and preservation procedures to support both its own digital collections (including digital surrogates and Australian digital publications), and a distributed national collection of electronic publications. These collections include both online and physical format digital resources. The Library shares relevant information freely with a number of other national libraries, consortia such as RLG, and digital archiving projects overseas, as well as with other Australian libraries and institutions, with a view to developing standards and best practices that will ensure the ongoing accessibility of digital collections.

In particular, the Library closely monitors the development of archiving models such as the Reference Model for an Open Archival Information System (OAIS). This emerging standard is being developed by the Consultative Committee for Space Data Systems on behalf of ISO Technical Committee 20, Subcommittee 13 (Space data and information transfer systems).

The Library is also working to develop best practice guidelines with an RLG/OCLC Digital Archive Working Group defining the attributes of a reliable digital archive, and with a special committee of the Council of Directors of

National Libraries (CDNL) on digital archiving issues.

The emergence of standards is likely to be slow in the area of strategies intended to maintain access to large collections of digital resources, such as migration and emulation. The Library monitors and when appropriate seeks to contribute to international research leading to a better understanding of these and other strategies. As best practices emerge, the Library plays a role in publicising them and encouraging their use, both through its PADI web site, and through published guidelines such as Safeguarding Australia's web resources: guidelines for creators and publishers and First steps in preserving digital publications.

Responsibility for this area rests with:

- Collection Management Division: Preservation Services Branch
- Technical Services Branch.

Preservation of Audio Resources

The Library takes an active role in developing informal standard procedures for sound archiving through the International Association of Sound and Audiovisual Archives (IASA), and applies best practice approaches in managing its analogue and digital audio collections. It monitors the activities of the RLG Working Group on Preserving Magnetic Media, and closely monitors the impact of Digital Video Disc technology on Compact Disc standards. However, as the Library moves its audio collections to mass storage systems over the next few years, CD standards are expected to become less important to the Library.

Responsibility for this area rests with Collection Management Division: Preservation Services Branch.

Metadata for Recording Preservation Information

The Library is developing systems for recording preservation information required to manage both its digital and non-digital collections.

The Library developed a draft set of preservation metadata requirements for managing all of its digital collections, designed to complement resource discovery, rights management and other administrative metadata. Building on this, the Library is a member of an OCLC/RLG Preservation Metadata Working Group developing international guidelines and recommendations which will be available for public comment by mid 2002. Responsibility for this area rests with Collection Management Division: Preservation Services Branch. The Library monitors standards in these areas but is not actively involved in their use at this stage. Responsibility for this area rests with Corporate Services Division.

5

Library Use and Users of Electronic Resources

OVERVIEW

Libraries of all sizes and types are embracing digital collections, although most libraries will continue to offer both print and digital collections for many years to come. New purchases and purchases of journals, magazines, and abstracting and indexing services are heavily weighted towards digital, while digital books (e-books) are only beginning to become a presence in library collections. Libraries prefer digital collections for many reasons, including, but not limited to, the following: digital journals can be linked from and to indexing and abstracting databases; access can be from the user's home, office, or dormitory whether or not the physical library is open; the library can get usage statistics that are not available for print collections; and digital collections save space and are relatively easy to maintain. When total processing and space costs are taken into account, electronic collections may also result in some overall reductions in library costs. Such a dramatic switch from print collections to digital collections has an impact on library users and users' perceptions of the library. Many researchers have attempted to predict or measure that impact through surveys, transaction log analysis, and other research techniques. Librarians would like to be able to use the information and conclusions generated by the many research studies, especially because it is time consuming to conduct good research on their own and because the best measures of impact come after decisions are al-ready made and collections are converted. Unfortunately, the conclu-sions of various studies sometimes seem contradictory, and it may be difficult to judge which research studies offer valid and reliable find-ings. The opinion literature outnumbers the research literature, and it may be a challenge to distinguish fact from opinion.

The purpose of this report for the Council on Library and Infor-mation Resources is to help librarians identify reliable research stud-ies, to provide a synopsis of the good studies, and to present an anal-ysis of conclusions. A subtitle of the report might well be the same as the CLIR symposium held March 28, 2003, "What Are Users Telling Us?" Or, "What do user studies tell us about how and why library constituents of all types use digital library resources and are likely to use them in the future?" The goal of this report is to provide in-formation that librarians can use to make important decisions about collections, services, and product design. Also relevant to this topic is CLIR's January 2002 report "Usage and Usability Assessment: Library Practices and Concerns" by Denise Troll Covey. Although this introduction refers to the resources as digital re-sources or digital libraries, the less precise, but more commonly used terms electronic resources or electronic libraries will be used throughout as synonyms.

REPORT OUTLINE

Hundreds of recent publications focus on how users interact with or how they feel about electronic library resources. It is important, therefore, to state clear parameters of what is included in this report.

Only publications or reports of studies that meet the following parameters are included and analysed:

- Studies must focus on the use of both electronic resources and libraries (electronic resources through the library, in addition to the library, or in comparison with the library). Studies that are mostly about the Internet, but include a substantive section on librar-ies (the Pew studies, for example) or those that are mostly about libraries in general, but include a substantive section on digital libraries (the LibQUAL+™ studies, for example) are also included. Internet use studies that do not focus on libraries are excluded.
- Studies or surveys that focus solely on librarians, library staff, library Web sites, or publishers are excluded; only those that study library patrons are included.
- Studies that are limited to the behaviour of authors rather than readers are excluded.
- Only research studies are included. Opinion pieces or descriptions of how a library converted their print collections to digital collec-tions are excluded.
- A wide variety of research methods are covered (including surveys, transaction log analysis, experimental). Because different kinds of research methods allow different types of conclusions to be drawn, this report describes the research method used in stud-ies and what types of conclusions made by the researchers are valid in accordance with the method.
- Studies are restricted to those conducted Since, 1995, or a post-Web world. Some studies compare recent findings with past studies (for

example, the Tenopir and King studies), so they may address how usage patterns have changed with the advent of electronic resources, but the main focus remains user behaviour in an increas-ingly digital age.

- Poorly conducted research from which valid conclusions cannot be drawn is excluded.

Applying the foregoing parameters resulted in a pool of more than 200 individual research publications. Some publications de-scribe different phases or parts of large, and often ongoing, research projects. A further distinction was made to separate these large or ongoing studies from the more limited studies and to describe each major study as a whole, rather than as separate publication parts. This led to a distinction between "Tier 1" and "Tier 2" studies. Tier 1 studies are those major studies that have many publica-tions, sometimes by many different authors.

The studies involve hundreds or thousands of subjects over multiple workplaces, work roles, or subject disciplines. Many important conclusions can be drawn from each of these studies and they are typically widely re-ported and discussed in the library community. Each Tier 1 study is actually a group of studies conducted by a research team. Tier 1 stud-ies are discussed in the greatest detail Since, they may use multiple methods and provide, at times, complex findings.

The designation as a Tier 1 study was intentionally highly se-lective. Only eight user studies (actually, groups of studies) were designated as Tier 1 studies, but they represent nearly 100 individual articles or reports.

Additionally, nearly that many other publications are designated Tier 2 studies. Tier 2 studies are not of lesser quality than Tier 1 studies; they are just typically smaller in scale or are one-time projects. Tier 2 studies may involve only dozens or hundreds of subjects. They may focus on a single workplace (for example, a single college campus).

They provide valuable insights into library user behaviour, but are best taken together as a whole to reach general conclusions. In addition to Tier 1 and Tier 2 studies, selected related materials are briefly described and are included in the bibliography. These in-clude bibliographies of writings about users of digital library materi-als and several important methods papers.

TIER 1 STUDIES

Eight groups of studies were identified as "Tier 1" or major recent research studies on how people use electronic library resources.

Tier 1 studies are (in no particular order):

- SuperJournal
- Digital Library Federation/Council on Library and Information Resources/Outsell (DLF/CLIR/Outsell)

- HighWire/eJUSt
- Pew Internet and American Life (with comparison to OCLC/Harris and Urban Libraries Council)
- OhioLINK
- Tenopir and King studies
- LibQUAL+™
- JSTOR studies

A synopsis of each is given first, followed by an analysis of the methods used, participants included, levels of conclusions, and find-ings for each group. In the bibliography, all of the publications that report on each study are listed together by the study group name.

SuperJournal

The SuperJournal project is a group of studies of e-journal use that began in 1995 in the United Kingdom in response to the information explosion and limited budgets. The researchers use a variety of research methods, including log file analysis, surveys, interviews, and focus groups, to study how academic users interact with e-journals and what features they value. Academic scientists and social scientists were studied, including both faculty and students in British universities.

Digital Library Federation/Council on Library and Information Resources/ Outsell (DLF/CLIR/Outsell)

Outsell, Inc., conducted a survey of information use for the Digital Library Federation and Council on Library and Information Resources in the fall of 2001 and early winter of 2002.

Some 3,234 faculty, graduate students, and undergraduate students across seven subject disciplines at private and public doctoral research universities and leading liberal arts colleges were interviewed over the telephone. They were asked about their use and preferences for both print and electronic resources from the library.

HighWire/eJUSt

The Stanford E-Journal Users Study (e-JUSt), published by HighWire Press, used a variety of methods to gain insights into the use of electronic journals, including qualitative user surveys, transaction log analysis, and an ethnographic study of scholarly e-journal usage.

The qualitative user surveys were done online with participants taken from subscribers to HighWire's medical and scientific journal Table of Contents service. The participants included graduate students, faculty members, and clinicians from universities, hospitals, and government and academic research institutes from 99 countries.

Pew Internet and American Life (also OCLC/Harris, and Urban Libraries Council)

The Pew Internet and American Life Project conducted two studies about how students use the Internet. In the "Internet Goes to College," 2,054 college students at two- and four-year public and private colleges completed surveys. In addition, graduate student researchers observed the behaviour of college students at Chicago area colleges and universities. In the other Pew Internet and American Life Project, "The Digital Disconnect: The Widening Gap between Internet Savvy Students and their Schools," middle and high school students were studied between November 2001 and March 2002. About 200 students wrote essays in which they expressed how they and their friends used the Internet for school and how they might use it in the future. Both these studies included how the students view the library.

OCLC/Harris and the Urban Libraries Council conducted similar surveys comparing library and Internet use by students and the public respectively. In the OCLC/Harris study, 1,050 participants were surveyed between December 11, 2001, and January 1, 2002. In the Urban Libraries Council study, 3,097 participants were surveyed by telephone between March and April 2000.

OhioLINK

The Ohio Library and Information Network is a consortium of Ohio's college and university libraries and the State Library of Ohio. The consortium serves in excess of 500,000 students, faculty, and staff at more than 80 institutions of higher learning. OhioLINK's Electronic Journal Center makes electronic articles and journals available to OhioLINK members. Transaction log analysis is used to measure the number of articles users download from the Electronic Journal Center. This programme, begun in April 1998, is ongoing.

Tenopir and King Studies

The Tenopir and King research studies are a series of surveys of more than 16,000 scientists, engineers, medical professionals, and social scientists in university and Non-university research settings. The surveys measure reading and authorship patterns of these subject experts through critical incident, demographic, and usage questions. Information-seeking behaviours, amount of reading, purposes of reading, and source of readings are all measured. Recent studies have focused on how reading patterns have changed over time with the adoption of e-journals and what role library-provided journals play in overall reading patterns. These ongoing experiments began in 1977.

LibQUAL+™

LibQUAL+ ™, conducted by the Association of Research Libraries (ARL) in conjunction with Texas A & M University, surveyed students, faculty, and staff at various community colleges, four-year colleges, and health science schools in the

United States as well as the New York Public Library and Smithsonian Institution during the spring of 2002. More than 70,000 faculty, staff, and students related how often they used the physical and electronic libraries. Furthermore, they answered questions about their library's level of service that they found minimally acceptable, the level they perceived, and the level they desired.

The results are presented by status of respondent and type of institution. Only those few questions that focus on desired levels for print and electronic collections and services are relevant and reported here.

JSTOR

The JSTOR system provides electronic archives of back issues of scholarly journals. JSTOR uses log analysis of both viewed and printed articles to characterise use of its materials. In addition, some JSTOR subscribing libraries have analysed their use of the JSTOR journals within their specific library environment.

In the fall of 2000, JSTOR surveyed more than 4,000 academic users of the collection in humanities, social sciences, and economics to discover usage patterns and preferences of university faculty.

PARTICIPANTS

Each of the eight Tier 1 studies examined a variety of participants, with college and university students and faculty members the most often studied, followed by practitioners and other subject experts in science, engineering, health, and social sciences. Table summarises the main participants included in each study.

Table. Tier 1: Participants

Study	Participants
SuperJournal	Students and faculty
DLF/CLIR/Outsell	Students and faculty
HighWire/eJUSt	Scholars and clinicians
Pew/OCLC-Harris/Urban Libraries Council	Middle, high, and college students/ general public
OhioLINK	OhioLINK users
Tenopir and King (academic and Non-academic)	Scientists and social scientists
LibQUAL+™	Library users at institutions of higher education (students and faculty)
JSTOR	JSTOR users (mostly faculty)

METHODS

The method or methods used in a research study determine what types of conclusions can be drawn about the sampled participants and what findings can be generalised to the population as a whole.

Wang provides an overview of methods for user behavioural research. An extension of her categorisation of methods is used here to describe Tier 1 studies. Tier 1 studies use one or more of the following methods:

- Surveying users
- Interviewing users (including focus groups)
- Observing users through experiments
- Observing users in natural settings (including keeping journals)
- Transaction log analysis

Covey also categorises usage studies to help librarians design the most appropriate studies for the type of information they hope to gather.

Covey's categories of research studies are similar to Wang's and include the following:

- Surveys (questionnaires)
- Focus groups
- User protocols (experiments and observations are both included here)
- Other (heuristic evaluations, paper prototypes and scenarios, and card-sorting tests)
- Transaction log analysis

Table summarises the methods used by the Tier 1 studies. Several use multiple methods for different phases of their projects; others rely on a single method.

Table. Tier 1: Methods Used.

Study	Methods
SuperJournal	Logs/surveys/focus groups/interviews
DLF/CLIR/Outsell	Interviews
HighWire/eJUSt	Surveys/interviews/logs
Pew/OCLC-Harris/Urban Libraries Council	Surveys/observation/focus groups/ journal keeping
OhioLINK	Logs
Tenopir and King	Surveys/critical incident
LibQUAL+™	Surveys
JSTOR	Logs

Surveys of users are typically done by sending a questionnaire by e-mail, the Web, or paper mail to a randomly selected percentage of the population under study. Tenopir and King, for example, survey samples of university faculty, members of professional organisations such as the American Astronomical Society, and scientists in companies and government laboratories. LibQUAL+ ™ libraries survey students and faculty within their own university community for comparison with other LibQUAL+ ™ libraries. Conclusions based on the responses are generalised to the whole using appropriate statistical tests. Care in selecting samples and a reasonable return rate are necessary to draw valid conclusions.

Almost all of the studies reported here that use surveys follow these basic precepts of sampling and analysis, but the types of conclusions that can be drawn vary by the types of questions that are asked. Among the Tier 1 studies that use surveys, the main distinctions in types of questions asked can be characterised as follows:

- Preference (focusing on what people want or think about a particular service; *e.g.*, LibQUAL+ ™, Pew)
- Reported behaviour (focusing on what people say they do in general; *e.g.*, DLF/CLIR/Outsell, HighWire/eJUSt)
- Critical incident questions (focusing on what people say they do in regard to a specific instance or reading; *e.g.*, Tenopir and King).

Table shows methods in more depth by looking at what types of questions were asked.

Table.Tier 1: Types of Questions

Study	Type of Questions
SuperJournal	Preference and reported behaviour
DLF/CLIR/Outsell	Preference and reported behaviour
HighWire/eJUSt	Preference and reported behaviour
Pew/OCLC-Harris/Urban Libraries Council	Preference and behaviour-reported and observed
OhioLINK	Log analysis
Tenopir and King reported behaviour	Critical incident, preference and
LibQUAL+™	Preference and reported behaviour
JSTOR	Preference and reported behaviour and log analysis

Together, the categories of participants and the methods used determine at which of three levels valid conclusions can be drawn:

- The "user level," that is, what do individuals or groups of individuals such as social science faculty say they do or prefer;
- The "group level," that is, what do groups of users at an institution do, without demographic differentiation; or
- The "readings or incident level," that is, what do specific users or groups of users do or prefer about a specific type of information or reading.

Table. Tier 1: Conclusion Level.

Study	Conclusions
SuperJournal	User level
DLF/CLIR/Outsell	User level
Study	**Conclusions**
HighWire/eJUSt	User level
Pew/OCLC-Harris/Urban Libraries Council	User level
OhioLINK	Group level
Tenopir and King	User and reading levels
LibQUAL+™	User level
JSTOR	User and group level

SuperJournal, for example, uses transaction logs, surveys with questions about preferences and behaviour, focus groups, and interviews to study faculty and graduate students. Demographic information is known for each user. These multiple methods allow conclusions to be drawn at the user level for both behaviour and preferences (what specific types of users do and what they prefer). JSTOR uses transaction logs separate from survey questions. DLF/CLIR/Outsell used interviews to gather information on what users say they prefer and say they do in general. Demographic information is known about each user. This allows conclusions to be drawn at the user level as well. Tenopir and King use critical incident questions in their surveys, which ask users to focus on the last article read. Together with demographic data, this allows conclusions to be made at the readings level (characteristics of the total amount of readings done by individuals and groups of individuals). Each of these methods has advantages and disadvantages.

According to Covey, problems or concerns with surveys include the following:

- General surveys are time-consuming and expensive to prepare, conduct, and interpret.
- Unless follow-ups are sent so longitudinal analysis can track changing patterns of use, surveys provide no baseline data.
- People receive many surveys, and it is difficult to motivate them to complete and return surveys.
- The usage information gathered in general surveys might better be gathered by transactional logs.
- Specific surveys are more beneficial, but must be repeated over time.
- User satisfaction surveys may not provide enough information to solve the problem, and service "gap" surveys are more difficult to administer and analyse.
- A survey is only as good as the wording of the questions and the response rate.

Problems or concerns with focus groups, according to Covey, include the following:

- A skilled moderator needs to direct the groups to keep discussions on track.
- An unskilled observer may fail to take adequate notes.
- The qualitative data gathered in focus groups can be time consuming and difficult to interpret.

Problems or concerns with experiments or observations (called user protocols by Covey), include the following:

- Librarians, if observing, have a difficult time not assisting the subjects.
- Librarians may not be trained to interpret and analyse the data from user protocols.
- Recruiting subjects, in particular subjects who are comfortable with the process of thinking aloud, is difficult.

Problems with transaction log analysis, according to Covey, in-clude the following:

- Deciding on the right and most useful usage statistics
- Collecting the right usage statistics
- Getting the right and consistent usage statistics from vendors
- Analysing and interpreting data (it can be time consuming and difficult)
- Presenting the data in a meaningful way.

In summary, the conclusions that can be drawn from each of the Tier 1 and Tier 2 studies depends on the methods used, including the overall method(s), types of questions asked, level of questions, and participants studied. It may be tempting for a researcher to draw broader conclusions than his or her methods justify—a failing that was found in more than one study examined. Only those findings that are justified by each study's methods are reported here. In general, the following types of conclusions can be drawn from each technique:

- *Transaction logs*: What groups do in general; for example, what the college or university libraries in the OhioLINK system do in general. Transaction logs do not show preferences; rather, they show action from which preferences are often inferred. Demographic data from individuals are usually not gathered because of privacy concerns. Instead usage is identified by IP address, location, or library, so conclusions about differences in work fields or status of user cannot be drawn. Transaction logs that result from an experimental design allow more finely tuned conclusions.
- *Interviews or surveys: preference questions*: Preference questions, or questions about what people want, show what people say they prefer or value. Demographic information is almost always asked, allowing conclusions to be made about groups. (For example, in HighWire/eJUSt, most science faculty members say their favorite e-journal feature is linking.) Preferences may or may not predict actual or future behaviour.
- *Interviews or surveys*: behavioural questions: Questions about behavior in general (for example, "Do you use the library's electronic journals?") show what people do at least some of the time. Demographic information is almost always gathered as well, allowing conclusions to be drawn about individuals or groups of individuals. (For example, the DLF/CLIR/Outsell study shows that most humanities fac-ulty members use the print collection for at least part of their work.)
- *Interviews or surveys*: critical incident questions: Respondents are asked to focus on a specific incident; for example, the last article they read or

the last article they authored. Specific questions about that incident are then asked. Demographic information is also collected. This allows conclusions to be made about the total amount of reading or for specific characteristics of users or readings. (For example, Tenopir report that 80 per cent of the articles astronomers read in a year are from electronic sources.)

- *Focus groups*: Focus group participants are not randomly selected; instead, individuals who can express opinions about a service or issue are invited to participate. Therefore, preferences and behaviours observed in focus groups must not be overly generalised to the population as a whole, nor interpreted as the only possibilities. (For example, from SuperJournal, faculty members report a variety of uses for electronic journals, including keeping current in their areas of research, gathering background information, and preparing for a specific event.) Focus groups are helpful as a first step or in conjunction with other research methods.
- *Observation*: experimental: Controlled experiments gather both quantitative and qualitative data on how users behave in a controlled environment, such as searching on a specific online system, and why they behave in a certain way. Demographic data are gathered, along with other data about individual differences, such as from controlled tests. Conclusions depend on the experimental treatment. (For example, log analysis in conjunction with experimental observation in the SuperJournal study shows that social scientists browse differently than scientists.)
- *Observation in natural setting*: journal keeping: Participants are asked to record their interactions with information systems or their research process. Conclusions can be drawn about types of behaviour, and models of behaviour can be derived. (For example, in the Pew Studies, students recorded using electronic resources more than print resources and felt they knew more about the Internet than do their teachers.)

TIER 2 ANALYSIS

How people use electronic resources or their preferences for print and electronic library services have been the focus of dozens of in-dividual research studies in the last few years. Surveys are by far the most popular method, with academic faculty and students the most popular participants.

Although participants include a variety of subject experts, scientists of various sorts have been studied most frequently. Not every study will be discussed in detail in this analysis, but both common threads and unique findings of the studies will be highlighted. Summary analyses of the methods used and groups studied are shown in figures.

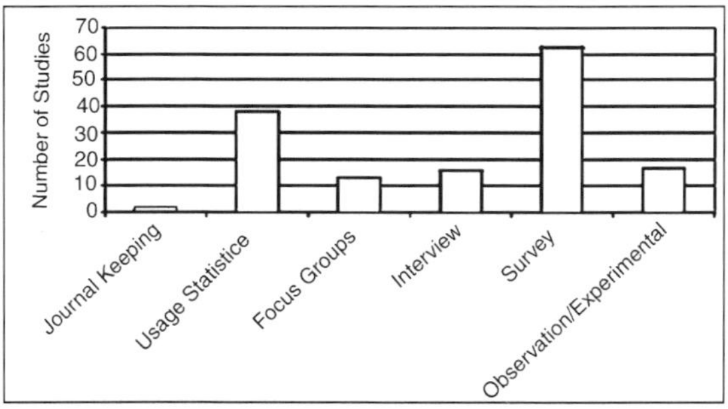

Fig. Methods Used in Tier 2 Studies.

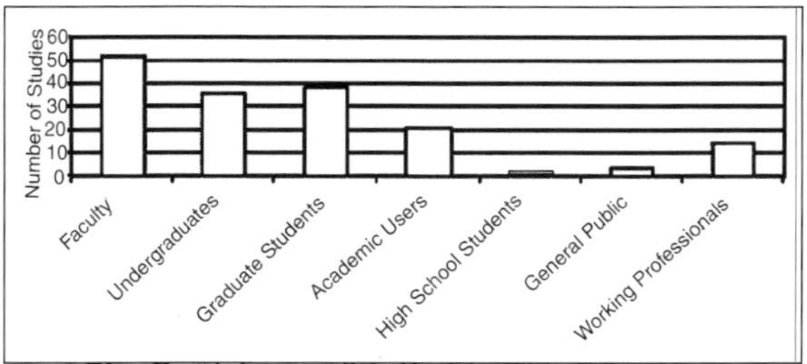

Fig. Participants Studied in Tier 2 Studies.

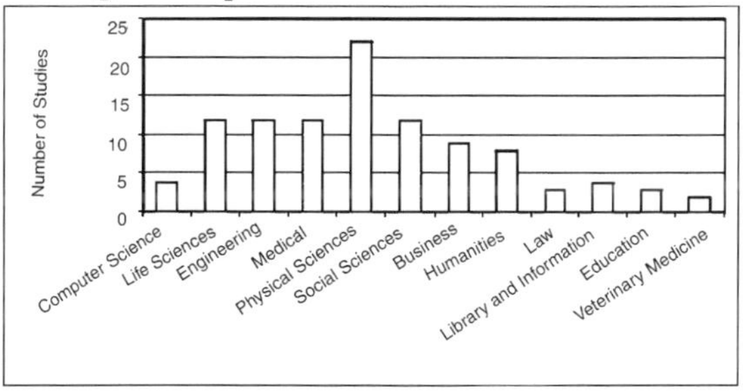

Fig. Workfields of Participants Studied in Tier 2 Studies.

The Tier 2 studies echo many of the findings of the larger Tier 1 studies, allowing some consistent conclusions to be drawn about user behaviour. This section is arranged by general themes that are found in many studies, and then further organised by specific themes, some of which emerge in only some of the studies, others that emerge consistently, but with contradictory results.

The general themes and specific sub-themes are as follows:

- Differences in behaviour or preferences that can be explained by differences among users. Differences include:
  - Differences by subject discipline
  - Differences by user status or workplace
  - Differences by task
  - Differences by age or gender
- Information-seeking behaviour and preferences, including differences between print and electronic resources:

- Browsing versus searching
- Preferences for print or electronic resources
- Awareness of electronic resources
- Search strategies
- Reasons for using the resources
- Sources of information about resources
- Self-evaluation of system navigation
- Perceived advantages of electronic resources and preferences, including:
  - How electronic resources improve workflow or save time
  - Preferred features of electronic information systems
  - Currency and timeliness of sources
- Perceived disadvantages or concerns about electronic resources, including:
  - Technological or service problems
  - Archiving
  - Problems or confusion with information systems
  - Preferred formats for reading
  - Electronic versus print resources
- Library policy and financial issues:
  - Willingness to pay for electronic information
  - Willingness to cancel print journals in favour of electronic
  - Other library budgetary issues that affect users

Differences in Behaviour or Preferences that can be Explained by Differences Among Users

The concept of a single typical "user" of information systems is clearly a fallacy. Scientists seek and use information differently than do social scientists or humanists; undergraduate students behave differently than do graduate students or faculty; searching for information for personal use is different from searching for work-related tasks.

Numerous studies have reached these conclusions. Faculty members and other professionals in the sciences, math, and medicine fields were early adopters of electronic journals and other digital library resources and remain the heaviest and most enthusiastic users. Lenares found as early as the late 1990s that 90 per cent of the physical science faculty used electronic journals at least part of the time, compared with 61 per cent of all faculty users in ARL universities.

The percentage of faculty using electronic journals for at least some of their readings increased from 1998 to 1999 and has continued to increase each year. By 2002 at the University of Maryland, more faculty members used electronic journals daily or weekly than they did print journals. This corresponds to the decrease in physical visits to the library by graduate students and faculty, especially in health sciences, science, and engineering. Enthusiasm for electronic journals and patterns of use vary even among fields of science. Chemists and physicists use them frequently, while earth scientists and mathematicians see fewer advantages.

Medical school users rely on fewer electronic journal titles for their downloads and readings than do other library users. These variations are also reported by Tenopir and King, who found physicists and astronomers to be among the most enthusiastic users of electronic articles, partly because the digital e-print archives, the Astrophysics Data System (ADS), and e-journals of the American Astronomical Society were designed specifically to facilitate their natural work patterns. Business school faculty members were also early adopters. Business school faculty reported the highest use, while Palmer and Sandler found economics faculty to be the most enthusiastic users of electronic journals. Speier and Hahn found that among business faculty, finance and management information systems faculty were more aware of electronic journals than those in other fields. Faculty members in history, education, and the arts have been slower to adopt electronic journals.

Among corporate users, investment and banking companies or departments spend a higher per cent of their budgets on electronic products than do other types of businesses such as pharmaceutical firms, legal services, food services, or telecommunications. Although high percentages of faculty members use electronic journals, they still use a variety of sources, including print, for their readings. In 1999, Lenares found that although 90 per cent of physical sciences faculty respondents at ARL libraries used electronic journals, half reported that they read articles from electronic journals infrequently.

Undergraduates in the life science disciplines were found by Whitmire to engage in more information-seeking activities than were students in other disciplines, including using the online catalog, asking librarians for help, using indexes, and browsing the stacks. Engineers engaged in the fewest information-seeking behaviours. Variations in information-seeking behaviour by individual groups make the task of designing an e-journal, user interface, or electronic library a challenge. One attempt to meet this challenge is to provide a "MyLibrary" feature on a library's home page. This allows users to customise their view of the electronic library and highlight the resources they use most often. Another solution is to maintain a balance between print and electronic collections, depending on the preferences of the main user groups.

Librarians must gauge their systems, collection development deci-sions, and instruction with user differences firmly in mind. No single solution will be best for everyone and the totally digital library is a long way in the future in many subject disciplines. Publishers also must design electronic resources that facilitate the work patterns of their target audiences. Differences in motivation or task also cause variations in information seeking and use. Nelson in a study of faculty and students at the University of West England, found that the greatest predictor of electronic use was whether or not the person was engaged in research. Researchers and academic staff were more likely to use electronic journals than were administrative staff. King and Mont-gomery found that more than half of the readings by faculty and doctoral students are done while conducting primary research. Faculty who publish more and those who had served on promotion and tenure committees were found to be more likely to be aware of electronic journals, and faculty with tenure are more likely to submit articles to electronic journals.

Scientists who win awards read more on average. Graduate students, particularly Ph.D. students, are often found to be heavy users of electronic journals, most likely in their role as researchers. As found in the SuperJournal projects, graduate students may be "binge" users, consulting electronic journals extensively for a short period when they are writing a thesis or dissertation. There are some exceptions—undergraduates were the most frequent users in an experimental study conducted by the American Chemical Society. Different workplaces or types of institutions have varying use patterns as well. Davis examined electronic journal user logs in libraries of the NorthEast Research Library Consortium and found that each institution has a unique pattern of use—medical institution users had higher use of a smaller number of journals, while users at large universities and smaller colleges downloaded articles from a greater variety of journal titles. Other differences are more controversial or less conclusive.

Some studies found differences in preferences or behaviour based on the age of the user. In the late-1990s, Researchers found that younger ARL university business faculty members reported that they read from electronic journals more often and were more aware of electronic journals than were older faculty. In a study done in 1996 and 1997, more than half of the faculty members under the age of 40 reported using electronic journals, as compared with only 14 per cent of those over 40, although more than 80 per cent of the total respondents indicated they would consider using electronic journals in the future. Antoir found that older people preferred print articles; Monopoli found that users between 21 and 34 used electronic journals most frequently. Older University of Michigan social sciences faculty members tended to prefer print more often than did younger faculty. Age made a difference in how faculty members, staff, and students at Colorado State University rated their computer skills, with more respondents under 30 rating their skills as good.

Differences in electronic journal use may be attributed to age, status, or rank. Tenner and Yang found that assistant professors are most likely to have used electronic journals (44.7 per cent), followed by full professors (34.5 per cent), and associate professors (34.2 per cent). Researchers found that undergraduates, medical students, and residents prefer electronic journals, while clinical and research faculty members prefer print. Researchers in other studies found no relationship between age and searching skills, although the researchers observed that younger users are more likely to browse on the computer, while older users prefer print journals for browsing. Researchers found no relationship between age and reading patterns among astronomers. Age differences should be studied more, at least for the next generation, Since, most college students now are computer literate and report that they use the Web frequently. This does not necessarily correlate with effective use, however. An experimental study found that faculty performed tasks requiring retrieval and use of journal and newspaper articles significantly better than undergraduates.

Researcher found that students had more confidence in their searching skills than did their faculty. Although lower division undergraduate students used the Web and Web search engines frequently, students are mostly unaware of the distinctions between material on the Web and peer-reviewed journals. Freshman psychology students with higher self-efficacy scores are more motivated to learn about electronic journals and find electronic journals easier to use, but they also visit the library more often. Gender differences are even more inconclusive. Only a few studies have examined gender as a factor in information use, beyond studies of recreational Internet use.

In teaching, men report significantly more use of a search engine to access e-journals than do women who access e-journals. Some individual differences may be a factor only in early adoption and, as electronic resources become familiar and ubiquitous through the library, these differences may cease to be important. Other factors, such as the way different disciplines do their work, may be more pervasive.

Researchers for example, found that biologists rely on print because of deeply ingrained work habits, and earth scientists fail to see work advantages of electronic journals. Part of the hesitancy of some may be a discomfort with technology, unavailability of technology, or insufficient knowledge of electronic journals, all of which are already changing. Physicists embrace preprints and have adopted e-print servers enthusiastically in part because their research tends to be highly collaborative and is conducted in large research institutions that have internal peer review.

ELECTRONIC RESOURCES

Electronic resources can be defined as resources in electronic format or computerprocessible format that provide information or an indicator to the information and are generally accessible over the Internet or stored on media like CD ROM/ DVD ROM or other storage devices.

The emergence of Internet and the World Wide Web (WWW) in early 1990s, as a new media of information storage and delivery, came as a real boon for evolution of electronic resources. While searching bibliographic databases became popular, it created demand for actual content in full-text that became difficult for libraries to obtain.

Coincided with evolution of World Wide Web (WWW), display technology evolved, cost of storage came down drastically and networks became faster. It became possible for publishers to deliver content, either as a bitmap page images or other structured formats such as HTML, PDF or RTF. Increasingly larger number of publishers started using the Internet as a global way to offer their publications to the international community of scientists and technologists given the fact that technology is in a position to deliver more content to more users at a significantly lower cost per user.

Electronic resources on the Internet manifest themselves in numerous flavours and categories, although most of them emulate the traditional publishing while others are revolutionary in their design and approach. While the present trend to imitate and emulate the traditional models of scholarly communication may continue for some time, eventually the capabilities added by the new media would be used in more innovative ways. Some of the important types of e-resources are described here.

ELECTRONIC DATABASES

An electronic database consists of electronic resources integrated in highly organised fashion so as to provide controlled access to it by their commercial providers. The first databases were bibliographic in nature and were online version of existing indexing and abstracting services such as Biological Abstracts, Index Medicus, Chemical Abstracts,,etc.

By the year 1988, only half of all databases were bibliographic in nature. With introduction of a number of online databases containing textual information, news, statistics, commodity prices,,etc.,, a third type of databases holding text of full-length documents started appearing. Several full-text of encyclopaedia, directories and articles from journals are now available online.

Most of the publishers now provide access to their full-text journals through their web site or through other electronic publishing platforms.

While there are a number of public-domain databases, most online databases require annual subscription for accessing them. Thousands of databases are now available on compact discs (CD-ROM) as well as on the Web.

ELECTRONIC JOURNALS

Electronic journals, or 'e-journals', are used for those journals and newsletters that are prepared and distributed electronically. Electronic journals may be defined very broadly as any journal, magazine, e-zine, webzine, newsletter or type of electronic serial publication which is available over the Internet and can be accessed using different technologies such as WWW, Gopher, ftp, telnet, e-mail or listserv. Several traditional journals are now being published both on the Web and in print.

Content lists for most of the journals are available on the Web or distributed to subscribers as an e-mail text messages or through technologies like RSS and Atom. Internet-based electronic journals started to appear in the beginning of 1990. These journals were mostly delivered as an attachment to e-mail while their back issues were mounted on anonymous ftp sites and users were required to download them from these ftp sites. The libraries and information centres made them accessible through their gopher site.

1995 witnessed peak of Gopher technology which then dropped suddenly and dramatically by 1997. With advent of WWW technology in 1993, electronic publishing became more than a novelty, the web as a means of delivery of electronic information has grown steadily Since, then. As publishers experiment with different publication modes and models, the very definition of a journal is undergoing change in the electronic environment.

New journals have evolved based on the graphic capabilities of the Internet that are available only in electronic form. Like print journals, current and archival issues of electronic journals can be browsed through their content pages. Moreover, e-journals can also be searched not only on their metadata but also in full-text through sophisticated search interface. Currently, there are more than 50,000 peer-reviewed, scholarly electronic journals that are available on the Internet.

ELECTRONIC BOOKS

An electronic book is digital reading material that a user can view on a desktop or Personal Digital Assistant (PDA), laptop or on a dedicated, portable device with a large storage capacity and the ability to download new titles via a network connection.

More and more traditional book publishers, as well as those catering to the professional and business communities, are launching their e-book collections. The electronic books market consists of two distinct components, *i.e.,* i) electronic books consisting of digital material or contents; and ii) electronic book hardware including ebook reading appliance, PCs, laptop or PDA.

The digital material or content that make an electronic book are simply textual and graphical files consisting of bits that can be transported any digital storage media or delivered over a network connection. It is designed to be viewed on some combination of hardware and software ranging from dumb terminals to web browsers, on personal computers to the new reading appliances. More and more books are now being released on the web through enhanced interfaces that offer features such as increased search capacity within a book or entire collection of books, ability to highlight and flag a page, ability to make notes on text without damaging the book, ability to e-mail quotes from the books to other colleagues, etc.

Most publishers like Springer, Wiley InterScience, Taylor and Francis, Cambridge University Press, Oxford University Press, etc., offer their e-book collections on subscription/ one-time purchase basis. Besides, there are a number of e-books aggregators that make thousands of books available online for libraries and individuals at relatively lower cost. Three major ebooks aggregators are Questia, Ebrary and NetLibrary. However, just like other e-resources, e-books come with restrictions such as limit on downloads, in terms of number of pages, *i.e.,* one page at a time or one chapter at a time or no download at all.

ELECTRONIC THESES AND DISSERTATIONS

Theses submitted to the universities as requirement for the award of Ph.D. degree constitute a useful source of information for the new and ongoing research. Doctoral dissertations submitted to universities and academic institutions are originally created in digital format using one of the word processing software packages like MSWord, LaTex, Word Perfect, Word Pro, etc.,

or one of the desktop publishing packages like Page Maker, Ventura, etc. These documents are undisputedly highly valuable collection especially in digital format that qualify to be an important component of a digital library. The documents composed on word processing packages/ desktop publishing packages can be easily converted into PDF, Post Script or XML using appropriate software tools so as to host them on the web.

Several universities and institutions have already implemented electronic submission of doctoral dissertations under the overall umbrella of an international digital library initiative called 'Networked Digital Library of Theses and Dissertations' (NDLTD).

AUDIO, VIDEO AND STREAMING MEDIA

Streaming multimedia is sequential delivery of multimedia content, including video, audio or some other learning objects, over a computer network that is displayed (or played back) to the end-user as it is being delivered by the provider.

The advent of the MP3 players and the iPod resulted in a greater effort to deliver downloadable media. Moreover, web documents are now coming with greater integration of text with media. Encyclopaedia now have articles with audio files, video clips and animation to illustrate a given topic. Media can broadly be categorised into three category, namely.

- Commercial movies that have greater copyright restrictions,
- Educational media typically are lesser controlled and many a time are made available free-of-cost; and
- Media targeted for individual users, such as movies and songs, that comes with restrictions in terms of copying and distributions.

SUBJECT GATEWAYS OR LIBRARY PORTALS

The web, being a hypermedia-based system, allows linking amongst electronic resources stored on servers dispersed geographically on distant locations.

The portal sites or gateways redirect a user to the holders of the original digital material. The librarians, being the earliest users of the web, started to gather and organise link to important web-based resources on various subjects. A subject gateway can be defined as facilities that allow easier access to web-based resources in a defined subject area.

The simplest types of subject gateways are sets of web pages containing list of links to resources. Some gateways index their lists of links and provide a simple search facility. More advanced gateways offer a muchenhanced service via a system consisting of a resource database and various indexes, which can be searched and/ or browse throughout a web-based interface.

Subject gateways are also known as Subject-based Information Gateways (SBIGs), subject-based gateways, subject index gateways, virtual libraries, clearing houses, subject trees, pathfinders,,etc. Subject gateway is an important component of a library web site designed for the library users so as to help them discover high-quality information on the Internet in a quick and effective way. In the traditional information environment human intermediaries, such as publishers and librarians, filter and process information so that users can search catalogues and indexes of organised knowledge as opposed to raw data and information. Subject gateways work on the same principle,, *i.e.,* they employ subject experts and information professionals to select, classify and catalogue Internet resources to aid search and retrieval for the users. Users are offered access to a database of Internet resources descriptions which they can search by keywords or browse by subject area. A description of each resource is provided to help users assess very quickly its origin, content and nature, enabling them to decide if it is worth investigating further.

In the process users get benefited from the expertise of librarians and subject experts with subject gateways rather than having to locate, evaluate, filter and organise the resources themselves. Specialised software are available as freeware or as priced software to create and maintain professionally developed subject gateways.

RECENT ELECTRONIC INFORMATION SYSTEMS

Some clues about how authors and readers might behave in digital libraries and hypertext publishing systems can be perceived by looking at how people currently use computer bulletin boards, computer data bases, and other information services and electronic mail systems. Instead of viewing these systems as technical precedents, it is instructive to consider them as experiments in developing appropriate models for intellectual property and reader/user/author behaviour that might be adapted for more ambitious applications such as Xanadu.

PRODIGY AND CompuServe

Prodigy and CompuServe are commercial services that provide a variety of bulletin boards, electronic mail, infor-mation services, and entertainment. They embody significantly different models of user behaviour, and their pricing strategies are markedly different. Prodigy targets the consumer and home markets, and treats its users as relatively passive information consumers who do not interact much with each other. Prodigy offers users access to many different kinds of information, as well as bulletin boards, electronic mail, and some entertainment. Its services are made available for a fixed monthly fee.

Usage-insensitive pricing is made possible by the paid advertising that Prodigy presents along with nearly every screen of information displayed to users. When Prodigy imposed a usage-pricing scheme for sending electronic mail, many users felt that their contract with Prodigy, as well as their "free speech fights," had been violated. In contrast, CompuServe has been oriented towards business and professional users and always had usage-based pricing based on connect time.

CompuServe information services are specifically focused, organized into a complex hierarchy of bulletin boards and data bases, many of which are moderated by an expert, who in some circumstances is compensated by CompuServe. This finer-grained categorization enables CompuServe to impose sur-charges for supposedly more timely or valuable information, but its user population is presumably used to paying for information according to its value. Users engage in heated electronic dialogues with one another on bulletin boards, commenting on and criticizing one another's postings. Both Prodigy and CompuServe place some limits on user downloading.

Some materials, such as shareware or public domain software from both sources, can be downloaded without restriction, but other materials are restricted. The two systems differ, however, in the locus of restrictions. Prodigy is a centralized service which means it sets and enforces the downloading policy. CompuServe, by contrast, has a more decentralized policy because it is essentially an umbrella organization for a number of information services, and these services often have their own downloading policies. Quite recently, however, both Prodigy and CompuServe have expanded user opportunities to download materials, although this adds to the cost of the service.

THE INTERNET

The Internet is a vast network of networks that inter-connect thousands of computing sites in government, industry, and academia. The Intermit has evolved from primarily providing electronic mail services to become the infrastructure for significantly broader services of information exchange and collaborative work. Like CompuServe, the heart of the Internet is a vast collection of newsgroups in which participants from around the world post and comment on messages. Some people take on the role of newsgroup moderators, but the overwhelming majority of newsgroups are unmediated.

Author and reader behaviour on the Internet are largely governed by norms or "netiquette" that have evolved over time and that are enforced both by system administrators and by the informal but effective sanctions of "flames" (critical messages) directed at violators. Included in these norms are rules about selecting newsgroups in which to post messages, sensitivity to authors of posted messages when citing or responding to them, and other matters that affect both authors and readers. Users of the Internet vary greatly in their perception of intellectual property laws as they apply to this new kind of publishing system. Some users, especially new users who are college students, act as if the Internet services and the information that can be had by exploring the Internet are completely free.

In fact, each host machine that serves as an Internet site has to pay a fee for the privilege. Institutions recoup these fees as well as other costs associated with use of host machines by passing them on, even if the costs are not immediately evident because they may be borne by a particular unit of the institution, rather than directly by those who use the machine for Internet services. Those who post information not authored by them on Intermit bulletin boards or in electronic newsletters delivered by Internet sometimes do so with a conspicuous notice that it is being posted without copyright permission, thereby asserting the poster's view of an appropriate scope of fair use.

But some who post materials on the Internet explicitly assert copyrights on the messages that they post. And it has become increasingly common for electronic journals distributed on the Internet to contain a notice that those who contribute items to the journals are responsible for obtaining whatever copyright permissions might be needed. Although "net" users generally regard it as fair to download items from the bulletin board for one's personal use, and even to send a copy to a friend who might otherwise not see the item, it is considered bad manners (or worse) to redistribute more widely someone else's posting without its author's permission.

Still, it is worth noting that because "the net" is so vast and the number of its users so large, it can be extremely difficult to police it for copyright purposes. Authors who distribute works on the Internet are generally not paid to publish, and receive no royalties. Nor do readers generally have to pay to read items on the Internet. But it is fair to state that many Interact activities are being paid for (or at least subsidized) by Interact participants' employers. Hence, it can be argued that anything posted on the Internet that is work-related is the intellectual property of the employer who provides access to the Internet by paying for the computers and telecommunications infrastructure.

Employers may feel that the value of the information their employees glean from the Internet outweighs the costs of the time to obtain it, but it is unlikely that many employers explicitly make this analysis. In addition to electronic mail and newsgroups, the Internet now supports several innovative services that enable it to function as a distributed digital library with vast holdings. If an Internet site chooses to make some of its information publicly available, a user on another site can use the anonymous FTP (file transfer protocol) mechanism to retrieve it.

Other experimental services, some with fanciful names like Archie, Gopher, and World Wide Web, build upon FTP to provide users with a worldwide index so that they can find sites that offer the information they seek. The WWW service allows users to retrieve what they want even if they cannot directly connect to the site that stores it. These new services are being enthusiastically embraced in the academic and research communities of the Internet, but they pose even more problems for intellectual property rights because they erode the boundaries between public and commercial information sources.

LEXIS ARM WESTLAW

Lawyers have had access to digital libraries of legal materials for well over a decade, thanks initially to the farsightedness of a paper manufacturer, which perceived a market opportunity for providing electronic access to judicial opinions, statutes, regulations, and other legal materials. This manufacturer formed Mead Data Central, whose Lexis data base lawyers use regularly. Like so many other print publishers, the major legal print publisher, West Publishing, did not see the market opportunity for electronic information services until after Lexis had become a major success.

Although a late entrant to the business, West has succeeded in designing a digital library of legal materials that offers some services, particularly the key numbering system that West had long used in print, that give it some competitive advantage. The initial pricing scheme employed by Lexis and by West was similar to that used by CompuServe: usage-based pricing based on connect-time. This pricing strategy worked particularly well because lawyers could typically pass these charges on to clients. Over time, both services developed pricing strategies for institutions, such as law schools, where connect-time charges could not be passed on.

Both services also now permit downloading of electronic versions of legal materials as well as printouts of selected materials. No special charges seem to be levied for these services, although usage-based charging would absorb the costs through connect-time, and institutional subscription pricing would be based on a predicted quantum of such uses. There is no technical reason why these two digital libraries could not become hypertext publishing systems. Their considerable financial success might suggest that this extension would be a natural one, and indeed, at least one author has tried to make them become so.

Professor Peter Martin of the Comell Law School sought to bring about this kind of expansion of legal data base functions by creating a hypertext treatise on Social Security Law on the Lexis system. Because Lexis had no particular incentive to promote its use, Martin eventually negotiated an arrangement by which he could "port" the treatise to a CD-ROM so it could be commercialized. Professor Henry Perritt of Villanova Law School has also proposed hypertext publishing systems built on top of digital libraries of legal materials as a way to produce electronic casebooks.

But except for the work of a few pioneers, such as Professors William Andersen of the University of Washington Law School, William Boyd of the University of Arizona Law School, and Ronald Staudt of the Chicago-Kent Law School, hypertext has yet to come to the field of law. The richly inter textual nature of law makes it a natural field for hypertext applications, and perhaps ways can be found to create them on top of a digital library of legal materials such as Lexis or Westlaw, and make them commercially viable.

INFORMATION-SEEKING BEHAVIOUR AND PREFERENCES

Students, faculty, and Non-university professionals now use a variety of sources for articles, including electronic journals, print journals, Web sites of professional organisations, author's Web sites, e-mail from colleagues, and e-print servers. Print remains important for at least some information for all subject disciplines and as part of the research process for undergraduates.

Even as early as 1996, academic users expressed dissatisfaction with library collections of printed journals, books, and conference proceedings. Both current and older materials remain important, as many of the Tier 1 studies found. At the University of California, Berkeley, 93 per cent of faculty members and 87 per cent of graduate students across academic disciplines reported that they use materials older than five years "sometimes" or "often." Most preferred electronic resources and often use the library from their desktops.

Faculty and other subject experts make a distinction between core journal titles and Non-core journals. At the University of Maryland, 70 per cent of the faculty want core journals in both print and electronic form, but the same number wanted Non-core journals only in electronic form. Although both browsing and searching remain important information seeking strategies, electronic journals are causing a decrease in browsing titles, while searching by topic has increased. Browsing of core journals by tables of contents remains important, but searching by topic for additional journals and articles is increasingly popular, particularly in large, mixed-journal title databases.

Most libraries offer a combination of these large full-text databases, which facilitate searching, and journal systems from publishers, which facilitate browsing. In systems restricted to journals from a single publisher, browsing through tables of contents remains important.

There was a dramatic increase in the number of articles viewed or downloaded between 1999 and 2001, but PDF remained a more popular format than HTML. Worlock found that articles recommended by colleagues were more often in print than in electronic format. Contradictory results were obtained by the researchers, who discovered that e-mail and listservs make it easier to share recommended articles with colleagues. University faculty members reported the ability to send articles to their colleagues instantly as being one of the major advan-tages of electronic journals. Use of online indexes and abstracts seems to have increased, particularly when there are links to full texts.

More than 80 per cent of veterinary medicine students at Iowa State University used online indexes in 1997, compared with only 16 per cent a decade earlier indicating a major shift to electronic resources during that decade. More than half of the medical faculty, residents, and students at a regional site of the University of Illinois report that they search MEDLINE at least weekly and much of their identification of journals comes from MEDLINE.

Awareness and use of other abstracting and indexing services or full text databases is low, however. The Pew studies and Graham clearly show that high school students, in particular, and undergraduate students prefer to search the Internet first for school-related tasks. When given a specific research task, only 2 per cent of undergraduates at Wellesley College's "Computers and the Internet" class included Non-Internet resources in their answers.

The students have extraordinary faith in their favorite search engine, even though they are unclear how it works. A nationwide survey of students and academics in the Neth-erlands found that 60 per cent of respondents in the humanities, 78 per cent of respondents in the social sciences, and 82 per cent of respondents in the sciences used the Internet for study or work and nearly all believed they had Internet skills. Still, when rating the importance of different means of searching, more than 88 per cent believed that subject searching of tables of contents databases was important or very important, followed by searching the OPAC, citations, and asking colleagues.

Nearly two-thirds believed searching the Internet or the Web were important or very important, and most perceived that their Web searches yielded enough or more than enough information. A vast majority reported they were self-taught Internet searchers, who rely on trial and error. Assistance from colleagues was the second most frequently cited means of acquiring searching skills; gaining the skills through library courses was far less commonly cited. Ninety-seven per cent of freshmen psychology students reported that they access the Internet at least weekly, about 44 per cent of the time for educational information. More than three-quarters say they begin their research through the Internet, and two-thirds say they find most of their information through the Internet. Still, two-thirds also report that they visit the physical library at least weekly, most often for studying.

The role of the library as a place to study and socialise was more important than as a place to get information. Half of the students access the library's electronic resources from home, and only a quarter said that use of the electronic resources was a reason to visit the library. Dilevko and Gottlieb report efforts to attract undergraduates to the physical library. Since, most undergraduates report that they turn first to online sources, and Since, turnstile counts were going down at the University of Toronto library, they surveyed students to find what role print materials still play for undergraduates. About 47 per cent of undergraduates reported that they began their assignments with online sources 90 per cent of the time, but printed journals and, especially, print books remain important in their research, particularly for humanities students. The authors conclude that print books are still vital and are associated with high-quality work. They recommend that librarians stress the value of printed materials in addition to online materials for the successful completion of assignments.

A teacher's or librarian's recommendation of specific sources, such as a library full-text database or a specific Web site, is reported to influence a student's choice of sources. At the University of California, Berkeley, the groups of faculty and graduate students that report the heaviest use of electronic resources also recommend the need for more library reference and instructional services.

Use of electronic books is also clearly course driven—books with the highest usage are those required in a class, and most users come to an electronic book collec-tion to use a single title. Researchers also found that most un-dergraduates in a composition class were always or almost always likely to use a recommended full-text database provided by the library as a first stop for information; the next largest group went first to the Web, and the smallest group went first to print.

When searching on a mixed full-text/bibliographic database, many said they always restricted their search to full text. Most students did not limit their research to a single source of information, but of those who did, the Web was the most popular single source for information, followed by a full-text database. Faculty members and librarians can influence students' choices of electronic resources, although faculty may not always be familiar with the range of sources available to them through the library.

Library instruction, with time for practice, increases college students' efficacy in online searching. Researcher found that students who had a more positive attitude Towards learning electronic information search skills had fewer negative emotions about electronic searching and performed better in assignments. Librarians should stress the importance of all library materials, including print and electronic resources, since, undergraduate students value recommendations.

The most effective way for students to learn about important resources in academic libraries seems to be for librarians to work directly with faculty to bring relevant electronic resources into the classroom. Students bring web searching habits to their use of electronic scholarly materials and seem to have difficulty adapting to different types of information resources, interfaces, or search systems. In a controlled study of 49 undergraduates, graduates, and faculty members, Researchers found that few undergraduates took time to read explanations or help screens, and that they give up easily and are not selective.

These findings are similar to the many Web use studies beyond the scope of this report that show Web users in general tend to enter only a single search term and seldom look beyond the first screen. Students claim to use evaluation methods for Web sites.

However, researcher found that students were susceptible to advertising claims on Web sites, government misinformation, and propaganda and could not consistently differentiate between advertising and fact.

Only a few students in this experiment double-checked the information they found on the Web.

There is some evidence also that college students have a low tolerance for system features that don't work or are too difficult. Bishop conducted user tests at the University of Illinois and found that if an abstract was missing when a student clicked on the abstract button, the student never again clicked on the button for abstracts.

Researcher concluded that one small system failure might have a long-term impact on student searching behaviour. Some college students report that they receive at least some training in evaluating library sources, but a sizable minority do not. Those with no training show a slight preference for the Internet over the library for research.

More than half of the undergraduate and graduate students from 97 different majors in a medium-sized Western university reported they use both the library and the Internet for research, while 21 per cent use the library exclusively, 21 per cent use the Internet exclusively, and 6 per cent use neither. Although this report does not attempt to cover the many studies of Internet-only use and Internet searching behaviour, these studies can provide some insights into the Web search patterns of children and adults who use the Web for both recreational and work-related purposes. To locate many of these studies.

PERCEIVED ADVANTAGES OF ELECTRONIC RESOURCES AND PREFERENCES

Users perceive electronic resources—in particular electronic journals and, for students, the Internet—to hold many advantages. Faculty members at ARL institutions cited convenience, timeliness, and the ability to search text as the most important factors in choosing electronic journals over print. Least important to them was animation of graphics, although others sometimes mention that as an important advantage.

In other surveys, graduate students said the top reasons for using electronic journals were the ability to link to additional information, the ability to search, and the currency of materials. The ability to search across a wide range of journal articles, search within an article, and interact with multiple levels of information objects were listed as the top three significant features sought in future electronic journals.Many studies have found that users believe the main advantage of electronic journals is convenience of accessing articles any time from their desktop computer. Experienced users also liked the ease of skimming and searching, the possibility of downloading or printing the desired document or segment, the currency of information, the speed of access, and the ability to send articles to their colleagues instantly.

Storing articles electronically, then printing out a portable print copy, appeals to frequent e-journal users. Convenience and speed of access are mentioned or implied repeatedly. Students reported the top three ways that access to electronic resources has improved their academic careers: access to a wider range of information, faster access to information, and easier access to information. In England, Tilburg University faculty members cite timely availability, easy access, full text searching, and access from home as factors that promote the use of electronic journals. Focus groups of engineering faculty members and students wanted to search electronic journals quickly and easily, but they desired interfaces that could be customised and the ability to create personal collections, while economics students and faculty want the addition of data sets.

The TULIP project, an early electronic journals study was a cooperative undertaking between several university libraries and Elsevier. It attempted to predict the potential use of electronic journals through log analysis, focus groups, and interviews, while making sample collections available to faculty members and graduate students.

The lessons from TULIP are incorporated into later commercial products, and the conclusions agree with later studies. Even in the early 1990s, faculty members and graduate students wanted electronic journal systems that are as intuitive as possible, preferably using a familiar interface, with access to all information from one source. They wanted high processing speed for downloading and printing, timely information, good image quality, many journal titles and sufficient dates covered, and linking.

Graduate students used the system more often than faculty members. At this early date, TULIP researchers noticed an emotional tie to paper and the library—something that has diminished fairly rapidly with today's convenience of electronic journals. Still, users liked the convenience of desktop access, but, consistent with almost all studies today, they preferred to print out a hard copy for reading. Promotion and training were both found to be crucial to develop a base of regular users. Familiarity, in the case of electronic journals, has bred continued use.

PROBLEMS OR CONCERNS WITH ELECTRONIC RESOURCES

Although the advantages are outweighing the perceived problems or concerns as use increases and more resources are available, users still express some concerns about the disadvantages of electronic library collections. Participants in several studies expressed the desire for more online materials, including additional journal titles, a wider variety of special or out-of-the mainstream materials, and complete volumes or back files of existing journals. Print is a proven archival format. Even those who prefer electronic access to journals, prefer that books remain in print format.

The most common complaint found in many studies is the dis-comfort of reading from the screen or poor graphic quality. Respondents consistently report that they prefer to print out articles for reading and do most of their reading from the paper printout. They prefer PDF format for printing, although the HTML format is better for skimming.Faculty members from ARL institutions said that the most im-portant characteristics that would lead them to choose print over electronic were ability to browse, portability, physical comfort, and convenience. In citing the chief reasons for preferring print over electronic journals, Vanderbilt University medical faculty and students said that print is an easier to read format, of better graphic quality, easier to browse, and easier to access.

Access to adequate technology may still be a problem for some; 22 per cent of science faculty respondents at the University of Michigan requested that procedural or technological barriers to access be removed. When asked to identify problems, only a small percentage of respondents to most interviews or surveys agree to the same ones. The response rate for any one concern or problem is rarely more than 20 per cent and "top problems" are usually expressed by less than 10 per cent of the respondents. Students at one university were asked how "access to electronic resources has hindered your academic career."Although not nearly as many agreed to hindrances as they did to improvements, the top three hindrances mentioned were that online access is time consuming (16.4 per cent), it detracts from doing work (13.5 per cent), and lack of information technology knowledge hinders effective use (11.1 per cent). The top category for disadvantages among faculty members and graduate students at Ohio State University was "don't know"; an additional 8 per cent of faculty and 6 per cent of graduate students saw no disadvantages.

A continuing problem is that users may be unaware of relevant resources in the library collection. In a survey at the University of Maryland, 31 per cent of the faculty members reported never using electronic journals; the reasons cited were unfamiliarity with how to access the journals and a lack of need because of personal subscriptions.In a study of computer engineering undergraduate students in Nanyang Technological University in Singapore, researchers discovered that more than one-third of the respondents had never accessed computer engineering databases available through the library and of those, half had never heard of them. Lower-division undergraduates in focus groups at the University of Tennessee report that they know the Web and major search engines such as Google, but unless a library resource is specifically named (and required) in a class, they are unaware of its usefulness. Although French research scientists are using electronic journals more often, librarians still need to promote the resources because scientists hesitate to use electronic sources when they feel they have insufficient knowledge of them. The perception that electronic journals are of lower quality than print is another problem that may be diminishing as a high percentage of peer-reviewed journals are digitised.

In the late-1990s, business school faculty members surveyed at ARL institutions reported that they did not perceive electronic journals to be of as high quality as paper counterparts; their responses changed, however, when they were asked to evaluate a well-respected print journal evolving to electronic format.

While more than 70 per cent of the faculty members in a British university believe the quality of articles in electronic journals is the same as in print journals, this same group of respondents cited the top disadvantage of electronic journals as being the impression that electronic publication is not "real" publication. On the other hand, faculty members at the University of West England reported that they believed electronic journal content generally to be of good quality, and in some cases, to have added value. They said that they would use more electronic journals as more were made available in their area of interest and would recommend them to students. Texas A&M faculty members also reported that they have no objections to students using peer-reviewed elec-tronic journals and that they would recommend electronic journals to students. The proliferation of sources for articles and the sheer amount of information now available may be confusing to some users. Retrieving too much information is a problem mentioned by some, as is getting lost on a tangent and not knowing when to quit searching.

The distinction between the "article" and the "journal" in full-text databases was unclear to faculty members and undergraduates surveyed in the Decomate study, although at Columbia University researchers found that students clearly understood the difference between electronic databases and Web sites.

In focus groups at the University of Tennessee, Tenopir found that students understand that information found on the Web is different from the resources provided by the library, but many are not fully aware of what resources the library offers.

LIBRARY POLICIES AND FINANCIAL CONCERNS

Decisions that libraries make based on financial concerns, such as pay per use, may have unintended consequences on user behaviour. Electronic journal collections in libraries are growing steadily and some libraries are formulating collection development policies that encourage lease of electronic journals over purchase of print journals.

Even as early as 1999, 29 per cent of ARL and 33.5 per cent of Non-ARL academic libraries reported cancellations of print journals in favour of electronic access, and more said they would cancel print in the future. There has been a steady increase in the percentage of acquisitions dollars spent on electronic resources in ARL libraries.

On average, ARL libraries spent 13.2 per cent of their acquisitions budget on electronic resources in 1999-2000, and several libraries reported spending more than 20 per cent. By 2000–2001 the average had grown to 16 per cent and some special libraries spend a far greater percentage. Investment banking and brokerage firms are reported to spend 40-100 per cent of their information budgets on online products, by far the highest of any type of company. Library policies that favour electronic journals over print are having an effect on user behaviour. Users are increasingly positive about electronic collections and visits to the physical library by faculty and graduate students are down in many libraries, replaced by visits to the virtual library.

At the University of Washington, between 1998 and 2001 graduate students and faculty in the health sciences, sciences, and engineering reported the most pronounced decline in visits to the physical library. The primary use of the library by undergraduates tends to be as a workplace, although science and engineering students say they visited the library most often to find journals. Libraries that report a decline in visits to the physical library as a decrease in library usage do themselves a disservice. Users enjoy the convenience and other benefits of electronic access and are adjusting their behaviour as encouraged by library collection development policies.

Total library use—physical plus virtual—is likely actually up in most institutions. Virtual library users are less likely to ask for help or communicate with librarians unless the library offers special virtual reference services. University faculty members report that an increase in their electronic journal usage is accompanied by a decrease in the frequency of their use of print journals. Surveys of Ohio State University users from 1998 to 2000 found a steady increase in acceptance of electronic journals and their reported use.

By 2000, almost two-thirds of faculty members and graduate students said it was important for OSU libraries to replace their print subscriptions with electronic journal subscriptions when permanent electronic storage is available. Users of the University of Southern California Norris Medical Library viewed approximately 28,000 electronic full-text articles in a six-month period, as compared with 1,800 uses of the corresponding print volumes.

Even considering that users might have read more than one article per print volume, the electronic viewings far outnumbered the print. Part of this may be explained by the availability of new titles in electronic form, but use of both print and electronic titles was concentrated on a small number of the most popular titles—just 20 of the titles accounted for 60 per cent of the total usage and the top 25 titles were common to both print and electronic.The most requested electronic titles at the Elektronishche Zeitschriftenbibliothek in Germany are major journals whose print editions are also heavily used.

Use is also higher for electronic versions of books at Columbia University compared with the same titles available in print, although the University of Pittsburgh Health Sciences library found that use of both print journal titles and electronic journal titles covered by the Ovid online system increased at a similar rate. This pattern of a small number of titles accounting for a large percentage of use is, of course, not new to electronic resources.

The so-called 80/20 rule has been well documented in library collections, where a large percentage of use is concentrated in a small percentage of the collection. Usage logs make the calculations of use much easier with electronic resources, and this 80/20 phenomenon is reported by many studies that use transaction log analysis. Interestingly, this rule may also hold true for users—a small per cent of total library users is responsible for most electronic journal use.

This is similar to the phenomenon of "binge" users in the SuperJournal project. Davis and Solla found that a vast majority of users of American Chemical Society journals at Cornell University download few articles and consult few journals.

They conclude that a small number of heavy users can have a great effect on the number of total downloads. Still, as the OhioLINK studies have shown, many of the remaining 80 or so per cent of the journals in an electronic collection will get some usage. In addition, Day found that at least one article was downloaded from 92 per cent of the journals available to users at the University of Manchester Institute of Science and Technology.

In his examination of NERL usage logs, however, Davis found that no institution uses every available title and some journal titles are used infrequently by all institutions. Overall, 90 per cent of the downloads came from 40 per cent of the collection.

Faculty and graduate students say 24-hour availability is a prime advantage of electronic journals, but even with 24/7 availability of the virtual library, most academic use follows the normal rhythms of the workweek and academic calendar. Just as turnstile counts mark the use of physical academic libraries, log data of virtual collections show peak use in March, November, and April and Monday through Thursday mid-morning to late afternoons, with a huge drop-off on Friday afternoons.

Although a user's institution pays for subscriptions or access to electronic journals, this cost is hidden from the user. Any overt charge or obvious pay perview has an impact on user behaviour. The "Pricing Electronic Access to Knowledge" (PEAK) project in the late 1990s was a major experiment with 12 libraries of varying size and type and the Elsevier journal collection.

It measured not only use of electronic journals by journal title and type of library, but also measured use under two different payment models for articles. Users of the subject libraries were provided with both "unmetered" access and "metered" access to journal articles. Although use increased from the first to the second year in the experiment, 60 per cent of accesses were for "unmetered" content, most of which was more than one year old.

The study concluded that the "user cost of access, consist-ing of both monetary payments and time or effort, has a significant effect on the number of articles that readers access". Pay per-view or pay per-use creates a barrier that affects the frequency of online access and downloads. Nicolas and Huntington found that users who entered an online journals system from a subscribing institution visited the collection more often than Non-subscribers.

Subscribers also spent more time viewing each article, viewed articles from more journals, and used a wider variety of journal titles and subjects than did non-subscribers. Although seven students studied at Central Connecticut State University found the enduser system Questia easy to use, only one of the seven thought "it is worth it to subscribe" on their own. Some users may be willing to pay for electronic articles, at least part of the time. Worlock surveyed 252 working scientists and social scientists in the United Kingdom to find out if they ever pay for articles. Nearly two-thirds of the respondents reported that, on average, they pay for between one and five articles per week beyond regular subscriptions. Still, two-thirds said they felt the articles were too expensive. Passwords can be another barrier to use, in particular different passwords for different databases or collections. Users want free access, without having to remember multiple passwords or logon protocols. In eliminating special access requirements, however, libraries may create a problem for themselves.

There is evidence that many faculty members and students do not realise that the numerous electronic journals they can reach from their office, dormitory, or home computer through their university user name or identification are actually paid for and provided by the library. If users are not aware what the library provides, they will be less inclined to advocate for the library at budget time. Users can help libraries set collection and service priorities, with no one best solution for all types of libraries, types of users, or all subject disciplines. They can help make decisions about licensing choices and be made familiar with relative costs and tradeoffs.

When asked to make choices about what they were willing to forego to get more electronic access, researchers from the Max Planck Society felt there were certain services or materials they could do without, including binding of journals, journals with low impact factors, and print versions of journals readily available electronically. Science, engineering, and health sciences faculty at the University of Washington favored canceling print journals in favour of electronic only, while humanities and social sciences faculty opposed this idea and responded that maintaining the quality of the print collection is their highest priority.

REVIEWS OF THE LITERATURE AND METHODS

Although this report summarises conclusions from recent research studies and highlights some conclusions about how people use electronic collections, there are individual and library-specific differ-ences that make it beneficial for many libraries to collect their own data. The last section of the bibliography in this report lists selected resources to help with this process and to identify additional usage studies. For several years, Charles Bailey at the University of Houston has maintained a comprehensive literature review of all types of articles about scholarly electronic publishing.

This monumental piece of work is the first place to look to identify articles on any aspect of the topic, including research and user studies. Since, the review is updated regularly, bibliographic information about new studies appears there frequently. Literature reviews by Kling and Callahan and Giangrande supplement Bailey; also, the Annual Review of Information Science and Technology occasionally publishes review articles that focus on electronic publishing or research techniques. Several recent relevant chapters from ARIST are listed in the bibliography.

ARIST typically is published every autumn, but the topics vary from year to year. Beyond general textbooks of research methods, several recent publications focus on research methods for library and Web usage studies. The ARIST chapter by Wang formed the basis for the categorisation of research methods in this repor. This method provides a richness in interview or survey data beyond opinions or reports of estimated behaviour by asking respondents to focus on details of a specific incident of research or reading. The Tenopir and King studies also use critical incident technique to draw conclusions about readings. Experimental tests are less often used in the library environment, perhaps because they are time-consuming and must use relatively small groups of participants. Usability tests allow specific system design features to be compared and measured and are particularly useful for testing library catalog and Web site design.

Think-aloud or verbal protocols provide information on why subjects pursue certain courses of action and how they react to systems at the time of use. Covey explains in detail when to use and how to design studies that gather data from surveys focus groups, user protocols transaction log analysis, and other research methods. In addition to excellent advice on conducting user studies, researcher presents a selected bibliography covering general research methods and specific articles through 2001 on each of the research methods she describes.

RESEARCH IN ELECTRONIC JOURNALS METHODOLOGY

For this research, the authors used Ithink modelling software. Ithink uses a mapping language designed to facilitate visualisation of the 'interrelationships which constitute a process, a strategy or an issue'. The key elements in an Ithink model are described below.

It is thaught to represent graphically the interrelationships that characterise each system modelled. The elements in the models then had numbers or ranges of numbers added and simulations were run. The models were deliberately made simple and aim to capture the essential features of the systems modelled.

They are intended as generic rather than specific examples. Many of the model elements are defined by equations which describe the relationship of that element with one or other elements in the same model. The relationships represented by the equations are generally informed by the literature. However, some assumptions are inherent in these relationships. The bases of the equations and the assumptions in each model are described in 'documents'. These documents may be viewed by double-clicking the element and selecting from the dialogue box a button labelled 'document*'.

The asterisk indicates that a document exists. Some elements are self-explanatory and so are not documented within the model. As these assumptions inform the results of the 'what if' scenarios and sensitivity analyses, they are most appropriately presented alongside those results.

Thus, the assumptions are documented in the Results and Discussion section of this report. Copies of the models described here are available from the authors and can be examined by using the free runtime version of the Ithink software package. This is available at the following URL: http://www.cognitus.co.uk/IS/IS.htm.

The runtime version of the software can be used to view and manipulate our models, but any changes that the user 64 makes cannot be saved. A brief guide for users of this modelling software is appended to this report.

The models were designed to facilitate greater understanding of the economic factors and the economic relationships between different stakeholders in each of the processes modelled. Model variables can be manipulated using so-called 'sliders', and the effects can then be monitored.

For example, in a model of electronic journal production and delivery any of the following elements could be varied using sliders: the number of subscriptions; the number of manuscripts submitted; the overhead rate applied to staff costs; the journal acceptance/rejection rate; or the profit margin applied by the publisher.

Holding all other variables equal, a user might, for example, vary the number of subscriptions and observe the effect on subscription price or individual article price. Similarly, in the model of an ER system, the user could vary the number and size of classes to establish how this would affect, for example, total cost, the institution fee, and the fee per student.

MODEL ELEMENTS

Stock

A stock represents an accumulation. For example, in the model of an electronic reserve system the repository of digitised materials is represented by a stock. The items accumulate by flowing into and/or out of the stock. The total content amounts to the inflow minus the outflow at each time period in a model simulation. In many of the stocks represented in the models described here the inflow and outflow are equal.

For example, a journal editor receives a number of manuscripts Stock 65 every year. Of those, she rejects a very small percentage and the remainder are sent for peer review. However, the repository in the ER system has no outflow as items must be stored for possible future use. Thus, its content increases annually.

Flow

A flow is like a pipe. It either fills or drains a stock in the direction of the flow arrow. A cloud at either end of a flow indicates an infinite source or destination of the 'stuff' flowing to or from a stock.

If the flow source were a stock and that stock were empty, the value of the flow equation would not flow into the destination stock. Thus, a cloud is a device which indicates that the source of 'stuff' passing through the flow is beyond the scope of the model.

For example, where the flow 'journal acquisitions receipts' flowing into the stock 'journal acquisitions budget' originates with a cloud, this means that the entire library or institutional budget is not represented. It is assumed that the library or institution provides funding to acquire journals.

Converter

A converter informs other elements in the model. It may contain a constant value, for example, VAT which is 17.5 per cent, or a variable value which may be manipulated by the model user by means of a slider.

Alternatively, it may represent an algebraic relationship between other elements in the model or it may represent an external input such as the rate at which items selected for digitisation in the ER model are duplicates of items already held in the repository.

The latter may be a ramp, *i.e.* the initial value is X% and it rises annually by Y%.

A converter may also be the repository for a graphical function which sketches the relationship between an input and an output. For example, the output may be the price of a subscription and the input the number of items in a database. A graphical functions can also be used to sketch non-linear relationships.

Connector

A connector is like a wire which transmits information between elements in a model, *e.g.* in Figure, the value of the flow labelled 'RDN staff' is determined by the product of the values of the two converters.

The value of the converters is conveyed to the flow by connectors. A connector can connect out of a stock and it can flow into or out of a flow or converter. It cannot connect into a stock as the value of the latter can be altered only by a flow.

EVALUATION OF ITHINK MODELLING SOFTWARE

Ithink was an effective tool for the research described here. It allowed the authors to map the interrelationships in a system before numbers were introduced.

The documentation supplied with the software is clear and comprehensive. Two versions of the software are available: Ithink Strategy and Ithink Analyst. The latter includes additional modelling features. These features were not required to build the models described in this report. Ithink software is available for educational use at half of the full price.

The educational RDN budget Emplmnt cos ts No employees RDN staff rate for Ithink Strategy is available for $299 and Ithink Analyst for £479. The price includes documentation. There were a few drawbacks. Among them were the fact that the software prohibits circular relationships. For example, in the model of a non-commercial journal, we wished to define the overhead applied when calculating total publication costs as a percentage of sales income.

However, as total publication cost is one factor determining price and price is one factor determining sales income, this relationship would have been circular and was prohibited. Another drawback for this project is the difficulty of printing the models. The software is designed as a learning tool. To be most effective models should be manipulated by users. Thus, prints of the models are considered to be of limited value. Nevertheless, the output of this research project had to be documented and published. Although the authors expect interested parties to request copies of the models, they also believe that illustrations would contribute to understanding of written reports and papers.

Unfortunately, several of the models would be illegible on anything smaller than an A2 sheet of paper. It is for this reason that we recommend that interested readers should download the runtime version of Ithink software and request copies of our models. Requests for discs with the models should be addressed to either of the authors of this report.

The authors built six Ithink models based on economic models of different aspects of the digital library. These include four economic models of electronic journal production and delivery. Development of electronic journals is more advanced than most other areas of the digital library. The selection of models evaluated here reflects this.

The other two models evaluated are a resource discovery network and a National Electronic Reserve Service (NERS). The former is based on a recent eLib supporting study of subject-based gateways and is informed by the JISC call for proposals to develop a Resource Discovery Network Centre (JISC circular 10/98). The latter model is based on the eLib-funded national electronic resource service, HERON and is informed by relevant eLib publications and by publications of other stakeholders such as the CLA and the PLS.

ELECTRONIC JOURNALS MODELS

There are four Ithink models of electronic journal production and delivery. The first is a model of a non-commercial electronic journal with traditional economic characteristics. In this model, costs are recovered from sales of subscriptions and individual articles.

A "Traditional model" is presented first to facilitate easy comparison with journal production and delivery in a print environment. The second model is based on the economic model proposed by Harnad and Hemus and is hereinafter described as the "Harnad model". The third is a 'market' model based on Fishwick *et al.*'s eLib supporting study on the economic implications of different models of publishing scholarly electronic journals and is hereinafter referred to as the "Fishwick model".

The fourth model is an alternative model, proposed by the authors, which is informed by the other three models. The Traditional model is presented first and assumptions informing different elements in the model are explained.

The Harnad model, the Fishwick model, and the authors' alternative model are then described. Where elements and assumptions in these models differ from those in the Traditional model these are documented.

The values of several elements in each of these models were varied and the models run to monitor the effects. The costs and benefits for different stakeholders of manipulating model elements was established and model sensitivities were identified. The results are described.

Non-commercial Electronic Journal with Traditional Economic Characteristics

The characteristics of this model are very similar to those of the scholarly print information delivery chain. Editors and referees are unpaid other than a contribution from the publisher towards editorial office costs.

A traditional pricing mechanism is applied, *i.e.* costs are recovered through sales of subscriptions and of individual articles. The model differs from the print system in that the entire editorial process is conducted electronically and the product is delivered in electronic form to libraries.

Libraries are free to obtain subscriptions/individual articles directly from publishers or to obtain them from an information broker. It is assumed, if a library chooses the former, that terms will be negotiated between the library and the publisher. The model consists of four interconnected sectors: content origination, publication, information brokerage, and the library function.

Content Origination

In this sector, manuscripts are first submitted to the editorial office for review. The number of incoming manuscripts is specified so that the number of papers published was limited to a realistic level. The model simulates production of a single journal. We assumed that the journal publishes approximately 120 papers per annum.

Theoretically, an electronic journal need not be constrained by a pre-determined limit on the number of papers that it can publish annually because distribution and storage costs are low. However, other resources required for production are related to journal size and these are likely to restricts growth in the short to medium term.

For the purpose of the modelling exercise, the authors assumed that the number of papers published per annum in an electronic journal is similar to the number published in a print journal. The rate at which manuscripts are submitted to any journal fluctuates. However, if an excess of manuscripts is accepted and, in turn, the publication delay is unacceptable, it is reasonable to assume that potential authors will be discouraged from submitting to that journal.

The editors also would regulate the number of papers accepted by increasing the rejection rate to maintain an acceptable publication delay. In the model, the number of papers submitted was specified with reference to the rejection rate to ensure that 120 papers were produced per annum. Most manuscripts submitted for publication are refereed but a small percentage is rejected immediately usually because the subject matter is unsuitable for publication in that journal.

The immediate rejection rate wan this model is 2 per cent and is based on an established print peer reviewed journal. The total rejection rate in the model is varied to monitor the effect. Rejection rates vary between journals, and vary significantly between disciplines (*i.e.* in the humanities 90 per cent is not uncommon whilst in the pure sciences 10 per cent is common). It is assumed that the editor spends a total of 30 minutes per paper.

This represents time spent scanning the manuscript content, deciding whether or not to have the paper refereed, selecting referees, and considering revisions and whether or not to return the paper to the referees. We assumed that all but 2 per cent of manuscripts are refereed, each of them by two peers. The average paper is revised once.

It was assumed that each referee spends two hours reviewing the manuscript in the first instance and that revision takes one hour. Thus, each referee spends three hours per paper and therefore, each paper takes six referee hours to process.

It was assumed that one hour of an average editor or referee costs £50 including full employment costs and overhead.

This is a conservative estimate which does not vary with overhead rate. The total cost to HE is calculated as the cost of editorial and refereeing work minus the contribution from the publisher towards the costs of the editorial office. This cost to HE is an opportunity cost as it is not accounted for in the financial transactions between different stakeholders.

It was assumed that the publisher contributes £160 per accepted manuscript towards the costs of the editorial office. This assumption is based on figures given.

The model includes no clerical administration cost, as most of the clerical administrative tasks are automated and journal production staff undertake what remains. Thus, the editorial and production functions are interlinked. This organisational model is based on that of the *Conservation Ecology* Project.

Publication

Production costs in the model vary with the overhead rate applied. It was assumed that overheads cost 120 per cent of production costs, but a rate of 60 per cent was also tested. The authors would have preferred to calculate overhead as a percentage of sales income because distribution incurs additional administration costs and thus costs vary with the size of the subscription base.

However, calculation of the overhead in this way would have required a circular connection between elements in the model which is prohibited by the software package.

As the model is non-commercial, it was assumed that the publisher does not seek to make substantial profits. However, some profit margin is required to develop the journal. We applied margins in the model at a rate varying from 0 per cent to 20 per cent. The journal is produced by a half-time production editor and a half-time systems administrator.

The cost per paper was estimated at £275. This is based on a part-time journal production editor and a part-time systems administrator each earning, pro rata, £25 000 who also cost an additional 20 per cent of that figure in national insurance contributions (NIC) and pension contributions.

This gives a total employment cost of £30 000. An overhead was not applied to staff costs in this instance. Assuming that these staff members can produce a journal consisting of 120 papers per volume (per year), the cost per paper is £250. An additional £25 was added to this figure to cover any other expenses. Subscription fees in the model vary with the level of use.

The price increases as the user base decreases because there are fewer subscribers or purchasers of individual documents to share the costs.

The price of an individual paper is double that of a paper sold as part of a subscription to reflect the increased risk to the publisher when she sells papers individually rather than in volume sized bundles. This price may be calculated by dividing the subscription price by 120 to generate a per-paper price and multiplying the resulting figure by two. All subscription and article prices include VAT at 17.5 per cent.

HEIs in the UK are currently required to pay VAT on purchases of electronic information, but not on print information. The authors acknowledge that it can take several years for journal start-up costs to be amortized and the duration varies considerably. In the interests of simplicity, the journal modeled here is assumed to be an on-going concern, *i.e.* start-up costs are not included.

The flow element 'other publisher income' represents sources of income derived from the journal publication other than sales of subscriptions and individual articles. Other source of income may include, for example, advertising or sponsored supplements.

This figure is calculated at 4 per cent of subscription and individual article income. This figure was derived from the journal costing form referred to above.

COST OF STORING DIGITAL JOURNALS

The cost of storing digital journals is currently very low and is falling. It is assumed that this cost is incurred by the publisher and that the work related to storage would be undertaken by the Systems administrator in the normal course of her duties.

The cost of storage space itself is based on a rough estimate that it costs £100 per gigabyte per annum to store digital content. It is estimated that an HTML journal volume occupies approximately 30 Mb. This is a liberal estimate based on figures supplied by Stuart Peters with reference to the electronic journal *Sociology Online*.

Thus, a volume costs £2.93 per annum to store. After 13 years the cost of storing that journal is £26 per annum. Storage costs are likely to decrease significantly over the period but no attempt is made to predict the degree of this decrease.

Information Broker Function

The information broker (subscription agent) undertakes administrative work that saves time and money for both the library and the publisher.

The various tasks involved are not represented. The information broker also generates management information which she supplies to both the publisher and the library as appropriate. As the type of information and thus its value and the cost of processing it are unknown as yet, this function is not represented. It is assumed that the information broker negotiates favorable licence terms for libraries. Libraries pay an annual fee to the information broker. In the model, this is based on the fee charged by NESLI. NESLI charges institutions a fee to use SwetsNet which amounts to £1 per title subscription up to a maximum of £560 (A. Prior, personal communication, 17 March 1999).

In the model, the fee paid by an institution is determined by the amount of service delivered to the institution as determined by number of subscriptions and number of individual articles delivered; the latter is divided by 120 as a proxy for a single journal title.

It is assumed in the model that when an individual at an HEI has received a document electronically, the document will then be available to other researchers at the institution free of charge. This assumption is based on the practice of Elsevier Science with regard to institutions participating in the PEAK project. Publishers pay for the services of information broker by supplying publications at a discounted rate. Generally, discounts from publishers to subscription agents are in the region of 7 per cent. This figure is used in the model.

It was beyond the scope of this study to explore the costs to information brokers of the variety of services that they provide. It was assumed that the discount from the publisher and the fee from the library is sufficient remuneration.

HE Library Function

The cost to the library of negotiating the licence terms on which journals and/or individual electronic articles are supplied is represented by a negotiation fraction for each of these resources. This fraction is based on the cost of an individual, professional negotiator working at full capacity plus the cost of 1 hour per week to five other senior staff members in HE.

This is a modest estimate of the cost based on current practice in the US where licence negotiation often involves a team of senior staff who sometimes meet as frequently as every week.

The hourly rate for employing a senior staff member (including employment costs and overhead) is £50. Electronic Individual Article Supply (EIAS) directly from the publisher is likely to be negotiated based on access to a bundle of titles, perhaps within a single subject area or perhaps the publisher's entire list. The negotiation process itself is likely to take longer than negotiation for a single title as both parties have more at stake. However, the cost of the negotiation may be spread across all EIAS acquisitions for, at least, a single year.

In the model, the cost of negotiation for EIAS directly from the publisher is based on 33 senior staff hours at £50 an hour (representing three 1-hour meetings attended by the negotiator and five other participants and 15 hours of negotiation and related tasks by the negotiator).

It is assumed that negotiation reduces the subscription cost and the EIAS cost to the library to 10 per cent less than the standard price. It was assumed also that the library acquisitions budget is £505 per active researcher.

This figure is based on SCONUL figures for an average academic library acquisitions budget and on the number of active researchers. It was assumed that an average institution has 1174 active researchers. This is a rough estimate based on SCONUL figures.

It includes the total mean number of teaching and research staff which is (arbitrarily) divided in half, the mean number of research only staff, and the mean number of postgraduate research students. In the model, the cost of licence negotiation is deducted from the library acquisitions budget.

This does not reflect reality. However, the cost of licence negotiation is directly related to the acquisition of journals and it is deducted from the acquisitions budget in the model so that the total cost of acquiring journals directly from the publisher may be compared with the cost of acquiring them from via an information broker.

It was assumed that the publisher commits as much time and effort to negotiating licences as the library. Thus, the negotiation fraction deducted from the library journals acquisitions budget is also deducted from the publisher gross income to indicate publisher spend.

COSTS OF PROCESSING, STORING AND ISSUING PRINT JOURNALS

The cost of processing, storing, issuing and other tasks related to print journals is included in the model for comparison. Odlyzko claims that these costs are the cause of the serials crisis and suggests that for every $1 that a library spends on journal acquisitions, it spends another $2 on these related activities.

He based this assertion on the fact that Association of Research Libraries (ARL) statistics consistently show that acquisitions represent approximately 30 per cent of the budgets of research libraries in the US and Canada.

The assumption is that if this material is acquired in digital form, these additional library costs can be eliminated. This assumption is, it must said, contentious. The cost of storing digital journals is likely to be much lower than the cost of storing print but the cost of maintaining that store and of technical migration to ensure that the content is available in the future will be significant. Furthermore, it is likely that in a digital library, the tasks currently undertaken by librarians will be as important as they are now.

These tasks may be undertaken by other stakeholders and the nature of the tasks will change to some degree. Nevertheless, the costs of undertaking them will be incurred and will be included in the price of scholarly literature. Figures used for calculating these costs are based on those calculated for use in planning the JSTOR project.

The cost of storing a single volume of the journal *Ecology* for 1 year is $3.07. This figure is used here as a basis for calculating storage costs for journals.

It has been inflated and converted at the current rate to give £2 per volume. Bowen estimated that circulation costs for current issues of journals amount to a total of $45 (currently £29) and that circulation costs for past issues also cost $45. In the model, the term 'current issue' refers to the current year and two previous years.

After that period has elapsed, the cost of circulating back issues will be added to library costs at the same rate as circulation of current issues. Bowen estimated that binding of current issues costs $20 (currently £13) and processing and check in a further $20 (currently £13). Finally, he estimated that the cost of conserving and preserving backruns is $5 (£3).

The total cost per title per annum ranges from £60 in year 1 to £113 in year 13. As a percentage of the current mean journal subscription fee in the UK this represents 58–109 per cent. These figures are lower than Odlyzko suggested, but are still significant when scaled up for a whole journal collection. For example, the cost of processing, storing and issuing a collection of only 1000 titles ranges from £60 000 in Year 1 to £11 3000 in Year 13. The mean number of titles held by a library is 4880.

The cost to the library of processing, storing and issuing a print collection of this size ranges from £292 800 in Year 1 to £551 440 in Year 13. As a percentage of total gross library expenditure, this represents 9–18

ELECTRONIC PUBLISHING

The electronic publishing has a very short history, compared to traditional form of publishing. The first known form of e-publishing is in the early 1980s when plain text e-mails were sent to the subscriber via a mailing list. But, the subsequent technological advancements made a tremendous impact on the information cycle process of creation, gathering/production and dissemination of information, which in turn hugely influenced the electronic publishing itself. In 1994-95 the first e-journal was published and the distribution of e-journal turned out to be an instant success. Majority of the journals are now made available in digital form. The publishers are now offering package subscription to electronic journals at highly reduced price as the publishing charges of e-journals have substantially come down, as compared to their print counterpart, which involved huge cost of printing and distribution.

Subsequently, even bibliographic resources were brought in electronic form. Soon, e-books also made their presence. These developments made the libraries to seriously rethink their collection development and information delivery policies. While moving totally to electronic may be a distant possibility, a progressive shift from print to electronic, is being noticed.

MOVING FROM PRINT TO ELECTRONIC

While the print and online versions have their own advantages and disadvantages. However, to put the subject in perspective, some critical remarks are made here. Print resources subscribed/ bought are physically available in the libraries and form an asset. Online resources subscribed/ bought on one-time purchase can only be accessed by users, as the digital content is held remotely at the publishers' end.

This raises the issue of ownership *vs.* access and is a well debated point in the user and the librarians' communities. The fact, however, is that, in case of online resources, the libraries are currently dependent totally on publishers to access the subscribed/ bought content. This situation made the libraries to think in terms of ensuring perpetual access to the subscribed/ bought content. Of course, publishers too have their own concerns of protecting their content from misuse. It is, therefore, a mutual interest of both the publisher and the end-user to enter into an Agreement protecting each other's interests. This agreement is generally known as License Agreement.

LEGAL DOCUMENT AND LICENCE AGREEMENT

A Licence agreement is a legal document and contract between the publisher and the institutional library. Both the parties agree to abide by the terms and conditions set in the agreement. There are basically three different kinds of site license agreements according to:

- The type of library,
- Product/ model, and
- Number of sites.

The agreements by the type of libraries include Academic/ Research, Government/ Corporate and Public and generally the variations are in terms of users, fees, etc.; The agreements by product/ model are based on the e-resources, such as E-journals, E-books and Bibliographic Databases. The agreements by site(s) are applicable according to the number of sites, such as single site, multi-sites and consortium. Although, the re-exist some Standard Licensing models, each publisher has his own Agreement and a close look at these indicate that there is a lack of consistency and standardisation. A few publishers have put up the copy of their site license agreement on their web site but others do not do so maintaining it as confidential document. However, signing of License Agreement has almost become mandatory. In fact, a well known publisher has a policy which stipulates that they will raise the invoice for an e-product only after the library signs the agreement. In a way, it is good that the library will know all the terms and conditions before buying the product. Other publishers send the agreement after the purchase order is raised and the payment is made. In such cases, it may be difficult to negotiate any changes in the clauses.

The terms and conditions of the site license agreement are heavily tilted in favour of publishers. However, except a few, the clauses in the Agreement are generally subject to negotiations. The job of dealing with such issues would be much simpler for those Organisations which have a Legal Cell. It is advisable to refer the document to that Cell. But, as is generally observed, many Organisations do not have such Units which make it imperative for the Librarian to take up himself the responsibility of examining the legal aspects in the Agreement. In that case, the librarian needs to be very cautious in studying various clauses in the Agreement.

He/ she must ensure that the interests of his/ her Organisation are protected to the maximum possible extent. After going through the Agreements carefully, one has to first seek clarifications from the publishers on those points which do not seem to be very clear. Possible changes may be suggested to bring in more clarity. If certain terms are unacceptable, it is essential to request for changes/ amendments in the Agreement. Sometimes, it needs a hard bargaining and the librarians need to have strong negotiating skills.

KEY ISSUES IN THE AGREEMENT

General Conditions

Some publishers incorporate a clause in the agreement, stating that the content of the Licensed Material is 'subject to change without notice'. If accepted, this allows the publisher to alter the subscribed/ purchased content without notice. In this case, subscriber will be totally in dark about the changes effected, including withdrawal of any content.

To avoid this, the librarians need to insist for change in the clause appropriately by changing it to 'subject to change with prior notice to the licensee' (*i.e.* library). This will protect the end-user from any loss of content, as the user will have time to copy and store the content locally. Some publishers also incorporate a clause that the contents of the License Agreement should not be disclosed to a third party without their consent.

While the publishers urging to maintain secrecy is understandable, it may be difficult for libraries to accept such a clause, especially for those organisations funded by State/ Central Governments, which, according to the Right to Information Act, may have to be disclose the content to those, who seek it. Therefore, it is essential that appropriate changes are demanded in the clauses.

Perpetual Access

Perpetual access is ensured by most of the publishers. But some publishers put a condition that the library should subscribe to at least one online journal or any online product of theirs. Otherwise, they will charge maintenance fee/ hosting fee. If the access is provided off-line, then they ask the libraries to bear the cost of production to provide the content on other electronic media, such as CDs/ DVDs, for local hosting. Some publishers prefer to use the term 'Continued Access' in place of 'Perpetual Access'. The terminological difference may have to be clearly understood. As one UK publisher puts it - the 'Perpetual Access' in their terminology refers to a limited period and the 'Continued Access' means indefinite period. Libraries need to ensure that their parent institution will not be put to disadvantage and take precautions to get inserted right terminology.

However, some publishers do not provide perpetual access at all to the subscribed content. If an online subscription is not renewed, the libraries will lose access even to the paid content. If that is the case, then the Licensing document must clearly state it. In such cases, the libraries need to think seriously about an alternative method of archiving either by continuing with print version or get archival year-end CDs/ DVDs, as offered by some publishers.

Withdrawal of Content

Publishers insert a clause that it reserves right to withdraw the content, which it no longer retains the right to publish or infringes copyright or defamatory, etc. While the last condition should be acceptable, the first two conditions may sometime put librarians in a fix. These situations may arise when a journal title is transferred to some other publisher. The new publisher may not permit the old subscribers to access this content, free. It is all the more critical if this content is substantial and/ or directly relevant to their users.

As a remedial measure, one can demand insertion of the following clauses - The publisher will make best efforts to convince the new publisher to provide access to the old subscribers or shall allow local hosting of such content. Also, if the withdrawal is substantial, then the publisher shall refund the amount proportionately.

Restrictions on Usage

Generally, publishers do not permit users to download entire journal issues and e-books. A standard condition to this effect may be found in License Agreement of all the publishers. There are publishers who even put a restriction on the number of pages and chapters printable from e-books. The decision of the libraries to buy ebooks from such publishers depends on how comfortable they are with the restrictions imposed by the publishers. A few publishers do permit the licensee to make an electronic copy and a hardcopy for backup purpose. However, the libraries need to create necessary infrastructure to preserve the content on their local computer server.

Access to Archives through Third Party

In the event of a publisher deciding to wind up his operations or merge with another publisher, it is an obligation on the part of the publisher to make alternative arrangements to provide access to archive of the licensed materials concerned. This is where the third party arrangement comes into picture. Many publishers have made arrangements with some external agencies for the long time preservation of their digital archive. Some examples are LOCKSS, CLOCKSS, PORTICO, and National Library of Netherlands. In a trigger event, it becomes the responsibility of these agencies to grant access to the content to the subscribers. The libraries should insist publishers to incorporate in the agreement a clause specifying the names of the agencies with whom the arrangements are made to provide access to the content in the event of publisher closing his business. Some of these agencies offer paid service, but since the subscribers have already paid for the content earlier, it becomes a debatable point whether the libraries can afford to pay again for the same content.

Inter-Library Loan (ILL)

Providing a copy of an article to another library (not-forprofit, non-commercial) under ILL is generally permitted by most of the publishers, but with varying conditions. While the publishers expect subscribers to observe normal Copyright rules, some put specific restrictions on document delivery system. While one publisher permits only to send copies in print format, the other allows electronic transmission through secure network, but insists that the recipient library delete the file after printing a paper copy. Such clauses are non-negotiable and the libraries need to accept them, so long some form of ILL is permitted.

Governing Laws

Business of digital content is only three decade old. Like any other business, there is a possibility that disputes might arise especially in terms of copyright rules, access problems etc. If such disputes remain unresolved mutually, the aggrieved parties have no option, but to approach Judiciary. This gives rise to the problem of jurisdiction as the two parties belong to different countries. The agreement is generally governed by the laws of the country of origin of the publisher. However, some publishers are flexible on this issue. While some agree to sort out the issue in the court of subscriber's country, others agree to the condition that the aggrieved party can approach their respective countries. Alternatively, some publishers also allow for an independent arbitrator mutually acceptable to both parties.

Fees

Fees charged by the publishers for e-books, online journal packages, etc. varies from library to library, depending upon size of the user community. However, publishers also offer price cap in case a library agrees to go for a multi-year agreement. The base price and the price cap shall form part of the Agreement and as such need to be stated explicitly.

Counter-signed Copy

Original copy of the agreement is generally in duplicate and the two signed copies are exchanged between the library and the publisher. However, the Agreements of some publishers have only the acceptance column which needs to be signed by the Library. In such a case, libraries should keep with them one copy of the agreement.

6

Measurement of Use and Performance Indicators in the Digital Library

INTERNATIONAL STANDARDS FOR PERFORMANCE MEASUREMENT

The ability to monitor use and interpret the results is essential if any information resource or service is to be deemed a success or otherwise. Internationally standardised performance indicators have been developed for traditional library services.

However, recent studies of usage measurement and performance indicators for digital libraries have found no evidence of standardisation and continue to recommend that international standards be developed and applied.

An initiative in this direction has been taken by the ICOLC who have published guidelines for statistical measures of usage of electronic resources. An eLib supporting study published in 1997 investigated Management Information Systems and Performance Measurement for the Electronic Library. The authors described a three-fold approach to library management with regard to performance measurement:

- The day-to-day needs of library managers;
- The need for information that can be used by planners for forecasting;
- The need for indicators of value for strategic review.

Although they found that some indicators used in traditional libraries can be adapted, it was necessary to devise other 57 new indicators. For example, the number of documents accessed was considered not to be important in an electronic environment; the range and depth of resources available was deemed far more important.

Furthermore, Brophy and Wynne identified a number of issues which must be addressed if progress is to be made in this area. While acknowledging the significant contribution of the eLib programme in this regard, they called for a clearer definition and understanding of what is meant by the term 'electronic library'.

Non-standard Usage Measurement

A requirement for international standards is clear but development of such standards is a lengthy process. While this process is ongoing, each individual digital library initiative requires feedback to inform development and, thus, must unilaterally adopt an approach to performance measurement.

Electronic library projects in the UK, Europe and the USA have used a variety of different definitions and methods of usage measurement and analysis. Thus, neither analyses nor data from different projects can be compared.

Most Internet usage analysis tools are applicable to digital library activities and WWW server log file analysis programmes still predominate. In 1997 the eLib supporting study referred to above found that most work in the electronic library field relied on transaction logging for management information.

If users are authenticated (*i.e.* have usernames and passwords), it is possible using these tools, to monitor individual use by logging the username alongside the URL. Hits can also be time stamped. In this way, an individual's progress can be tracked from page to page. It is possible also, using cookies, for a service supplier to track an individual's movements on the Internet beyond that supplier's site. However, this is likely to be considered a breach of privacy and librarians 58 make it an issue in negotiation with content suppliers.

To comply with the library ethos, performance indicators should not rely on information about individuals' reading habits. Many academic subscription services authenticate whole sites by registering and restricting access a list of IP addresses.

Not only does this overcome privacy issues related to individual users as names and time stamps cannot be recorded on accesses, but it also removes the need for costly password management. An alternative means of reducing the cost of authentication in the UK is use of the ATHENS service which provides an individual with a username and password which may be used to access a variety of services.

Unfortunately, use of ATHENS greatly reduces the management information that can be gathered by individual service suppliers. This is deliberate to protect the privacy of individual users. For example, it is not possible for a supplier to monitor use of her service within a specific discipline if neither individuals nor even whole classes are identifiable by user ID.

Limitations of Current usage Measurement Tools

It is important when designing performance measurement activities that they be justified in terms of the benefits derived. Because it is automatic, transaction logging is a cheap way of gathering data in an electronic environment.

Unfortunately, the type of data that can be collected is often restricted by the delivery format. In 1996, when Michigan University intended to test economic models during the TULIP Project, it was unable to do so because 'the Web does not support the kind of data collection required to test economic models'.

Project MUSE is still unable to distinguish between downloading/printing and browsing as the Web is a stateless environment. SuperJournal know that although users claim to prefer HTML documents for onscreen viewing, given a choice of formats, a large majority 59 chooses PDF over HTML. As most users print documents if they intend to read more than a few lines, it can be assumed that they select PDF as a superior format for printing.

Unfortunately, SuperJournal cannot verify this assumption by monitoring use as it is not possible to differentiate downloading from printing. Thus, although data gathering is cheap, as yet, it is also limited. Furthermore, analysis of such data tends to be time consuming and thus expensive and interpretation is not always straightforward.

For example, it may be assumed that more hits indicate a better service, as a high number suggests that users return and that they recommend a site to others but, of course, this may not always be the case. A subject-based gateway which generates search results that closely match a users needs will record very few hits before that user leaves the site satisfied with the result.

If the search results supplied are poor and include a number of extraneous links or if the user is required to conduct several searches before she retrieves useful links, the gateway will record many more hits before the user leaves.

However, if a subject-based gateway offers not only access to a database of catalogue records but also holds a local archive, it should record a larger number of hits as users are likely both to search the database and to retrieve local resources. Furthermore, attempts to make more efficient use of internet bandwidth by caching and mirroring can subvert attempts to monitor use. Access to resources from site A from a cache or mirror held at site B will not be included in usage measurement unless site B informs site A about the cache and agrees to supply site A with use data. This type of shortfall makes WWW statistics unreliable or, worse, misleading.

Inferring user Behaviour from Transaction Logs

Use of transaction logs for performance measurement requires digital library practitioners to infer meaning from specific types of user act in a digital environment. For example, A. Dawson of the BUBL service (http://www.bubl.ac.uk) suggests that to view a list of journal issues with dates and contents is the equivalent of browsing a library shelf. He also asserts that searching is a deliberate activity which is not easily mistaken and that to access full-text is a likely indication that the user is reading the article.

The latter assertion is qualified by the acknowledgement that the reader may access text to scan for relevance rather than, necessarily, to read the article.

However, Dawson argues that this ambiguity need not influence the accuracy of any performance measure as it applies to all journals.

This type of inference helps digital library practitioners to make sense of quantitative data. However, knowledge of user behaviour in the digital environment is limited and it can be dangerous to base inference entirely on assumptions and prior experience.

For example, Dawson's assumption that the frequency with which a reader accessing full text is in fact scanning for relevance will apply equally to all journals is contradicted by the findings of the SuperJournal project.

SuperJournal found evidence that the way in which scientists and social scientists use journal elements differs. For example, scientists are more likely than social scientists to identify a relevant article from its title and to print it on that basis. Social scientists more often read the abstract to establish relevance because article titles in the social sciences can be more ambiguous. There may be similar differences in the way that scientists and social scientists approach full text.

It is clearly difficult to derive qualitative research findings from quantitative information. Qualitative methods such as interviews and 61 observation should be used to inform assumptions about the meaning of quantitative information and for triangulation.

Training and Awareness

Some of the eLib projects in the Training and Awareness programme area have now migrated to a service model and offer training courses in the use of new technologies for teaching and learning. HEIs are likely to continue to pay for this type of training from staff development budgets.

Training of users in the use of IT is unlikely to fall within the remit of libraries although libraries will probably continue to offer training in information skills and the use of specific resources.

It is beyond the scope of this project to explore the economics of this activity and compare the costs and benefits of training academics and students in the use of electronic and print resources. Clearly, the transition from a traditional to a digital or hybrid library involves dramatic changes in the infrastructure that supports the production and use of information resources. At present people prefer not to read on screen so they print articles from electronic journals.

As resources for teaching, learning and research are increasingly delivered in electronic form there is likely to be a mass shift from photocopying to printing; the latter is more expensive than the former but the total opportunity cost of an individual operating a photocopier is not incurred so costs are probably very similar.

As people become more familiar with technology, users may no longer need print copies.

This could lead to a net reduction in the cost of using information. The report of a recent study on the impact of electronic journals on networked printing suggested that one of the reasons for printing material from the Internet is to ensure future access; networked access is not always reliable.

In effect users create a personal print cache of networked resources. The report predicted that improved access to networked resources would 62 reduce the need to print but suggested that it may also increase use of the network, which in turn would increase the print load. The net effect of a combination of such changes is virtually impossible to predict.

Another factor impacting on the economics of digital information is the pace of technological change; new technologies become obsolete at an alarming rate, making it expensive for organisations to meet the changing needs of users. However, technological advances are reducing some costs, for example the cost of storing digital resources.

It is not possible within the scope of this project to estimate the infrastructure costs associated with delivering electronic resources in such an unstable and unpredictable climate. Investment in infrastructure that effectively enables all stakeholders to conduct much of their business electronically will be required.

The models described here will be based on the assumption that the HE sector will invest in sufficient infrastructure to support digital/hybrid library activities.

At present there is no coherent model of the digital library, nor is there yet any developed model of the hybrid library. Furthermore, economic issues tend to be tested after solutions have been found to the more pressing technical, cultural and legal issues. Many specific digital library activities are insufficiently mature to have generated economic models. Where a model exists it has been evaluated and where alternatives exist these have been compared.

It is clear that a great deal of progress has been made over the last decade towards a greater understanding of how digital library activities may be integrated in HE. Nevertheless, a considerable amount of work remains, specifically in the areas of preservation and archiving and in standardisation of usage measurement and performance indicators. Conclusions regarding specific issues relating to digital library activities are outlined in the remainder of this report.

DIGITAL LIBRARY SERVICES

Always library services are followed by library works. But now the advancement in information technology has brought changes in the concept of traditional library work as well as service. The recent trend and change in the information related field especially in collection, storing, processing and dissemination of information have resulted in to the evolution of digital libraries. Now most of the reference books like encyclopaedias, dictionaries, directories, hand books, etc. are published in electronic form.

Similarly about 50 per cent of the existing secondary resources like abstracting and indexing services are available in electronic form for example, Chemical Abstracts Service, Index Medicus, Engineering Index. At present most of the digital libraries have been highlighted mainly on providing access to diverse digital information resources. The provision of personalized reference and information services is considered as one of the important characteristics of the library and information profession.

However reference services include:

- Either finding the required information on behalf of users, or assisting users in finding information themselves;
- Instruction in the use of library resources and services, and
- User guidance in which users are guided in selecting the most appropriate information sources and services.

In this changing scenario, reference works of modern libraries are influenced by a set of related technical and economic factors, especially the increasing use of technology and techniques. To cite some examples, the recent developments in the INTERNET and in Web Technologies have brought significant changes in the concept of traditional reference services and a number of web-based "expert services", that are now offered by many non-library organisation.

Information services are provided to the users on demand as well as anticipating the user needs including various forms of current awareness and selective dissemination of informa-tion services. Such services are provided to the users to keep them abreast of the latest developments in their field of interest through on-line search services in digital information environment, even by the non-library organisations like Dialog.

DIGITAL REFERENCE SERVICES OF ACADEMIC LIBRARIES

Web based reference services are also now being provided by academic libraries, Recently a study report on web-based reference services reflects the current practices of digital library services in seventy academic libraries of USA. The study shows that university libraries allow their patrons to put reference questions in a variety ways: 99 per cent offer e-mail reference, 96 per cent offer reference services by appointment while 29 per cent of the libraries offer real-time virtual reference. These libraries use *customer relationship management* (CRM) software packages for providing web-based reference services in the virtual reference environment.

CO-OPERATIVE DIGITAL LIBRARY SERVICES

The rising cost of digital reference sources and its proper processing by the trained manpower and also the initial infrastructural investment for introducing new services in libraries have influenced different organisations to choose a co-operative model of digital reference services. As a result some co-operative projects have been launched for providing web-based reference services to the users who can ask for such services from a remote location at any time. The Library of Congress, USA has launched the collaborative digital reference service with a mission to provide the users, anywhere anytime through an international digital network of libraries.

This network has three main components consisting of:

- Member Profiles
- Request Manager-Software for entering, routing and answering reference queries; and
- Knowledge Base-a searchable database of questions and answer sets.

In this network a participating library sends a question to the system on behalf of a user and the system looks in to the knowledge base for a match. Then a reply is sent to the relevant library through e-mail. Incase the question and its corresponding answer is not found in the knowledge base, then it is passed on to the Request Manager where using the profiles of participating libraries and their information resources collection, expertise etc, relevant query is passed on to an appropriate library.

This library receives the query, finds an answer and sends back reply to the results store and answer to the knowledge base. Thus the Knowledge Base and Request Manager become able to provide reference service in digital environment. However, the Library of Congress and OCLC have developed a co-operative "Question Point" the advanced generation of *collaborative Digital Reference Service* (CDTS) in June 2002 which integrates local as well as global electronic reference networks.

PERSONALIZED SERVICES

Most of the researches on digital library development have focused on access to and retrieval of digital information but they have overlooked the personalized service aspects, as primary goal of library information services. However the technology and information resources, on their own, can not make up an effective digital library. On priority basis the personalized services in a digital library environment would help the users to find information resources available in a digitally chaotic world.

In a Delphy study it was revealed that:

- The primary roles library professionals play in digital libraries include organization of macro and micro-documents, selection and acquisition and acting as gateways to the provision of information services, and
- The best reasons of developing a digital library include: increasing access to information serving and users needs and bringing organization to the unstructured universe of electronically available information.

However there is a demand for end-user instruction on the use of digital libraries and the digital library professionals who are subject specialists should help users to formulate disciplinary search strategies and provide assistance in developing new digital information resources.

Web-based reference and information services

Several reference and information services are now available on the web and many of these services are provided by non-library organization. Also a web site that provides a categorized listing of libraries that offer real-time reference services using specific software, live interactive communication tools, call centre management software, bulletin board services and other INTERNET technologies.

Of course, most of these services are designed for registered users of some specific libraries in-digital information environment. HodgKin has made an aggregation approach to reference and information services. According to which more than one reference sources is made accessible digitally and also it is more practicable in terms of visibility and profitability than a single reference source.

Further:

- It's reference service becomes much better known to professional users and thus easier to find, by providing access to several reference works,
- By tackling a number of reference works at a time, the publishers can achieve economics of scale in production and development
- The user's search session is likely to be much more powerful and fruitful.

Online reference and information services can be broadly categorized into three groups:

- Those from publishers, database search services and specialized institutions
- Those provided by libraries and/or experts through the INTERNET and
- Where the users need to conduct a search and find information through the web.

Also they have listed several online information services that belong to the first category comprising various current awareness, and SDI services, for example:

- Contents pages services from commercial publishers, such as Elsevier's Contents Direct Service and IDEAL Alert from Academic Press.
- Information on new books available for free from publishers and vendors, such as Wiley Book, Notification Service from Wiley, and Amazon.com.

- SDI services from online search services providers, such as Dialog (Dialog Alerts)
- Current contents and ISI Alerting Services from ISI and so on.

However some of these services, particularly the contents page services from publishers of journals, are free, while for others, such as Dialog Alerts, or Current Contents from ISI, users need to register and pay for the services. There are also some web-based reference services where users need to conduct a search in order to answer their reference query.

For example:

- The Internet Public Library,
- Britannica,
- The Electric Library and
- The Internet Library for librarians.

Most of these web-based reference services are available free of charge but some charge a small amount as fee. For example, the Electric Library charges an annual subscription fee.

SEARCH ENGINE SERVICES

Sherman made a comparision among three web-based reference services like:

- Ask Jeeves basically a search engine, is useful for complex questions and is a good choice for searchers who lack Boolean or other searching skills, because of its strong natural language parser and question-and-answer template structure. The users can ask a question on a given topic and it comes up with a list of questions on the same or similar topics; the users can select any of those predefined questions and then it provides further answers. It processes each query syntactically and semantically and then its answer processing engine provides the question template response. When the users click on a response, the answer-processing engine retrieves the answer template that contains links to the answer locations. Thus Ask Jeeves can help users to select a query from a pre-defined set of queries on a given topic. So it is considered as a useful model for reference and infor-mation services in digital libraries.
- The Electric Library is an excellent choice for a serious researcher in need of timely content from a wide array of otherwise unavailable sources. It provides access to various on line reference sources and allows users to either select a specific source or conduct a search on a range, or all, of the sources.
- Information please is a suitable tool for students and other researchers, as an authoritative source of facts and pointers for further investigation.

Moreover Chowdhury and Chowdhury have suggested some other useful search engine services like:

- Web help.com that claims to offer real time search assistance with a real live expertany time, day or night,
- About.com is a service that shows a number of pre-defined categories related to a search topic given by the user.

For example, a simple search on 'e-commerce' not only produces a list of sites, but also provides a set of topics related to e-commerce, such as e-commercedefinition, e-commerce security, the advantages and disadvantages of e-commerce, e-commerce statistics and so on.

DIGITAL LIBRARY INFRASTRUCTURE

A digital library has certain technological requirements such as:

- Locally developed database
- Local library system with adequate personal computers having LAN and CD-ROM Drives.
- Electronic mail service
- Network connection to have access to other data bases
- Various functions to coordinate, manage the entry and retrieve data.
- Multimedia Kit
- Well trained manpower
- Computer Hardware with Audio-Visuals, Video Conferencing Kit, Pentium Web Server, Laser Printer, Scanner, Barcode Scanner, Barcode Printer, Digital graphic printer and UPS.
- Software and its accessories.

The super structure of digital library rests on some important factors like:

- The human need for information especially that is timely and relevant and
- Accumulation of information, and all the supporting infrastructure that includes research community, professional associations, libraries and publishers, advances in methods and technology leading to developments in net working, information science, information storage and retireval, hyper-media, human-computer interaction, artificial intelligence and other areas of computer science that make digital libraries a possible proposition.

DIGITAL REFERENCE SERVICES FOR GENERAL PUBLIC

Today web-based digital reference services are being provided by a network of public libraries. The users make their query on an enquiry page and it is automatically routed to one of the participating libraries which records it as an e-mail message to the user containing necessary and available information.

For example, the British Library, London provides special reference services for business, scientific, technical, medical, patent and environmental information which range from answering simple queries up to complex questions involving on line data base searches. Of course some of these services are free if users put simple queries, but for complex queries users need to pay at the prescribed rate which covers the costs of staff time, on-line searching and value added tax (VAT). The British Library provides STM (Science, Technology and Medicine) Search Service for which users need to pay. Similarly New York Public Library (Digital Library), American Library of Congress, Alexandria Digital Library, Berkeley Digital Library, Bibliotheque Nationale de France, Victoria State Library, Vatican Library, etc. are some other libraries which provide digital reference services for users.

PRESENT SCENARIO IN INDIA

All the six IITs (Indian Institute of Technology) created as centres of excellence for higher training, research and development in science, engineering and technology, have automated their libraries and now they have access to more than one thousand electronic journals. The Central Library IIT, Delhi has switched over to the Silver Platter's Electronics Reference Library (ERL) technology for providing access to bibliographic databases subscribed on CD-ROM.

The technology facilitates simultaneous and integrated access to ERL complaint reference databases to multiple users across the LAN/WAN Via TCP/IP. This library offers network-based CD-ROM search services from the CD-ROM databases subscribed in the central library. Most of its databases have now been transferred to ERL technology and its CD-NET system has been installed for searching of CD-ROM databases on the campus intranet. This Library has started subscribing to the web-based full-text electronic journals with availability of high speed INTERNET connection and about 1330 electronic journals are accessible full text.

In most of the higher learning and research institutes in India such as:

- The Regional Engineering Colleges (RECs),
- Tata Institute of Fundamental Research (TFIR),
- Indian Institute of Science (IIS),
- Indian Statistical Institute (ISI),
- Indian Agricultural Research Institute (IARI),
- Institute of Veterinary Research of India (IVRI),
- All India Institute of Medical Science (AIMS),
- Indian Institute of Management (IIMs),
- Institute of Physics, Institute of Life Science,
- Shaha Institute Nuclear Physics,
- The Medical College Libraries etc., have automated their library systems.

Some of them are in the process of digitization of rare and valuable documents. Digital library services in India are in developing stage. At present most of the university libraries have taken steps to provide web-based reference and information services in digital environment in addition to their traditional library services.

These services include:

- Access to library catalogues and union catalogues.
- Access to bibliographic databases
- Access to subject gate ways in specific disciplines
- Providing links to web sites
- Accessing and procuring e-reference sources
- Subscribing to e-journals
- Reference services provided by librarians and experts on the web
- Document delivery services
- On-line current awareness services
- Digitization of library resources, considering their intellectual value.

The University Grants Commission (UGC) of India has launched the major initiative for setting up nation wide communication network for Indian universities called UGC-Infonet. Each university was to establish a LAN in its campus linking all the teaching departments including library. ERNET of India and INFLIBNET Centre, Ahmedabad are conducting a series of training programmes for technical staff of each participating university library for managing and maintaining the network at their premises. The INFLIBNET Centre will administer and monitor the E-Journal programme and will have independent electronic access to all the publications to help with the process.

The INFLIBNET Centre has carried out training programmes in various places to spread awareness and to develop expertise in the University community in the use of E-Resoures under the networked environment. The INFLIBNET Centre has developed and also recently released library automation software package new version for university libraries (SOUL) for building up digital library services. Soul is Windows based user friendly software, based on client server architecture with multi-user and multi language facilities which supports internationally known standards such as CCF, AACR-II andMARC-21, etc.

Thus INFLIBNET centre is patronizing for digitization of college and university libraries and encouraging e-subscription and e-learning in Indian Universities and colleges. The DELNET (Delhi Library Network) created as a metropolitan network in 1988, has changed its name to Developing Library New Work (DELNET) in 2000. The main objectives of DELNET are to promote resource sharing among its member libraries, develop a network of member libraries, collect store and disseminate information, offer computerized information services in digital environment

The DELNET presently avails the high speed satellite communication facilities of NIC spread across the country and its 620 member libraries can access about 35 lakh bibliographic records in machine readable form. Also it maintains an online union catalogue of books available in its member libraries in CCF format. Its union catalogue is continuously updated. DELNET has been networking the libraries of about 400 affiliated institutes of AICTE, New Delhi. DELNET presents two management software packages *i.e.* DELMARC and DELPLUS.

CO-USAGE OF DOCUMENTS IN A LARGE DIGITAL LIBRARY

Creating relationships between similar documents is an activity that has a long distinguished history in Information Retrieval. In his textbook on the subject Korfhage (1997) writes "Probably the single key concept behind information storage and retrieval is document similarity". A practical motivation for the search for similarity is to improve information retrieval. When users have found one document they can be directed to similar documents that may be worth their attention.

A more theoretical motivation is the discovery of patterns of thought within a body of knowledge that is dispersed across a collection of documents. There are, of course, many ways in which similarity between documents can be assessed. One way is to use the judgement of an expert.

This is typically done by classifying documents according to a subject classification. This is a tried and trusted method. However, it requires human expertise and labour. These do not come cheap these days.

Therefore many collections have no classification data. Within the collection of documents that we study in this paper, three in four documents do not have a subject classification. Other classic measures of relationship between academic papers are the strengths of co-citation and bibliographic coupling. Such an analysis presumes that a citation index for the papers is available. Producing one manually is even more expensive than subject classification.

It is possible to use recently available software for autonomous citation indexing. Barrueco Cruz and Krichel report on on recent effort s using the same digital library that we study here. In this paper, we introduce a completely new concept of similarity that is user-centered.

We start with the idea that two documents are similar if they respond to the same information need. Thus roughly speaking we can think of two document as similar, if many users will withdraw the papers together while they are working on the system. Provided that we have a digital library with a long log of usage, we can find which papers have frequently been used together. This is what we will refer to as "co-usage" in the following. We are not aware of a study that has developed and tested this concept within a digital library context. We are, of course, aware that commercial systems use a related concept. Amazon.com, for example, suggests to a customer who is considering to purchase an item x that other people who bought x also bought item y. But since users are anonymous in our digital library, within the scope of our collection, the evidence on common usage is more difficult to gather.

MEASURING CO-USAGE

Our dataset comes from logs of the usage of the RePEc digital library. We have built this library over many years. RePEc is the largest free distributed academic digital library in the world. It is a pioneering effort in three respects.

First, RePEc pioneered the business model of the Open Archives Initiative distinction between data providers and service providers. RePEc has grown over 200 archives that are used in 10 different user services.

Second, RePEc is more than a collection of data about documents. RePEc offers a comprehensive picture of academic output by describing collection of documents, persons that are involved as authors of documents or editors of collections, and the institutions to which they belong in a relational database scheme.

Third, RePEc is essentially volunteer driven and has no owner. It is a public good much like the Internet. The data that we examine comes from the WoPEc user service. This service, founded in 1993 is available on the web at three locations since 1994.

These are Hitotsubashi University in Tokyo, Japan, Manchester Computing in the UK, and Washington University in St. Louis in the USA. The web site has static pages for each paper. In addition, there are a number of pages that link different papers together.

There are pages that list papers that have been issued within same series, and there are pages that group papers with the same subject classification. The log data also contains indication about what searches users have been making. However, as far as we are concerned, only the access to the description of the individual papers is relevant.

To begin with, recall that WoPEc is a non-commercial service. WoPEc does not enter into a contractual arrangement with a customer, with or without an exchange of money. Contractual arrangements with customers are expensive to arrange because they involve complicated negotiations, privacy issues etc. On the other hand contractual arrangement—even without exchange of money—generate customer data. The customer data itself has considerable value, see Shapiro and Varian for an illuminating discussion.

In the period that we examine, cookies have not been used. Therefore we need to wade through the log to find traces of usage by the same persons. All that the log offers is a trace to the Internet address (*i.e.* IP number) of the client machine, a file or action performed, and a time when this happened. Over recent years, the Internet is more and more accessed through personal computers rather than through multi-user systems.

However, we can not be completely sure that an IP number corresponds to the machine of an individual user, because there are caching sites. Therefore we must be watchful of IP addresses that appear particularly frequently. Let us for the moment make the assumption that the usage data from one single machine comes from one single user. We are then in the happy situation that we have identified the user.

However, to be able to claim that papers that are appearing together are joined together because they correspond to the same user need, we still have to assume that the information need of the user remains the same throughout the period of observation. This is problematic. Typically users will regard WoPEc as a reference source, and therefore naturally turn to it with different information needs. Therefore it is likely that the log contains material that corresponds to different information needs, even if they are expressed by the same user.

Therefore, we have chosen to think of users using the system within sessions. We typically think of a session as an academic, using a web browser on a desktop machine, going to the WoPEc site, make a few searches and look at a few results. Or we can think of it as a student, walking into a computer lab, uses a search engine, finds a page on the WoPEc service and navigates it for further data.

Technically, we define a session as a subset of the total log that comes from the same IP address within a certain time frame. In fact we assume that there must not be more than one hour between two consecutive log entries for them to qualify to be within the same session. In addition, we do not consider repeat access to the same paper as two different accesses to that paper. Such access is likely to occur mainly for technical reasons, such as that the user did not have time to read the article at the first discovery.

Under these restrictions it appears to be convenient to model sessions as sets of papers. We can now proceed to a formal definition of co-usage. Let D be the set documents in the library and S be the set of sessions. Each session s contains a subset of the set of documents, *i.e.* s Ì D. Introduce | · | as as notation for the number of elements in a set. Let there be two documents di and dj. Let u(di, dj) be the set of all sessions that contain both di and dj. For convenience of notation, write u(di) = u(di, di). Then we propose to call the co-usage coefficient c(di, dj) as follows

$$c\left(d_1, d_j\right) = \frac{\left|u\left(d_i, d_j\right)\right|}{\left|u\left(d_i\right)\right|\left|u\left(d_j\right)\right|}.$$

The motivation for introducing the product in the denominator is to ensure that we do not have situations where one paper appears frequently with another by the sheer size of its own usage. It also leads c(di, dj) to gain the attractive properties that 0 <= c(di, dj) <= 1 and that c(di, di) = 1. It is clear that the measure that we propose here is an intuitive one. It is not a scientifically developed metric of the likelihood that, whatever size the session is, we will see the two papers appearing together in the session.

It is possible to evaluate that probability. However that calculation is not attempted here. It is left for future work. Even if we can theoretically ascertain how to calculate the probability, we can not in practice calculate it for all possible document couples, because of the amount of calculations that would have to be made within a large digital library as ours.

Results

We ran a programme to search for co-usage on a log for three years 1999–2001. There are 102551867 lines in the log. We discarded 24836221 requests for images, 401614 requests for CSS files, and 9315 contained another error. 3164598 requests contained a 404 error and were omitted. Most of them went to robots.txt. 3966837 distinct hosts accessed the system.

We exclude all accesses from hosts that accessed robots.txt. In addition, there are cache and proxy sites that we would like to remove as well. This is a more difficult terrain. The rule that we chose was to look at each day's log, and detect all hosts that issued more than 100 requests. In total, we detected 23068 such hosts, and discarded 17484961 lines because they were made by these hosts. This left us with 23413849 to analyzed. We detected 5251337 sessions.

We limited ourselves to sessions that had more than 3 accesses and less than 100, and that included at least one search. There were 69179 sessions that remained for analysis. We can not make the results available here, for obvious reasons of space. Therefore we have placed them at http://openlib.org/home/krichel/kumegawa/report.htm. We print the top couples that have the highest co-usage, up to a rounded coefficient of 50 per cent. The following results appear when we look through the data.

First, papers in the same series seem to be much more prone to co-usage than papers from different series. It is often papers by the same authors, over different periods of time, available in the same working paper series or journal that appeared to be co-used a lot. This observation suggests that the original split of the data in different series does not only provide an organizational layer to the data, but also a semantic one. Second, from reading through the related couples, it appears that a key concept that appears in the title immediately explains the co-usage. Thus, it should be possible to gain insights into key concepts that are of user interest by looking at the title data of papers that are co-used, and find the common words. This would be an interesting subject for further research.

This paper has introduced co-usage as a means to make document to document relationships. The concept of co-usage has been found to lead to excellent empirical results. Our results suggests that the concept of co-usage is a valid and interesting one.

Any remaining problems that we are experiencing to make it work in practice are consequences of poor measurement of usage, rather than flaws in the underlying theoretical reasoning. Just in the case of co-citation and bibliographic coupling, there will be a debate on how useful co-usage analysis really is. We have opened that debate with this paper.

There are two further consequences from this paper. In the short run, we intend to incorporate co-usage similarity into future developments of WoPEc, to build links from the description of one paper to the description of another as suggested by co-usage analysis.

In the longer run, we believe that our work can be seen as simple, but pioneering step towards information retrieval systems that are learning. Instead of having a system that has a fixed procedure that is applicable whatever the query an the collection, we can imagine that future information systems will learn from past user behaviour to better serve the present user. Co-usage appears as a key concept to move things forward in that direction.

DESIGN OF DIGITAL LIBRARY MEDIND WEB SITE

The medIND project is having its own domain name at the Internet. It has pneumonic value and stands for Medical Journals on Internet [from India]. Home page gives details of the project listing of the participating journals.

This listing is hyperlinked to each participating journal home page at the medIND web site. The site provides two approaches to access the journal articles.

Browsing

Journals are hyperlinked and arranged in alphabetical order. Such hyperlinked list leads to pages giving details of selected journals such as editors, instructions to authors, contact address, parent body etc.

Further, this leads to listing of issues of the journal by years/volume wise. The content page provides hyperlinks to the individual article.

Searching

The searching is being provided through the bibliographic database IndMED. Each record of the IndMED has been linked to the individual article in the MedIND site. The searching of the articles can be achieved through from http://indmed.nic.in as well as from http://mednic.nic.in web sites.

The references will display icons indicating the availability of the full text. In developing digital collection, issues of intellectual property rights have been dealt to strengthen the cooperation between editors and content service provider to facilitate access to digital content through Internet to end users in the area of biomedicine on non-commercial basis.

The design of digital collection should be usable, flexible and simple enough to accommodate future changes and also enables other applications to utilize data for development of future applications.

The naming convention of digital collection is acted as bridge between metadata base and full text of content. This project fulfills the demand of providing full text of documents to health professionals free of cost throughout the world.

It serves as a model for the development of similar collections in others S&T areas, medIND is a step in the process of making it as an open archive source where Indian journals covered in Medline database as well in IndMED database will be stored and will be provided access free of cost to health professionals throughout the world.

This will give enough visibility and exposure to Indian biomedical journals and demand for Indian literature would be met through the medIND project. In future, more visibility to articles included in medIND journals would be provided by adopting and exposing metadata in OAI-PMH and RSS protocols.

LOCATING QUALITY DIGITAL INFORMATION

Providing mechanisms for information seekers from academe to locate quality information resources in a particular subject area is also a challenge for libraries—a very important one. Many academic libraries provide "library guides" or pathfinders to quality information resources, available through the library Web site, but typically they are not heavily used. A limited number of subject disciplines have developed coordinated Web guides to information resources; a notable example is AgNIC, serving the field of agriculture. Some libraries are developing mechanisms to link subject pathfinders into course management systems for every course at the institution.

This useful strategy brings the information to the place where students will be actively engaged in academic work. Librarians at the University of Rochester looked for new ways to bring quality subject resources to the attention of students. They recognised that "undergraduate students' mental model is one focused on courses and coursework, rather than disciplines." Therefore, they developed a mechanism to incorporate pathfinders into every course at the institution using the course management system. Both students and faculty believe that the library is doing a poor job with helping them discern which Web resources are suitable for academic work. Libraries are addressing this concern by developing portals to catalogs, licensed databases, and Web sites that would meet the kinds of criteria used in building academic library collections and by working with such projects as Google Scholar.

LIBRARIES AND INFORMATION SERVICE

Librarians often take great pride in the personalised information services they offer to their constituencies and the classes they teach to incorporate information literacy into the academic curriculum. While many of today's Net Gen students have grown up with technology, they do not necessarily have the requisite knowledge or skills to use technology and digital information in ways appropriate to the academy. Librarians should persist in their efforts to find ways to help students learn about digital information, including important policy issues in this arena, such as privacy and intellectual property. They should consider updating some of their methods for teaching students, incorporating gaming technology, or developing more visually oriented instruction aids, for example. One-on-one services offered electronically should be tailored to students' characteristics, such as their propensity to work late hours and use a variety of technologies, including laptops and cell phones.

Designing Web pages that are responsive to Net Gen students' style would also help guide students to appropriate content or help them when they have problems with searches. A study of high school students' Web searching revealed that students relied heavily on information displayed in graphic form on Web pages and often relied on graphics and visual cues to interpret the relevance of such pages. Libraries and information service providers generally do not design their resources with such criteria in mind. Incorporating students on design teams and giving them the go-ahead to re-envision the way the library displays its resources would be a useful method of developing information that resonates better with Net Gen students.

To summarise, Net Gen access services will:

- Continue to integrate library information into Google or other popular access mechanisms
- Offer simplified and graphic ways for students to approach subject searches
- Integrate subject guides or pathfinders into CMS or other locations conducive to use
- Integrate searching of "open" Web resources and materials owned or licensed by the library

FLUENCY WITH TECHNOLOGY AND INFORMATION LITERACY

Are Net Gen students already so technology literate and information savvy that they have no need for instruction or personal assistance in using technology and library and information resources? We know that Net Gen students come to campus having played hours of video games, having spent much of their spare time surfing the Net and instant messaging their friends, and having used multiple electronic devices simultaneously. On the other hand, we hear complaints from faculty that students use inappropriate sources from the Web to support their ideas in term papers instead of peer-reviewed academic resources; that they submit multimedia projects that are superficial and full of glitz, not substance —and that they no longer read, period.

When students graduate, their faculty in graduate degree programmes and their employers expect that they will have a facility with technology and with digital information that the older generations do not have. New office recruits are often hired because of their Internet skill and are given projects that exploit their technology and information skills, developed during their college years.

In addition, today's college graduates live in a world where it is important to understand key information policy issues. Intellectual property, privacy, and First Amendment issues are fundamental to operating as an informed citisen in today's information society and directly affect the work of individuals who create, as well as use, networked information. While Net Gen students generally can multitask, learn systems without consulting manuals, and surf the Web, they lack technology and information skills appropriate for academic work. Higher education institutions do not integrate or package technology and digital information skills instruction into the mainstream curriculum.

A National Academies report described a model set of skills for "fluency in information technology," which incorporates both information technology and literacy skills. The report's authors divided skills into three categories: foundational concepts, contemporary skills, and intellectual capabilities. They recommended that each university's subject area curriculum develop ways to incorporate instruction in these topics; however, they lamented that this is not currently the case.

The Association of College and Research Libraries (ACRL), a division of the American Library Association, has also developed guidelines for information literacy, but they have not been widely implemented by universities. Technology and information literacy are generally perceived to be "library" or "IT" problems, not overall curricular issues.

At Southwestern University, a team of IT professionals, librarians, and faculty developed a student survey based on both the National Academies' fluency with information technology principles and the ACRL Information Literacy Competency Standards. Their findings revealed that while students rated themselves highly in their ability to find information on the Internet, they recognised that they floundered when they attempted to find materials appropriate for their research and wasted much time in the process.

The students also expressed a desire for more technology applications to be integrated into their courses. This model is being explored through a Mellon Foundation–sponsored project at the University of California, Berkeley, where selected faculty and librarians are working in partnership to incorporate information literacy skills and undergraduate research into large-enrollment courses with the goal of assisting students in developing skills that will serve them throughout their coursework at the institution.

PUBLISH/SUBSCRIBE FUNCTIONALITIES FOR FUTURE DIGITAL LIBRARIES

We are interested in the problem of *distributed resource sharing* in future digital libraries. We adopt a pure P2P architecture but our ideas can be easily modified to work in the case of hierarchical P2P networks, as in. *Information providers* (DLs) and *information consumers* (users) are both represented by peers participating in a peer-to-peer (P2P) overlay network. There are two kinds of basic functionality that we expect this architecture to offer: *information retrieval (IR)* and *publish/subscribe*. In an IR scenario a user poses a *query* and the system returns information about matching resources.

In a pub/sub scenario a user posts a *subscription* to the system to receive notifications whenever certain events of interest take place. In this extended abstract we concentrate on the latter kind of functionality and sketch how to provide it by extending the distributed hash table Chord. *Distributed Hash Tables (DHTs)* are the second generation *structured* P2P overlay networks devised as a remedy for the known limitations of earlier P2P networks such as Napster and Gnutella.

We present a set of protocols, collectively called *DHTrie*, that extend the Chord protocols with pub/sub functionality. We assume that resources are annotated using a well-understood attribute- value model called *AWPS* in. Thus publications and subscriptions will also be expressed in *AWPS*. *AWPS* is based on *named attributes* with value *free text* interpreted under the Boolean and vector space (VSM) models. The query language of *AWPS* allows Boolean combinations of comparisons *A op v*, where *A* is an attribute, *v* is a text value and *op* is one of the operators 'equals', 'contains' or 'similar'. The following is an example of a publication in *AWPS*:

$$\{ (AUTHOR, \text{"John Smith"}),\ (TITLE, \text{"Information dissemination in P2P ..."}),\ (ABSTRACT, \text{"In this paper we show that ..."}) \}$$

The following is an example of a query:

$$(AUTHOR = \text{"John Smith"}) \wedge (TITLE \sqsupseteq P2P \wedge (information \prec_{[0,0]} alert)) \wedge (ABSTRACT \sim_{0.7} \text{"P2P architectures have been..."})$$

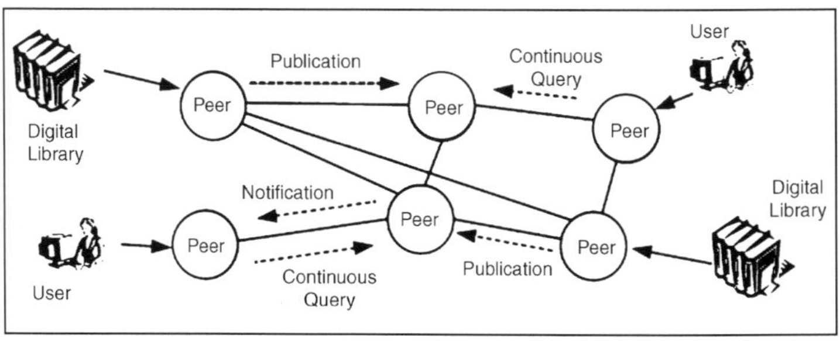

Fig. Distributed Resources Sharing in Future DLs

This query requests resources that have *John Smith* as their author, and their title contains the word *P2P* and a word pattern where the word *information* is immediately followed by the word *alert*. Additionally, the resources should have an abstract similar to the text value *'P2P architectures have been...'* with similarity greater than 0:7. The contributions of this abstract are the following.

The research presented in this abstract is a continuation of our previous work on the DL information alert architecture DIAS and the system P2P-DIET. The main contribution of our current work is that our protocols are extensions of DHTs and achieve much better scalability, robustness, fault-tolerance and load balancing. The rest of this extended abstract is as follows.

THE DHTRIE PROTOCOLS

We implement pub/sub functionality by a set of protocols called the *DHTrie protocols*. The DHTrie protocols use *two levels of indexing* to store queries submitted by clients. The first level corresponds to the partitioning of the global query index to different nodes using DHTs as the underlying infrastructure. Each node is responsible for a fraction of the submitted user queries through a mapping of attribute values to node identifiers. The DHT infrastructure is used to define the mapping scheme and also manages the routing of messages between different nodes. We use an extension of the Chord DHT to implement our network.

The second level of our indexing mechanism is managed locally by each node and is used for indexing the user queries the node is responsible for. In this level, each node uses a hash table to index all the atomic queries contained in a query by using their attribute name as the key. For each atomic Boolean query the hash table points to a *trie*-like structure that exploits *common words* and a hash table that indexes text values in equalities as in. Additionally for atomic VSM queries an inverted index for the most 'significant' query words is used as in. In this abstract as suggested, focus on the first level of indexing and present the sub- scription, publication and notification protocols that regulate node interactions.

Protocols for query updating and removal are omitted due to space. The local indexing algorithms we use and their experimental evaluation are thoroughly discussed in.

The Notification Protocol

When a message FwdResource containing a publication *p* of a resource arrives at a node *P*, the queries matching *p* are found by utilising its local index structures and using the algorithms. Once all the matching queries have been retrieved from the database, *P* creates notification messages of the form notification and contacts all the nodes that their queries where matched against *p* using their IP address associated with the query they submitted. If a node *P0* is not online when *P* tries to notify it about the published resource, the notification message is sent to the *successor*. In this way *P0* will be notified the next time it logs on the network. The modifications to the join and leave protocols of Chord to achieve this functionality originally presented in the non-DHT system P2P-DIET are omitted due to space considerations. To utilise the network in a more efficient way, notifications can also be batched and sent to the subscribers when traffic is expected to be low.

Frequency Cache

In this part, we introduce an additional routing table that is maintained in each node. This table, called *frequency cache* is used to reduce the cost of publishing a resource by storing the IP addresses of the nodes responsible for frequent words contained in published documents. FCache is a hash table used to associate each word that appears in a published document with a node IP address. FCache uses a word w as a key, and each FCache entry is a data structure that holds an IP address.

Thus, whenever P needs to contact another node $P0$ that is responsible for queries containing w, it searches its FCache. If FCache contains an entry for w, P can directly contact $P0$ using the IP stored in its FCache. If w is not contained in FCache, P uses the standard DHT lookup protocol to locate $P0$ and stores contact information in FCache for further reference. Using FCache the cost of processing a published resource p is reduced to $O(v + (h — v) \log N)$, where v is the number of words of p contained in FCache. FCache entries are populated as follows.

Each time a resource p is published at a node P, P contacts the nodes responsible for storing queries with words contained in p. After this process is over, P knows the contact information of those nodes, and stores it to FCache along with the word each node is responsible for. After that, for each publication taking place at P, P maintains this routing information for the most frequent words contained in resources published to it. Notice that the construction and maintenance of FCache is based only on local information and that the only extra cost involved is FCache misses and the routing information discovered is also cached for further reference).

BRIEF PRESENTATION OF EXPERIMENTAL RESULTS

We have evaluated DHTrie experimentally in a distributed digital library scenario with hundreds of thousands of nodes and millions of user profiles. For our experiments we used 10426 documents downloaded from CiteSeer and also used in. The documents are research papers in the area of Neural Networks and as suggested, refer to them as the NN corpus. Because no database of queries was available to us, our queries are synthetically generated by exploiting 2000 documents of the corpus. The remaining 8426 documents are used to generate publications. Our experiments show that the DHTrie protocols are *scalable*: the number of messages it takes to publish a document and notify interested subscribers remains almost constant as the network grows. Moreover, the increase in message traffic shows little sensitivity to increase in document size.

We demonstrate that simple data structures with only local information can make a big difference in a DHT environment: the routing table FCache manages to reduce network traffic by a factor of 4 in all the alternative methods we have studied. Since probability distributions associated with publication and query elements are expected to be skewed in typical pub/sub scenarios, achieving a *balanced load* is an important problem. We have studied an important case of load balancing for DHTrie and present a new algorithm which is also applicable to the standard DHT look-up problem.

7

Semantic Research for Digital Libraries

During the DLI, which ran from 1994 to 1998, significant research was conducted at all six projects in the area of semantic retrieval and analysis for digital libraries. Among the semantic indexing and analysis techniques that are considered scalable and domain independent, the following classes of algorithms and methods have been examined and subjected to experimentation in various digital library, multimedia database, and information science applications:

OBJECT RECOGNITION, SEGMENTATION, AND INDEXING

The most fundamental techniques in Information Retrieval involve identifying key features in objects. For example, automatic indexing and natural language processing (*e.g.*, noun phrase extraction or object type tagging) are frequently used to extract meaningful keywords or phrases from texts automatically.

Texture, colour, or shape-based indexing and segmentation techniques are often used to identify images. For audio and video applications, voice recognition, speech recognition, and scene segmentation, techniques can be used to identify meaningful descriptors in audio or video streams.

Semantic Analysis

Several classes of techniques have been used for semantic analysis of texts or multimedia objects. Symbolic machine learning (*e.g.*, ID3 decision tree algorithm, version space), graph-based clustering and classification (*e.g.*, Ward's hierarchical clustering), statistics-based multivariate analyses (*e.g.*, latent semantic indexing, multi-dimensional scaling, regressions), artificial neural network-based computing (*e.g.*, backpropagation networks, Kohonen self-organizing maps), and evolution-based programming (*e.g.*, genetic algorithms) are among the popular techniques.

In this information age, we believe such techniques will serve as good alternatives for processing, analyzing, and summarizing large amounts of diverse and rapidly changing multimedia information.

Knowledge Representations

The results from a semantic analysis process could be represented in the form of semantic networks, decision rules, or predicate logic. Many researchers have attempted to integrate such results with existing human-created knowledge structures such as ontologies, subject headings, or thesauri. Spreading activation based inferencing methods often are used to traverse various large-scale knowledge structures.

Human-computer Interactions (HCI) and Information Visualization:

One of the major trends in almost all emerging information systems applications is the focus on user-friendly, graphical, and seamless Human Computer Interactions. The Web-based browsers for texts, images, and videos have raised user expectations of rendering and manipulation of information.

Recent advances in development languages and platforms such as Java, OpenGL, and VRML and the availability of advanced graphical workstations at affordable prices have also made information visualization a promising area for research.

Several digital library research teams including Arizona/Illinois, Xerox PARC, Berkeley, and Stanford, are pushing the boundary of visualization techniques for dynamic displays of large-scale information collections.

The Illinois DLI Project: Federating Repositories of Scientific Literature

The Artificial Intelligence Lab at the University of Arizona was a major partner in the University of Illinois DLI Project, one of six projects funded by the NSF/DARPA/NASA DLI (Phase 1). The project consisted of two major components:

- A production testbed based in a real library
- Fundamental technology research for semantic interoperability (semantic indexes across subjects and media developed at the University of Arizona).

The Testbed

The Illinois DLI production testbed was developed in the Grainger Engineering Library at the University of Illinois at Urbana-Champaign (UIUC). It supports full federated searching on the structure of journal articles, as specified by SGML markup, using an experimental Web-based interface.

The initial rollout was available at the UIUC campus in October 1997 and has been integrated with the library information services. The testbed consists of materials from 5 publishers, 55 engineering journals, and 40,000 full-text articles. The primary partners of the project include: American Institute of Physics, American Physical Society, American Astronomical Society, American

Society of Civil Engineers, American Society of Mechanical Engineers, American Society of Agricultural Engineers, American Institute of Aeronautics and Astronautics, Institute of Electrical and Electronic Engineers, Institute of Electrical Engineers, and IEEE Computer Society.

The testbed was implemented using Soft Quad (SGML rendering) and Open Text (full-text search), both commercial software.

The Illinois DLI project developers and evaluators have worked together very closely on needs assessment and usability studies. The production testbed has been evaluated since October 1997.

Six hundred UIUC user subjects enrolled in introductory computer science classes have used the system; and their feedback has been collected and analyzed. We expect to have collected usage data for about 1500 subjects at the end of the study. Usage data consists of session observations and transaction logs.

After four years of research effort, the testbed successes include:

- Willingness to build custom encoding procedures for SGML. This enabled the testbed to succeed in federating journals from different publishers with differing use of SGML, where Elsevier and OCLC failed.
- Canonical encoding for structure tags. The testbed can federate across publishers and journals.
- Willingness to build custom software for searching. The Illinois DLI system is able to show multiple views on the Web and has advanced structure search capabilities.
- Production repositories for real publishers. The project became the R&D arm of several scientific publishers and generated valuable contributions to the scientific publishing industry.
- Changing the nature of libraries with research. The project enables a research prototype to become a standard service capability for engineering libraries.

However, in the nature of research, we also have experienced many testbed difficulties:

For the user interface, the project originally planned to modify the Mosaic Web browser (which was developed at UIUC). When the Web became commercial, Mosaic was quickly taken out of the control of the developers. Custom software is hard to deploy widely: the Web browser interface has widespread support, but the functionality was too primitive for professional full-text search and display.

Several practical difficulties were found in using SGML for this project. Plans to use standard BRS as full-text backend had to be abandoned. It proved essential to use an SGML-specific search engine.

Good-quality SGML simply was not available. We had to work with every publisher, since nothing was ready for SGML publishing.

SGML interactive display proved not to be of journal quality. Physics requires good-quality display of mathematics, which is very difficult to achieve.

As the project comes to its end, several future directions are being explored:

- Technology transfer to publisher partners: Several partners have expressed interest in receiving the testbed technologies. A contract has been developed with the American Institute of Physics to clone the testbed software and processing. A similar contract is under development with American Society of Civil Engineers.
- Testbed continuance by university library: An industrial partnership programme has been established between the UIUC Library and publishers. A UIUC spin-off company has been formed to provide software and future services.

Semantic Research in Illinois DLI Project

The University of Illinois DLI project, through the partnership with the Artificial Intelligence Lab at the University of Arizona, has conducted research in semantic retrieval and analysis.

In particular, natural language processing, statistical analysis, neural network clustering, and information visualization techniques have been developed for different subject domains and media types.

Scalable Semantics become Feasible

Statistical and neural network clustering proves useful and feasible interactively and for large-scale collections. Specifically, the AI lab has developed a noun phrasing technique for concept extraction, a concept space technique for building automatic thesauri, and a self-organizing map (SOM) algorithm for building category maps. More details are provided below.

Semantic indexes for large collections

Two large-scale semantic indexing simulations were performed in 1996 and 1997, respectively. We analyzed 400,000 Inspec abstracts and 4,000,000 Compendex abstracts to generate about 1,000 engineering-specific concept spaces (automatic thesauri) using the NCSA supercomputers (Convex Exemplar and SGI Origin 2000). Results of such computations could be used for semantic retrieval and vocabulary switching across domains.

USING OPEN SOURCE SOCIAL SOFTWARE AS DIGITAL LIBRARY INTERFACE

This article investigates the use of social software applications in digital library environments. It examines the use of blogging software as an interface to digital library content stored in a separate repository. The article begins with a definition of digital library approaches and features, examines ways in which open source and social software applications can serve to fill digital library roles, and presents a case study of the use of blogging software as a public interface to a project called Digital Forsyth, a grant-funded project involving three institutions in Forsyth County, NC. The article concludes with a review of positive and negative outcomes from this approach and makes recommendations for further research.

A significant portion of digital library literature focuses on issues such as document/technology heterogeneity and the relationship of users and communities in digital libraries. While applications such as MediaWiki and WordPress have been built primarily to support specific types of Web-publishing, they also include a number of structures common to the digital library community, including storage, preservation, and access models. For this reason, MediaWiki and WordPress can be investigated as acceptable platforms for digital library applications. Some library applications have already been developed using these platforms including Scriblio from Plymouth State University, and The Polar Bear Expedition digital collections. Both of these sites demonstrate the benefits of the incorporation of user services into digital library software.

There are a number of possible approaches to using social software in digital library environments. Downloadable applications such as MediaWiki or WordPress blogging software lend themselves to data and interface customization. Other sites, such as Flickr, support data storage and application programming interface functions that could be used to create a digital library application.

Through working with WordPress in the digital library application presented in this article, a number of challenges to using social software were discovered including:

- The ability/inability to crosswalk data between the social software application and the primary repository
- A lack of emphasis on metadata by default
- A lack of searching algorithms by default

The remainder of this article presents how a specific social software application (WordPress) was used to implement a public interface to a specific digital library. The article looks at the advantages and disadvantages of this approach as well as what its future potential there may be.

CASE STUDY PRESENTATION

Digital Forsyth is a grant-funded digital library project involving the Forsyth County Public Library, Winston Salem State University, and Wake Forest University.

The project is supported by grant funds from the Institute of Museum and Library Services under the provisions of the federal Library Services and Technology Act (LSTA), administered as a multi-year grant by the State Library of North Carolina, a division of the Department of Cultural Resources. The purpose of the grant is to create a digital repository for the historic photographs and collections of Forsyth County, NC institutions. In the first two years, a primary focus of this project has been the digitization and collective categorization of photographs from the archives of each of the institutions.

This process has involved the creation of a digital library using Qualified Dublin Core (QDC) as the metadata standard, with extensive description using a faceted categorization system. Each photograph is described with QDC elements and has faceted analysis completed on the elements and context of the photograph. On average, each photograph has 11 faceted descriptors.

The faceted taxonomy is developed from the 'bottom-up' using the photographs and archival information and is managed using Protégé, an open source ontology management system developed by Stanford University. As the Digital Forsyth project evolved, community participation emerged as one of the goals of the digital library. The resulting definition of the user interface included goals of community participation in the content, description, and organization of this digital library. While the back-end of the digital library employs a commercial digital library system that enforces authority control and manages metadata well, it did not include a public interface that met the community goals of this project. For this reason, we began looking at alternative platforms that would both allow us to present and manage our data easily and provide a robust community experience.

In short, the basic functional requirements of the software were to have the ability to:

- Store and display QDC metadata
- Store and display hierarchical facets
- Allow user-contributed content, including comments, description, and tags
- Permit the import and export of data in bulk
- Be customized easily both for user-interface and data management purposes

The project team considered several social software or Web-publishing applications including MediaWiki, WordPress, Flamenco, and Flickr. We chose blogging software as a platform because it fills many of the needs of the project, including photo representation, metadata support through use of special fields, category support, and embedded social tools.

While the idea of hosted blogging software was discussed, we felt that a local solution was required in order to achieve the level of customization and data access needed. We ultimately chose WordPress due to our prior experience with the software, which is hosted by one of the project partners for its own user community. The next section includes a discussion of some of the issues and solutions that we encountered.

SOLUTIONS

Using WordPress as a digital library application required the Digital Forsyth team to solve a number of problems related to metadata management, data migration, and user interface management.

Modifying WordPress for metadata representation

In order to work as a digital library interface, WordPress needed to support some level of detail for QDC metadata and provide the capacity to use our hierarchical facets as tags. To achieve this, we utilized custom fields in WordPress, post categories, and manipulation of the WordPress searching and browsing functions.

One of the strengths of WordPress is its support for custom fields that can be used to satisfy rudimentary metadata. We were able to configure these fields to match the Qualified Dublin Core metadata standard and move much of the content out of the blog posting text to these custom fields. In addition, we were able to load the Protégé-based taxonomy of the faceted categorization system into WordPress categories. This allowed us to preserve the relationships of the taxonomy while making terms easily usable in the blog interface.

For loading blog posts using both custom fields and categories, we modified the blog loader scripts to accommodate the new fields. We were able to use internal Protégé IDs to match on category assignments in the metadata records themselves, enabling permanent URLs to be created to point to different sections of the taxonomy. While this provides a unique, customizable link, it does not give the interface 'clean' URLs that would be easily remembered by a user.

The use of clean URLs is a popular feature in many social software platforms including Flickr, Del.icio.us and MediaWiki, and allows a user to navigate to different parts of the site using common words rather than cryptic strings.

In order to enable more granular searching of these new fields and categories, we used a pre-developed WordPress searching plug-in called AdvancedSearch. This gave us a suite of defined functions that supported category and custom field limits, which allowed the users of the interface to limit their search/browse experience by institution, date, or other metadata fields.

While the plug-in was modified to support local needs, the existence of the library allowed us to quickly develop search and limiting functionality. While in some cases, we altered specific components of the plug-ins, we avoided making modifications to the core WordPress software. This has allowed us to patch the software several times without negatively impacting local customizations. While future upgrades (particularly the implementation of WordPress 2.3) will require an evaluation of local modifications, the use of locally written plug-ins and minor modifications to third party plug-ins is expected to minimize development required for upgrades.

METADATA ISSUES

While initially we had standardized on Qualified Dublin Core, moving forward with WordPress required us to make two substantial modifications, one to the metadata itself and the other to the WordPress functionality. First, although the libraries had followed the recommended QDC date format wherever possible (but had created non-standard dates when days/months/years were not known specifically), WordPress required a well-formed date value. Because of this, we had to zero-fill any un-specified values. This allowed WordPress to make decisions and appropriately place non-specific dated posts.

The second major issue we faced occurred due to the size of some areas of the taxonomy. The standard functionality of WordPress categories includes a retrieval of all the related child categories when a user is interacting with the category browse interface. While this is preferable in some cases, database response times for our project were leading to time-out issues whenever category values exceeded several hundred.

In order to solve this issue, the category retrieval functions had to be re-written to make this process more efficient and to pull child values only when they were needed.

WordPress allows local implementations to make modifications like this using a local functions file that is related to specific interface themes. While this will require us to re-examine these functions with each WordPress upgrade, it also allows us to continue expanding the use of the taxonomy to create new relationships between the images in our collection.

In general, we used the following four approaches to modify WordPress in the Digital Forsyth project:

- First, the implementers downloaded pre-developed plug-ins. These plug-ins allowed us to quickly extend or modify the functionality of WordPress without significant effort.
- Second, we modified existing functions to fit our local needs. While using pre-defined functions makes these modifications much simpler to do, they can also affect the system when upgrades are made to WordPress.
- Third, in some cases we chose to modify the core functionality of WordPress.
- This was required in special cases where the WordPress default behaviour was not in sync with our expectations for Digital Forsyth. A simple example of this is the fact that blogging software by default returns posts in reverse chronological order. However, for our project

we wanted posts to be returned in increasing chronological order; therefore, in such cases we modified basic WordPress functions accordingly.

- Fourth, we created new local functions. While this approach was not used extensively, in the case of category retrieval new functions were required to make data retrieval more efficient. This final approach is probably the most susceptible to issues related to system upgrades.

As the Digital Forsyth project moves into its third year, we are looking towards merging the library cataloger experience with public feedback and tagging experience. This may allow us to stop using a back-end digital library for record creation and simply use it for archiving, which will significantly simplify the processes of data creation, loading, user-tagging, and updating currently in place.

Creating a user Interface using Themes

We were able to use the theme platform in WordPress to easily create a custom look and feel for our digital library. Two of the major modifications required were modifying the theme to display hierarchical tags more prominently and including our custom metadata fields at the correct place in the blog posting. Other modifications included style and layout customization. Some high level uses and benefits of themes are:

- Enabling multiple user/organization centric views of the data
- Enabling rapid prototyping of interfaces during initial development
- Using splash pages to provide deep links to searching and browsing interfaces.

In general, Word Press themes provide a simple platform for creating user interfaces, and involve approximately 8-10 files. Themes can be based on templates and specific pages where required. In some cases, we found ourselves deciding whether to use external plug-ins for themes or to develop them locally. An example of this is the development of 'photoblogging' style functions without using the photoblogging plug-in that comes with Word Press.

While we found the use of local functions was appropriate at the time we made our decision on this matter, being willing to re-investigate/re-develop this area as upgrades occur is an important component of using social software. Because so many possible features exist and are developed in the blogging user community, deciding which features to include and use can be challenging. Here again, the presence of such a large community of developers and users means that we are able to embed and deploy new services quickly, without a large amount of local development.

We found that using the WordPress software allowed development to start at a much deeper level. For example, rather than writing a batch loader or indexer, we were able to make small modifications to the WordPress software using existing modules. A prime example of modification is the revision to the tag-cloud plug-in. While traditional tag-clouds emphasize the most popular terms, with regard to our project we found that emphasizing the un-common facet categories in the tag cloud using a Term Frequency/Inverse Document Frequency (TF/IDF) approach yielded a more relevant and usable interface.

We accomplished this by creating a function that counted the number of times a facet was used in the corpus of blog posts and comparing those counts against the facets in the individual post. Based on the assigned weights using class definitions in the HTML, the interface uses CSS (Cascading Style Sheets) to modify the style of the resulting tags.

Data Migration

In order to load data from the digital library system to WordPress, we modified the existing RSS loader to support Qualified Dublin Core tags. The RSS loader was used because it already had a framework to support XML and employed a generic approach to the import functions. By adding control structures and modifying the mapping approach of data, we were able to map QDC fields to the appropriate custom fields and categories in WordPress. We also modified the loader in a few ways, such as excluding certain records and category matches in order to ensure that existing records are not overwritten and that duplicate categories are not created. In order to handle record updating, a separate update script was written.

As we begin to collect user-contributed data, data export and archiving is becoming a more significant problem. We are looking at different approaches for exporting and preserving this data, including extending the Qualified Dublin Core data in the back-end digital library system to support new blog-centric fields and storing data in archival packages.

Two fundamental questions arose while we worked on data loading and exporting. First, while we were committed to using external standards to represent and store data, it became obvious that it might be just as useful to define a local standard and then rely on mapping applications to make data available to external systems. Using a locally defined standard could have allowed us to approach some fields (such as record state, cataloger) more specifically while preserving the standard descriptive fields.

A related need to add qualifiers to different types of links could have been achieved via either a local standard or simply a different approach. As the project moves into its third year, we are considering different metadata standards or approaches that might allow more specificity at the administrative levels. Second, we found that the blogging software had sufficient functionality to support all of the data creation, management, and social-contribution needs of the project. It became obvious that using a digital library system for archiving rather than data creation might be a more efficient approach.

While we adapted the WordPress import/export functionality to suit the needs of our digital library, the issue of scalability might make it necessary in the future to take different approaches with large metadata batches. While current loading practices for our project are acceptable, loading larger batches through direct database interaction could lead to more flexible system interoperability.

The Content of the Blog Post Record

For our project, we use the blog record to represent an individual photograph. The QDC record title is mapped to the blog posting title. Post content contains the QDC identifier field mapped to the image HTML element, and the QDC description field is mapped to a Paragraph.

The Post excerpt contains an image element referencing a thumbnail representation of the photograph. The rest of the blog posting uses custom fields to store the rest of the QDC elements. By making extensive use of WordPress's custom fields to store QDC metadata, the interface and search functionality is enhanced.

OBSERVATIONS AND DISCUSSION

Many of the main benefits of using WordPress or other social software as a digital library interface have already been mentioned. Using a pre-developed system can enable rapid and flexible system development, enables the project to be more focused on user-driven functions, and benefits from the development focus of a larger community.

ISSUES

Data Management

One of the primary issues with the use of social software applications as a digital library interface is data management. While digital libraries have multiple goals (including creation, management, and preservation of digital objects and their metadata), the goals of social software are often focused on ease of content creation, user-friendly interfaces, and data presentation.

Making sure that digital objects are accurately represented and displayed means: utilizing primary identifiers from the core digital library system; taking steps to ensure that metadata is accurately represented in the social software application to ensure no degradation of accuracy or specificity; and accurately managing metadata and digital object versions to ensure that the most accurate data is preserved.

While WordPress required us to manipulate some functions to ensure that these goals were met in our project, its flexibility as a content creation and display system has resulted in a significant reduction in the amount of work required to create and manage our user interface. Future developments in the use of WordPress as a content creation and management system are expected to save time and allow Digital Forsyth to employ systems that can focus on metadata management and preservation.

Technical Skills

A common criticism of social software is the skill level required to implement and manage these applications. Using social software in a custom environment such as the one described in this article exacerbates this situation, as specific skills are required to make the software work in specific ways. In general, programming skills, XML skills, metadata skills and digital object skills are essential for a project like ours. In addition, some specific skills are required to work with WordPress and common digital library applications, including skills using:

- PHP
- SQL
- CSS/HTML
- Web server software
- JavaScript

Two issues that took time for us to work through were:

- Lack of familiarity with the WordPress programming framework
- Lack of documentation of software

In addition, while theme creation is relatively straightforward, customizing a theme beyond simple colour and layout decisions required more extensive work. WordPress is rather complicated software, so finding the appropriate function can be difficult at times. Working with these functions can get confusing, regardless of the extent of documentation provided.

SUSTAINABILITY

Project sustainability should be a key concern when selecting software for a digital library project. Commercial systems can have a host of sustainability issues, including vendor support, ease of system use and customization, and system flexibility. Social software and open source software applications have other sustainability issues to consider as well.

These include the inability to guarantee service stability and permanence. While commercial systems typically have market permanence or vendor-supplied migration options, open source and social software is often only as permanent as the user community surrounding it. This means that an organization must be willing to find new solutions when required, and it also means that these organizations will have to carry the burden of system migration on their own.

Further, while there are many hosted low cost and free options for digital libraries (including hosted blogs/wikis, hosted image sites such as Flickr), the system being considered should be compared against the needed stability and uptime of the system. In short, it does not make sense to base key parts of a digital library on a free, hosted service if the digital library cannot sustain itself outside of that service.

In choosing the approach we took for Digital Forsyth, we found that the implementation of the user interface was accomplished quickly and with community-centric features that serve as the centerpiece of the project site. Despite the issues that we experienced with metadata management, system assumptions/limitations, and interoperability, overall the use of WordPress lowered our development and maintenance costs.

We are hopeful that the system will benefit from increased sustainability and portability as future releases of WordPress are installed, and as special functions are developed and deployed. In selecting an existing open source application to serve as an interface to your particular digital library, some key questions to ask are:

- Will the system scale to the level that your data requires?
- Are the data models used in the system compliant with your digital library metadata structure?
- Is migrating data between the applications sustainable?
- What needs can be filled with these social software/open source applications? Is the software appropriate just for user interfaces or can it serve other functions of the digital library system?
- How will system sustainability be ensured with the selected options?
- Will developing the customized parts of the software be more manageable than other solutions?
- What core functional requirements exist, and is this application the best approach?

By choosing the solution we did, we hope to be able to incorporate a number of approaches to public interfaces while keeping our digital library applications centralized and focused on key functions of storage and preservation.

SEMANTIC QUERY ROUTING AND PROCESSING IN P2P DIGITAL LIBRARIES

The digital library community envisions the availability of digital content on a global scale through Digital Libraries (DL) that can be accessed, integrated and individualised for any user, anytime and anywhere. A key point in such a vision is the interaction with multiple DL nodes to support integrated access. We believe that such interaction is far beyond the traditional information integration technologies, which impose restrictions on representation and communication languages used at both the semantic and the structural levels, since:

- DL nodes should be autonomous. Ideally, a node must not have restrictions on how to organise its data and what kind of query capabilities to offer.

- DL services should support decentralised sharing and management of data through a network of DL nodes. In such a network, a DL node must be able to provide data to other DL nodes and, at the same time, to have access to data of other DL nodes.
- The diversity of DL nodes in terms of availability, processing power and interface options, makes a DL network a highly heterogeneous environment in terms of hardware/software setup in addition to the data being provided.
- Finally, the system needs to be evolving in the sense of DL nodes joining and leaving the network at their own will. DL node arrivals and departures affect the data that is available.

Our work explores the application of the peer-to-peer (P2P) paradigm in DL technologies. In particular, schema-based P2P systems exploit schema information to specify what kind of data is provided by the involved peers. The advantages of this approach lies to the fact that:

- More sophisticated than keyword-based queries can be posed and
- More efficient approaches can be developed for identifying peers that are capable of answering the queries.

A natural candidate for representing descriptive schemas of information resources is the Resource Description Framework/Schema Language. RDF schemas offer rich semantics. The primitives of RDF schemas are classes and properties. Classes describe general concepts or entities. Properties describe the characteristics of classes or the relationships between classes. RDF/S:

- Enables a modular design of descriptive schemas based on the mechanism of namespaces;
- Allows easy reuse or refinement of existing schemas through subsumption of both class and property definitions;
- Supports partial descriptions since properties associated with a resource are by default optional and repeated and
- Permits super-imposed descriptions in the sense that a resource may be multiply classified under several classes from one or several schemas.

These modelling primitives are crucial for schema-based P2P systems where monolithic RDF/S schemas and resource descriptions cannot be constructed in advance and DL nodes may have only incomplete descriptions about the available resources. The advanced structuring and retrieval functionality of schema-based P2P systems raises new challenges for view integration, query routing and processing over autonomous, distributed and dynamic networks of DLs. The main contributions of our work presented in this paper are:

- The design and implementation of effective and efficient query routing in P2P DLs, exploiting intensional indexing of DL node views and

- The study of interleaved query routing and processing algorithms in P2P DLs in order to produce as quickly as possible the first query results.

Related Work

Several projects address query processing issues in general P2P systems. However, they require a priori knowledge of the relevant to a query peers. Mutant Query Plans (MQPs) implement efficient query routing. Unlike our approach, MQP reduces the optimisation opportunities by simply migrating possibly big XML fragments of query plans along with partial results of sub-queries. In indices are used to identify peers that can handle containment queries. However there are no details on how a set of semantically related peers can actually execute a complex query involving vertical and horizontal distribution. RDFPeers is a scalable distributed RDF/S repository which efficiently answers multi-attribute and range queries. This approach ignores RDF/S schema information during query routing, while distributed query processing and execution policies are not addressed.

In, a P2P architecture is introduced, based on the extension of an existing RDF/S store. Although schema information is used for indexing, RDF/S class and property subsumption is not considered. A schema-based P2P infrastructure for the Semantic Web is described in. Their approach involves exact matching of basic class and property pattern and does not consider run-time adaptability of query plans.

P2P DIGITAL LIBRARIES

In order to design an efficient P2P DL infrastructure we need to address the following issues:

- How DL nodes advertise their bases?
- How DL nodes formulate queries?
- How DL nodes route queries? and
- How DL nodes process queries?

Advertisements of DL Nodes

A schema-based P2P DL infrastructure requires that each DL node advertises its local base content to other DL nodes. Using these advertisements, a DL node becomes aware of the bases hosted by other nodes in the DL. In our approach, we assume that there are global RDF/s schemas for various communities, in which DL nodes have access through the mechanism of namespaces. However, a global RDF/S schema may contain numerous classes and properties not necessarily populated in a DL node. Therefore, we need a fine-grained definition of schema-based advertisements. We employ RVL views to specify the sub- set of a community RDF/S schema(s) for which all classes and properties are populated in a DL node base. These views may be broadcasted to other DL nodes, thus informing the rest of the P2P DL of the information actually available in the DL nodes.

Query Formulation in DL Nodes

In this work, queries and views in a P2P DL are formulated by nodes in the RQL/RVL language. RQL is a typed functional language in the form of OQL. It uniformly queries both RDF data descriptions and schemas. RVL ex- tends RQL by supporting views on RDF/S. In RQL/RVL, class and property path patterns allow users to navigate through the RDF/S schema of a DL node to retrieve resources. RQL queries allow us to retrieve the contents of any DL node base, namely resources classified under schema classes or associated to other resources using schema properties. It is worth noticing that RQL queries imply both intensional and extensional filtering conditions.

Query Routing in P2P Digital Libraries

Query routing is responsible for finding the relevant to a query DL nodes by taking into account data distribution of their bases committing to an RDF schema. The query-routing algorithm takes as input a query and the available DL node views and detects which DL nodes can actually answer the query as a whole or fragments of it. The latter is important, since there might be answers that can be received by joining partial answers from different DL nodes. Our approach exploits query/view sub- sumption algorithms to check whether the classes or properties of the view are subsumed by the respective classes or properties used in the query. In this way, query routing takes into consideration semantic information from the RDF Schemas of the involved DL nodes. Specifically, a fragmentor breaks the given query into subqueries, whose number is bounded by an input variable. The query/view subsumption algorithms of are employed to determine which part of a query can be answered by a DL node view. For maintaining a distributed catalog of views published by the DL nodes in a P2P DL, appropriate DHT structures have been designed.

Query Processing in P2P Digital Libraries

Query processing is responsible for generating query plans according to the results returned by the routing algorithm. If more than one DL nodes can answer the same query fragment, the results from each. "The results obtained for different query fragments that are connected at a specific domain or range class are rejoined". The generated query plan reflects the data distribution of the system and uses it for obtaining at execution time both complete and correct results. The resulting query plan can be optimised. Compile-time optimisation relies on algebraic equivalences and heuristics allowing us to push, as much as, possible query evaluation to the same DL nodes. Additionally, cost-based optimisations based on statistics about the DL node bases enable to reorder joins and choose between different execution policies for the query plans.

A key feature of our approach is that query routing and processing are interleaved in several iteration steps. This leads to the creation and execution of multiple query (sub)plans that when 'unioned' offer completeness in the results. Specifically, starting with the initial query, at each iteration step, smaller sub- queries are considered in order to find the relevant DL nodes that can actually answer them. The routing information, *i.e.*, remote DL node views, is acquired by the lookup service offered by the system on top of intensional DHT structures.

The interleaved query evaluation terminates when the initial query is decomposed into its basic class and property patterns. The main advantage of the interleaved query routing and processing algorithm is that the query results are collected as quickly as possible since they require fewer intra-DL node joins. More precisely, each query fragment is looked up as a whole and only DL nodes that can fully answer it are actually involved in each query processing iteration step.

OPEN DIGITAL LIBRARY DESIGN

ODLs are guided by a set of design principles and operationalized with the aid of a set of OAI-PMH extensions. By analyzing some of the emerging aspects of Internet development, a set of basic design principles have been extracted to guide the construction of new protocols so that they are consistent with proven techniques in networked information systems.

The observed factors that influence these include: simplicity of protocols, openness of standards, layering of semantics, independence of components, loose coupling of systems, purposeful orthogonality, and reuse wherever possible. Based on these ideas, a generalization of the OAI protocol is possible so that it may be used for purposes that go beyond its original intention, namely to provide higher-level DL services. Formally, these principles are stated as follows:

1. All DL services should be encapsulated within components that are extensions of Open Archives.
2. All access to the DL services should be through their extended OAI interfaces.
3. The semantics of the OAI protocol should be extended or overloaded as allowed by the OAI protocol, but without contradicting the essential meaning.
4. All DL services should get access to other data sources using the extended OAI protocol.
5. Digital Libraries should be constructed as networks of extended Open Archives.

Each DL service is then designed as a self-contained component that communicates with other services using a protocol that is an extension of the OAI-PMH. A typical example of how this works in practice is illustrated, which shows a search engine's relationships to its data source and the interface that uses it as a service component.

In this case, the OAI Harvester is used to obtain a stream of data which in turn is used to create indices for searching. Queries are then submitted through the OAI Data Provider interface. These queries overload the semantics of the OAI-PMH, by using the OAI notion of sets to correspond to the dynamically generated result sets of a search engine. Analogously, when such a request is submitted, the query is mapped to the name of a set. Thus, without making any changes, the OAI-PMH can be used to serve as the interface to a search engine. With a few minor additions to the OAI-PMH, information such as cardinality of result sets also can be returned.

An example of such an OAI request, with overloaded semantics for a search component is:

verb=List I dentifiers and set = odl search 1/computer % 20 science/1/ 10

This query specifies that the response should contain the identifiers of the first 10 most relevant documents with respect to the query "computer science". The response generated by the component is in the standard format returned by OAI-compliant archives.

To use this component in a typical ODL network, it must be connected to a source of metadata and a user interface, much in the same manner as UNIX pipes and filters are used to connect cooperating processes together.

Implementation and Analysis

To test the feasibility of ODL design, a suite of components was specified, implemented, integrated into a network, and assessed for their ability to replace existing systems. These components and their functionality are specified.

Component

Function

ODL-Union

Combine metadata from multiple sources

ODL-Filter

Reformat metadata from (non-OAI-Conforming) data sources

ODL-Search

Provide search engine functionality

ODL-Browse

Provide category-driven browsing functionality

ODL-Recent

Provide a sample of recently-added items

Components Used in Prototype Systems

The components were implemented individually, tested using the Repository Explorer [Suleman, 2001], and combined into an ODL network to provide DL services over the union archive of metadata maintained by the Networked Digital Library of Theses and Dissertations (NDLTD) [Suleman, et al., 2001]. Then, to illustrate reusability, some components were integrated into the production server for the Computer Science Teaching Centre [CSTC, 2001]. A system architecture for the former of these systems is depicted.

There were seven source archives from which data was harvested through OAI-PMH interfaces, one of which required a filter because of minor differences in implementation from the others. The data was aggregated into a central archive for use by local services.

Three high-level services were provided using this data: Search, Browse, and Recent. Search indexed the data and exposed an OAI-like interface for specifying keyword queries. Browse sorted the data and exposed a slightly different OAI-like interface for accessing items by controlled vocabulary elements. Recent stored recent items and upon request returned a random sample of those.

The user interfaces were created using minimal scripts to translate HTML form elements into ODL requests and then convert the XML responses into human-readable displays using XSL stylesheets.

The design and implementation of the NDLTD ODL system conformed to the design principles stated earlier and thus provide an extensible framework for future expansion. Initial reactions to the design have been positive, with simplicity cited by some users as a motivation for using such a system.

Equivalence of the ODL network to a monolithic system is an important criterion for acceptance. Work has already been done on techniques to improve speed and reduce redundancy in storage. Substantial speed improvements were realized by using caching and persistent CGI script facilities provided by Fast CGI and Speedy CGI. Storage requirements were reduced by obtaining records on demand from co-located metadata archives. Network performance was tuned through some initial studies of the complexity of the OAI approach to harvesting. The net result of designing by principle and implementing for real-world scenarios is that the resulting system provides the expected level of service while still abiding by the principles of software engineering as applied to networked information systems, and the design and development of Digital Libraries in particular.

Future Work

It is hoped that the results of this ongoing work will change the way people build Digital Libraries. The evaluations and feedback received from users and colleagues strengthen the case for building on the OAI protocol to support high-level services, and composition of those services into complete Digital Library systems.

Building upon a foundation of extensibility, it then will be possible to work on providing more interesting services to users, thus bridging the wide gap between current research and production systems, and ultimately making information more accessible to more people.

CURRENT DIGITAL LIBRARY RESEARCH ON PERSONALISED SERVICES

Researchers have recently reviewed the status of some digital libraries from around the globe. These reviews reveal that while the digital libraries have very good information access and retrieval mechanisms in place, there is almost no provision for quality reference and information services.

However, these studies show that there is a trend towards the personalisation of digital library service, as in case of HEADLINE and GEMS (presently called iGEMS, a digital library developed at Nanyang Technological University in Singapore). Some recent research efforts have been directed at building personalised digital library environments. These studies can be grouped into three categories: user needs assessment, personalised user interface and personalised digital library, researchers reviewed literature on user interfaces, particularly in a digital library environment, and suggested the need for a task-based digital library.

Researcher discussed the personal digital library (PDL) that acts as a front-end to other electronic library systems and manages the user's information needs. Barry and Barbara discussed the creation of personal digital libraries. The North Carolina University Library developed MyLibrary @NCState as a portal application to the NCSU Library's information resources. This portal allows user profiling to build a dynamic, customised gateway to both general and discipline specific resources. MyLibrary is a Cornell University Library initiative to provide personalised library services to their students, faculty and staff on the basis of a focus group study to gauge library users.

The MyLibrary project has two components, MyLink and MyUpdate. MyLink allows patrons to save useful information resource links that they found themselves or those suggested by the librarians via a targeted notification in their personal space. Users can access this personal space from any place. MyUpdate periodically queries the online catalogue and notifies users, utilising a pre-defined user profile. Headline is one of the eLib Programme's Phase 3 projects, developing a hybrid library system called the HeadLine Personal Information Environment (PIE), This PIE uses portal-type technology to present an information environment that is personalised to the user's needs and allows user customisation. This project presents users with pages of resources relevant to their courses/department. PIE users are also provided with an "all resources" page that contains all the library resources.

Users can create their own lists of resources on their own pages. Meyyappan reported on ongoing research at Nanyang Technological University in Singapore on the design and development of task-based digital library organisation and a digital work environment (DWE). The major objective of these research projects is to allow users to personalise digital library access so that they can view their preferred resources, and hence, information is automatically filtered. These projects aim to select automatically a subset of the DL collection based on the nature and characteristics of a user.

The user then can add new resources, or delete recommended resources, to his or her page. The DWE project is somewhat different from others in the sense that the main objective of the DWE is to provide filtered access to the local digital library collections, to remote digital libraries, as well as to traditional libraries, and,most importantly, to the vast information resources on the university intranet. The system also allows users to create their own personal workspace to store selected information resources for future use.

CURRENT DIGITAL LIBRARY PROJECTS ON DIGITAL REFERENCE SERVICES

Some research projects aimed at providing reference and information services as part of the digital library services have recently begun. The most prominent is the Collaborative Digital Reference Service (CDRS) project launched by the Library of Congress.

CDRS

Researcher commented that "by applying the best of what libraries and librarians have to offer to the labyrinthine universe of unstructured and unverified information on the Internet, we can begin to bridge the gulf that exists between providers and users of information". With this end in view, the Library of Congress has launched the Collaborative Digital Reference Service, the mission of which is to provide "professional reference service to users, anywhere any time, through an international, digital network of libraries".

The CDRS is a library to library network for asking and answering reference questions. It has three main components:

- *Member profiles*: That contain information on member strengths and features.
- *Request Manager*: A software for entering, routing and answering reference questions.
- *Knowledge base*: A searchable database of question and answer sets.

The system is designed to work in a very simple manner. A participating library sends a question to the system on behalf of a user. The system looks into the knowledgebase for a match. If the answer is found, a response is sent to the querying library by e-mail. If the question is not found in the knowledgebase, then it is passed on to the Request Manager, which forwards the query to an appropriate library selected from the profiles of the participating libraries and their collections, expertise, etc. This library receives the query, finds an answer and sends it back to the results store, which then sends the response back to the asking library, and stores the query and the answer in the knowledgebase. Hence, the strength of the system lies in the knowledgebase and the Request Manager. Since, June 2000 CDRS has been a "working" pilot with a current total of 220 active members who are routing real questions and answers. The next generation on CDRS is being co-developed by Library of Congress and OCLC. It will integrate local and global e-reference networks, and will be released as a full production service in June of 2002.

AUTOMATIC REFERENCE LIBRARIANS FOR THE WORLD WIDE WEB

The Automatic Reference Librarians for the World Wide Web, a DLI-2 funded project at the University of Washington. The central objective of this project, according to them, "is to create software agents that posses reference intelligence I a limited understanding of complex technical topics, but a very sophisticated understanding of how and where to find high-quality information on theWorld Wide Web". Etioni and Weld reported the basic working principles of the proposed system, which works on a wrapper technology.

The basic steps involved are:

- The user asks a question;
- The Query Router assigns a topic to the query;
- The topic maps to a number of relevant wrappers;
- The parallel Web search module sends requests via wrappers to the sites;
- Responses from the sites are obtained and sent to the fusion engine for collation;
- User gets the response.

SIFTER is an interdisciplinary research collaboration among faculty and students in the Computer and Information Science Department and the School of Library and Information Science at Indiana University. The broad aim of the project is to develop information agents that would perform a number of functions such as culling information from complex resources residing in diverse locations, and conducting analysis, synthesis and customisation according to the requirements of the user.

The specific objectives are:

- Dealing with heterogeneous information sources that may change over time;
- Handling shifting requirements and interest of users with minimal human involvement;
- Creating a robust agent architecture for reactive, proactive and collaborative filtering;

- Supporting agent collaboration based on natural or artificial economic frameworks for multi-agent tasks.

VIRTUAL REFERENCE DESK

The Virtual Reference Desk (VRD) is a project sponsored by the US Department of Education, and its objective is "the advancement of digital reference and the successful creation and operation of human-mediated, Internet-based information services". VRD defines a digital reference service as Internet-based question-and-answer services that connect users with experts. The basic idea of VRD is that when a given user asks a question that cannot be answered by a participating centre, it is forwarded to the VRD network for assistance.

VRD services include the following:

- *Collaborative AskA Service*: A network of AskA services and volunteer information professionals.
- *The Learning Center*: A Web site for the K-12 community with curriculum-related Web sites, frequently asked questions, and other previously asked questions.
- *AskA+ Locator*: A searchable database of high-quality K-12 AskA services.

VRD also supports research on interoperability standards, metadata and other aspects of digital reference services.

LEVERAGING THE DOCUMENT SELECTIONS OF EXPERT PROBLEM SOLVERS

This is a DLI-2 project at the Oregon Health Sciences University and Oregon Graduate Institute. The goals of this project are "to understand how experts select information in a large and complex information space and to develop tools that assist them in this process", The project aims to capture the trace of information used by experts in the health field, for example medical doctors. The basic idea is that as medical experts traverse the large and diverse collection of documents, they make explicit choices about which information resources to examine more carefully and which ones to ignore.

These choices create a subset of documents relevant to a given problem and this subset of documents may be of interest to other users concerned with the same or similar problem. Thus, by capturing this information that is inherent in the selection of appropriate information resources for problem solving, this project aims to come up with models that may be useful for other users.

The project proposed to develop:

- A trace that describes the path taken by an expert in solving his/her problem by using the available information resources;
- A precis of information about each document, its content, and the history of its use by experts; and

- Navigation tools that would assist subsequent problem solvers using the collection by exploiting the knowledge inherent in the existing traces.

Though the project specifically deals with medical experts and looks into their problem-solving processes, the project team expects that the resulting technology will be scalable, because the value of a set of precis and bundles within a collection should increase as the document collection grows and as more experts use the collection.

DEFINITION OF DIGITAL LIBRARIES AND PERSONALISED SERVICES

While reviewing the definitions of digital libraries, Borgman noted that "in general, researchers (who primarily come from computer science and/or engineering backgrounds) focus on digital libraries as content collected on behalf of user communities, while librarians focus on digital libraries as institutions or services"'. She further stressed that the current state of digital library research and development, especially in the USA, is influenced by the research definition of digital libraries.

The emphasis on the "enabling technologies" for access to digital resources rather than on the services traditionally provided by libraries becomes quite evident when one looks at the two special issues of the *Journal of the American Society for Information Science*, The two issues contain excellent articles reflecting the state of digital library research but none focus on digital library services *per se*. Even the editor of the two special issues did not discuss reference and information services. He mentioned that "digital libraries have the ability to provide a previously unattainable level of service". He emphasised access to information and suggested the various methods, tools and techniques that facilitate improved access to information in digital libraries. However, this is in sharp contrast to the views of the two editors of the special issue of *Information Processing and Management* on digital libraries. Marchionini and Fox in their editorial stated that "digital library work occurs in the context of a complex design space shaped by four dimensions: community, technology, services and content".

The fact that digital libraries should not be regarded only as point of access to digital information was emphasised by a definition of digital libraries given by Borgman as early as in 1992 whereby she contended that a digital library are:

- A service;
- an architecture;
- A set of information resources, databases of text, numbers, graphics, sound, video, etc. and
- A set of tools and capabilities to locate, retrieve and utilise the information resources available.

The definition of a digital library that came up in the March 1994 Digital Library Workshop emphasised that a full service digital library must accomplish all the essential services of traditional libraries and also exploit the well-known advantages of digital storage, searching and communication.

There are many other definitions of digital libraries that mention the services aspect, either explicitly or implicitly. Pointing out the lack of emphasis on reference and information services, Sloan lamented that "human interaction in the digital library is discussed far less frequently. One would almost get the impression that the service tradition of the physical library will be unnecessary and redundant in the digital library environment". He emphasised the point that "technology and information resources, on their own, cannot make up an effective digital library".

Emphasising the need for personalised services in digital libraries, Lombardi mentioned that, "helping clients find resources in a digitally chaotic world is the first priority". In a Delphi study of digital libraries it was revealed that "the primary roles librarians play in digital libraries include organisation, selection and acquisition and acting as gateways to the provision of services involving information". This study also revealed that "the best reasons for developing a digital library include: increasing access to information, serving end users' needs and bringing organisation to the unstructured universe of electronically available information".

Thus, this study shows the importance of "serving end users' needs", and the need for the librarians to act as "gateways to the provision of services involving information" in a digital library. Another study conducted by Downs and Friedman indicated that "in the absence of human intermediaries, there is a need for end-user instruction on the use of digital libraries". Covi pointed out that "digital libraries will be used only when workers can readily integrate into social legimitated and legitimatable ways of working". She further suggested that subject specialists, as digital library service providers, help users formulate disciplinary search strategies and provide assistance in developing new resources.

Arms, while trying to answer the question "whether or not we need reference librarians in a digital library", pointed out that automatic tools are steadily reducing the need for reference librarians in fields like medicine that required a significant amount of intermediation in information searching. The essence of Arms' paper is that while computers can do a lot in performing most of the traditional jobs of reference librarians, their skills may be required in case of complex information searches.

Arms, however, believes that there have been significant improvements in the end-user search facilities, provided by electronic database search services and Web search engines, and hence, the need for human intermediaries in information searching has reduced significantly. Perhaps the most comprehensive view of the need for and the nature of personalised services in a digital library has been delineated by researchers.

They maintained that:

- Services reflect the functionality afforded by systems serving the community of users. Access services that facilitate search and browsing have been central to digital library research thus far, but there is great need for attention to reference and question-answering, on-demand help, and fostering of citisenship and literacy and mechanisms to simplify participatory involvement of user communities.

REFERENCE AND INFORMATION SERVICES ON THE WEB

A number of reference and information services are now available on the Web. Interestingly, many of these services are provided by non-library and commercial organisations. While some are free, others need payment.

Detailed discussions on such services are available in a number of publications, McKiernan maintains a site that provides categorised listing of libraries that offer real-time reference services using chat software, live interactive communication tools, call centre management software, bulletin board services and other Internet technologies. Most of these services are designed for registered users of the libraries concerned.

Researchers categorised online reference and information services into three broad groups:

- Reference and information services from publishers, database search services, and specialised institutions;
- Reference services provided by libraries and/or experts through the Internet; and
- Reference and information services where users need to conduct a search and find information through theWeb.

Researchers discussed several online information services that belong to the first category.

They have listed various current awareness and SDI services such as: the contents page service from commercial publishers, such as Elsevier's

- Contents Direct Service, IDEAL Alert from Academic Press, and so on;
- Information on new books available free from publishers and vendors, such as the *Wiley Book Notification Service* and Amazon.com;
- SDI services fromonline search service providers, such as Dialog;
- *Current Contents* and *ISI Alerting Services* from ISI, and so on.

Some of these services, particularly the contents page services from publishers of journals, are free, while for others, such as *Dialog Alerts* or *Current Contents* from ISI, users need to register and pay.

Table provides a quick overview of some online reference and information services currently available. This is not an exhaustive list, but the table shows the different types of services and some of their characteristics.

It provides the following facts about theWeb-based reference services listed there:

- The listed Web-based reference services are offered by dotcom companies;
- These services use the Web only for communication between the user and the system/answer provider, while the information service is provided by a human expert;
- While most services are free, some charge as high as $250 per question;
- in many cases services are provided by (self-proclaimed?) volunteer experts;
- There are some services offered in specific subject fields.

In addition to those in table, there are also some Web-based reference services where users need to conduct a search for a reference query. Such services provide free access to various online reference sources, and allow users either to select a specific source or conduct a search on a range, or all, of the reference sources.

Examples of such services include the following:

- Internet Public Library.
- Infoplease
- Britannica
- Bartleby Reference.
- Internet Library for Librarians.
- Electric Library.
- Mediaeater Reference Desk.
- ReferenceDesk.
- Xrefer.

While most of these Web-based reference services are available free, some charge a small fee. For example, the Electric Library charges $79.95 for an entire year of unlimited access. Janes *et al.* reported a study of 20 Web-based "expert services". By asking 240 questions to 20 selected expert services, they noted that the sites gave verifiable answers to 69 per cent of factual questions. An interesting observation of this study was that the kind of reference interview that takes place in traditional reference service environments is non-existent in Web-based reference services.

In fact, the sites did not come back for any discussion or clarification after receiving the initial queries. As a justification, the authors suggested that Web-based information services have been built mainly to answer factual questions, and therefore the experts concerned do not need to go through the reference interview process. Nevertheless, the high rate of success of factual questions shows that more and more end-users will move towards these expert services rather than to libraries for answers to simple types of questions.

SEARCH ENGINE SERVICES

Although Ask Jeeves is basically a search engine, many researchers also see it as aWeb-based information service because of two reasons:

- Unlike in other search and metasearch engines, users can ask a question in Ask Jeeves, and in many cases can get an answer right away; and
- Users can ask a question on a given topic, and Ask Jeeves comes up with a list of questions on the same or similar topics; the user can select any of the those predefined questions, and then Ask Jeeves provides answers to that.

This is an interesting service and may be considered as a useful model for digital library reference and information services.

The Ask Jeeves site maintains that:

- Ask Jeeves is a unique question-answering system that allows users to ask questions in plain English, and then delivers the answer. As one of the most sophisticated navigation systems on the Internet, Ask Jeeves combines a unique natural language engine with a proprietary knowledgebase.Taken together, this mechanism processes the meaning and grammar of real questions in plain English; provides intelligent responses for user confirmation; links directly to relevant, high-quality answers; and, perhaps most exciting of all, becomesmore intelligent as its knowledgebase expands with each question asked and each answer delivered.

The site further says that Ask Jeeves processes each query syntactically and semantically, and then Ask Jeeves' answer-processing engine provides the question template response. When the user clicks on a response, the answer-processing engine retrieves the answer template that contains links to the answer locations. Thus, Ask Jeeves helps users select a query from a pre-defined set of queries on a given topic.

However, there is a debate on whether the kind of service provided by Ask Jeeves matches reference services provided by libraries. Kresh reported an interesting finding: "One consortial system in northern California conducted an informal test of Ask Jeeves by sending it 12 questions its libraries had answered. There were no trick questions, none were arcane, just questions typically received by those libraries. Jeeves was unable to answer any of the questions".

Nevertheless, the techniques and the technology used by Ask Jeeves may be very useful for introducing reference services in digital libraries. Webhelp.com is another service that claims to offer "real-time search assistance with a real live expert I any time, day or night". About.com is a service that shows a number of pre-defined categories related to a search topic given by the user. For example, a simple search on "e-commerce" not only produces a list of sites, but also provides a set of topics related to "e-commerce", such as e-commerce definition, e-commerce security, advantages of e-commerce, e-commerce disadvantages, e-commerce statistics, etc.

DIGITAL REFERENCE SERVICES AND LIBRARIES

A number of libraries have now begun to offer Web-based reference services and a number of recent studies report the current practice of reference services provided by libraries. Although this is not an exhaustive review of all the Web-based reference services provided by libraries, the following section provides a quick overview of some that are currently available.

DIGITAL REFERENCE SERVICES FOR THE GENERAL PUBLIC

Ask A Librarian is a Web-based reference service, primarily designed for UK residents, provided by a network of public libraries in the UK. The site says: "Mail us your factual question and we'll send you an answer within two working days, if not before". A user has to put the query through an enquiry page, which is automatically routed to one of the participating libraries, which receives it as an e-mail message. Within two days the library sends an e-mail message to the user with its response to the enquiry. The British Library provides special reference services for business, patent, scientific, technical, medical and environmental information. These services range from answering simple questions to finding answers to complex questions involving online database searching, etc. While some of these services are free, for others users need to pay. For example, users can ask simple business questions using a form, and can expect an answer within ten working days. Similarly, users can send
e-mails with simple environmental queries.

A typical answer in such a case may include:

- A list of bibliographies from a British Library catalogue literature search; and/or;
- A list of organisations to contact for more detailed information, and/ or
- Information retrieved from Internet sources.

Users are not charged for this kind of service. However, for complex queries users need to pay.

For example, the British Library provides a Science Technology Medicine (STM) search service for which users need to pay at the following rate:

- J 82.00 per hour of staff time divided into 15-minute periods;
- Plus costs of online searching;
- Plus Value Added Tax (VAT).

As stated in the Web site most searches take at least 30 minutes and therefore cost J 41.00 for staff time + costs for online searching + VAT. The site also mentions that the average list of references costs J 80.00 for medical subjects, and between J 100.00 and J 150.00 for other subjects.

Users are also charged a fee if the results are to be faxed. In order to obtain an STM search service, the user has to fill in a form that has three parts. In the first part users need to fill in their personal details, etc., in the second part, users need to enter the query, and in the third part they need to specify the modes of delivery, payment, etc. In the second part of the form, users can enter the detail specification of the query using Boolean operators and specifying date, language, etc., as limiting factors.

COLLECTION CONFIGURATION AND DOCUMENT REPRESENTATION OF DIGITAL LIBRARY

Before describing the process by which collections are built, we will show how the collection-building process is configured, and how documents are represented internally within the system. In we described our "plugin" mechanism and showed how it provides great flexibility for such varied tasks as ingesting both document files and metadata files, extracting text and metadata from different file formats, and expanding compressed files.

It has proved so successful that we have adopted it in the new framework. However, we depart radically from our earlier system by using the METS framework (which postdates that system) throughout for internal document representation.

Configuration

Collections are designed individually, and the structure of a collection is encapsulated in an XML file called the "collection configuration file." Its contents include build-time configuration options such as:

- The document types that the collection should recognise
- The metadata access structures or "classifiers" that are to be provided for users to browse the collection, such as by Titles A–Z
- The full-text indexes to build for searching the collection. The configuration file also contains run-time information about the collections, for example display options.

The bulk of an example configuration file can be seen in Figure—all that is omitted is the part concerning the purely runtime configuration. It defines a simple collection of HTML pages and plain text files, along with XML files that define metadata that is to be associated with these documents.

A document may consist of several separate files—for example, in this collection any images associated with the HTML pages will be contained within the HTML document rather than being identified as documents in their own right. Or a document may comprise complementary pairs of files—like a Word file and matching PDF version.

A collection configuration file

```
<documenttypes>
<document type="HTML">
<document type="Text">
<document type="MetadataXML">
</doctypes>
<search type="mg">
<index name="dtx" level="document" field="text">
<displayItem name="name" lang="en">entire documents</
displayItem>
<displayItem name="name" lang="fr">documents entiers</
displayItem>
<displayItem name="name" lang="es">documentos enteros</
displayItem>
</index>
<index name="stx" level="section" field="text">
<displayItem name="name" lang="en">chapters</displayItem>
<displayItem name="name" lang="fr">chapitres</displayItem>
<displayItem name="name" lang="es">cap?tulos</displayItem>
</index>
<index name="stt" level="section" field="title">
<displayItem name="name" lang="en">section titles</displayItem>
<displayItem name="name" lang="fr">titres des sections</
displayItem>
<displayItem name="name" lang="es">t?tulos de las secciones</
displayItem>
</index>
<format>
<gsf:template match="documentNode"><td
valign="top"><gsf:link><gsf:icon/></gsf:link>
</td><td><gsf:metadata name="Title"/></td></gsf:template>
</format>
</search>
<browse>
<classifier name="CLSubject" type="Hierarchy" file="subject.xml"
field="Subject"/>
<classifier name="CLTitle" type="AZList"/>
<classifier name="CLOrganization" type="Hierarchy"
file="organization.xml"
field="Organization"/>
```

```
<classifier name="CLKeyword" type="List" file="howto.xml"
field="HowTo">
<displayItem name="name" lang="en">HowTo</displayItem>
</classifier>
</browse>
```

The search block in Figure defines the full-text-searchable indexes that will be built. In this case the MG indexer will be used to build document-level and section-level indexes of the main text, and a section-level index of Title metadata. The browse block defines the metadata-based browsing mechanisms through which users can access the collection.

This configuration file specifies a hierarchical subject browser by defining a Hierarchy-type classifier of each document's Subject metadata, and the file that defines that hierarchy is named.

Other browsing classifiers are also defined. Run-time configuration items can be seen in both the classification and indexation parts of the file. For example. the "displayItem" nodes give names for the indexes (in English, French and Spanish) and for one of the browsers.

The Greenstone 3 building programme reads this file and configures the components to be used by the collection-building process. Many default options are implied. For instance, this collection would automatically expand Zip files—because the Zip expansion plugin is enabled by default. The process followed during building will be described later.

METS and Document Representation

We were eager to adopt an open, standard form for modelling the content and metadata of a document. The METS framework supports a free selection of metadata formats and avoids duplicating data that is already stored in constituent files. Using this standard, open framework should facilitate interoperation with other digital library systems. These are the METS Header, Administrative Metadata, Descriptive Metadata, File lists and Structural lists.

The structural content is the only required section, and the content of the remaining sections is mapped onto the encoded structure. For the sake of clarity, this example shows only the connections between sections and the descriptive metadata and files.

A document is encoded into METS form by a plugin that corresponds to the type of the document. Each such plugin extracts any appropriate metadata from the document files (*e.g.* title), catalogues the files that comprise the document, and extracts the document text in subsequent phases.

In other words, it encapsulates the document content and acts as a standard gateway to its METS representation. This means that other phases of the building process are able to access data without having to understand the particulars of each file format—even if the data is stored as a binary object.

Document text can be provided in one of three ways, as the processing component requires. Plain Unicode is a simple baseline recognized throughout the system. At a higher level of sophistication, an XML representation is supported.

Finally, indexers can use the underlying binary files if they so desire. A complete document plugin provides all these formats, though the XML representation is optional. In any case, a document may have no textual content whatsoever (in which case all forms are empty).

For example, a PostScript file can be translated into an XML format. The PostScript plugin allows a plain-text reduction of this, but if an indexer wishes to treat PostScript files in a special way, it can access the original files directly. METS documents are partitioned into several components, the most common elements being structure, files, administrative metadata and descriptive metadata. A given document may form part of a single file, or be an agglomeration of individual files and parts of files. Metadata can be associated with a document as a whole or with any part of its structure. A document may also have more than one structural form.

For instance, it may have both a page based structure and a logical chapter-and-section based structure. Metadata may be provided in several different formats and standards, and this allows for the native coding of metadata on the document in different formats—for instance RFC1807 and Dublin Core.

When a document first enters the library, it is given a unique identifier. That identifier will remain with the document throughout any subsequent revisions, and is recorded within the METS framework. Having described the configuration controls and document representation that underpin the new collection-building architecture, we now describe the building process itself.

Building Digital Library Collections

In our new architecture, collections are built in several distinct phases, which occur in sequence.

- *Expansion*: Compressed files such as Zip archives are expanded, and links to web sites are expanded into lists of constituent web pages.
- *Recognition*: All files are sent to the Recognition Manager, which identifies groups of files as documents.
- *Encoding*: All the recognised documents are catalogued for the subsequent phases of building.
- *Extraction*: Every document is passed through extractors, which use special processing algorithms to extract information from the document (*e.g.* title, keyphrases) or add metadata stored in special files.
- *Classification*: Documents are assigned to classifiers (*e.g.* topical classifiers, ordered list classifiers) depending on their inherent and extracted metadata.

- *Indexation*: Documents are sent to indexers to build indexes that support later searching.
- *Validation*: Post-building checks are carried out on the collection as a whole, and on its constituent documents.

Expansion

Before any individual documents are identified, any files that are compressed, or refer to external sources, are expanded. The case of a Zip archive has already been mentioned; other cases include OAI repositories, and links to web sites via a file of URLs.

The purpose of this phase is to create a complete list of all files that are available for building the collection. These raw files are then passed to the next phase for grouping into documents.

Recognition

The relationship between files and documents is complex. A file of e-mails may be seen as one file that contains many documents. Conversely, a JPEG image and a plain text file that describes it may constitute a two-file document. Our architecture uses special "recogniser" plugins to address the problem of distinguishing documents from files.

When the building process is initialised, all plugins listed in the collection configuration file are registered by a "Recogniser Manager." When the Expansion phase terminates, this Manager is handed each file in the collection in turn. It sends these files to each plugin.

For some simple cases—like a plain text document comprising a single file—the plugins are trivial. However, in other circumstances conflicts can emerge, and the Recogniser Manager includes a scheme for resolving these. For example, suppose a collection includes both web pages and digital photographs. A single JPEG file may be a document in its own right, or form part of a web page. By default, JPEG files that are referred to by web pages, being constituent parts of a larger whole, are not treated as documents in their own right, while JPEGs that do not appear in the web pages are identified as separate, discrete documents. This default behaviour can be adjusted, if desired, to allow all JPEG files to be treated as documents, even ones that also appear in a web document.

The same issue arises with any image file on a web page. Furthermore, such a file (for instance a logo) could well be part of more than one document. In this case it is treated as a subcomponent of all the documents in which it appears. A web page and associated files cannot form a strict subset of another web page, because the.html files must necessarily differ. The same strategy is used in other cases.

Once the Recogniser Manager has taken a pass through the entire inventory of files and identified the documents, it resolves any conflicts that occur and hands the output on to the Encoding phase.

At this stage all that is known of a document is the list of files that constitute its content. No metadata has yet been assigned—even that found within the document itself. The content and representation of any metadata internal to the document is identified in the next phase.

Encoding

Documents appear in a wide variety of forms, textual encodings and file formats. The Encoding phase creates the document framework that is used throughout the remainder of the building process.

This framework supports the retrieval of the full text of the document. It contains metadata defined within the document, and will also contain any metadata added to it. Finally, it binds the document, with its representation, into the classification and indexation structures.

The METS document framework is used to encapsulate the files, metadata and structure of each document. At the end of the Encoding phase, documents are ready to be processed by extracting further metadata, indexation and storage.

Extraction

The Extraction phase is controlled by the Extraction Manager, which filters the documents through a series of extraction plugins. These can have one of two origins:

- Metadata-only files identified in the recognition phase above
- Explicit mention in the collection configuration file

The former method is typically used for files of descriptive metadata that are provided with the documents. The latter is used to invoke automatic extraction tools such as the KEA Keyphrase Extractor.

At the conclusion of the Extraction phase, all metadata has been collected and stored in the METS document representation. The next two phases place the documents into the context of the collection as a whole.

Classification

The Classification phase uses each document's metadata to site it within the browsing structures, or "classifiers," that are supplied by the collection to access the documents it contains. Each classification is represented by a plugin specified in the collection configuration file.

There may be more than one instance of any given classification type, achieved by initiating a separate copy of the plugin for each classification. Classifications are stored in a database, and when a document is matched to a node in a classification, this fact is recorded in both the document and the classification node.

Indexation

Indexing follows classification. To support the widest range of indexing systems, indexers are also treated as plugins. Again, the indexer—or indexers—used when building a collection are determined by the collection configuration file. For each indexer, parameters can be supplied that control its behaviour.

Indexers can build several different indexes, each with its own parameters. In the case of MG, for example, the structure level (*e.g.* document, section) and field (full text, title, etc.) can be controlled.

Validation

Validation plugins are used to control the quality of the collection by checking the final form of each document, and the collection as a whole. For example, a collection may insist on a complete metadata set—that is, all compulsory fields must be present.

Or the databases may be checked for empty classification nodes, which may be suppressed. Validation could be done in earlier phases, but we separate it into a final phase for architectural clarity.

8

Training and Support to Users in Library

The importance of the library as a resource centre and the endeavor of the management to exploit the resources gathered over the years with a lot of investment, need not be over emphasized. However, it has been the experience of many a library, especially those attached to organisations, the use of their resources appear to be little compared to the efforts put in building up the resources. As such there appears to be a constant need to initiate outreach programmes in order to enhance the usage of the library to the maximum extent. Library is looked upon as a centre for learning. The Library has to strive to repackage the material that is received in the library in the form of Alerts, reviews, digests, abstracts and databases to enhance library utilization and improve readership. Also, in view of the rapid developments in Information and Communication Technologies, the role of a librarian is not like what it used to be a few decades ago. Added to IT, satellite communication systems, networking, Internet and intellectual property rights, have all made the library environment more complex. Further, the budgetary constraints, inadequate infrastructure, falling standards in human resources are all compelling the librarian to change his attitude from a mere custodian of information to that of a facilitator. As the library is a service institution there should be close interaction between the information providers, processors and users to enhance the effectivity of any resource centre Keeping in view the above factors, National Institute of Rural Development (NIRD) conducted a learning programme on. This programme provided a forum for the users of information and the library personnel to come together, to understand each others way of dealing with information and how the information barriers can be overcome and what best practices are to be adopted to increase the utilization of the resources of the Library through various training programmes.

LIBRARY UTILIZATION AND READERSHIP ENHANCEMENT (LURE)

When CORD conducted the one-day programme LURE I in 1991, had a modest goal to find out the ways and means to increase the library utilization by adopting innovative methods tolure the readers. This was based on a feeling that we have been investing in the library huge amounts of money year after year, trying to equip the library with more relevant reading material and also recruit trained personnel to make the resources more useful. While we are trying to build up a tempo, we had a feeling somewhere along the line that the readers or users are still not coming along with us. This feeling lead us to an introspection which gave rise to the impetus for conducting a programme for the first time on LURE in 1991. As stated earlier, the learning programme provided an opportunity for interaction between the library professionals and our own users in understanding the lacunae in promoting exploitation of library resources. In the first workshop on LURE in 1991 several issues were thrown up such as the following:

ISSUES FOR CONSIDERATION

As the reader is reluctant to come to library, it may be necessary that the library has to go to the reader. Naturally, that situation will determine the kind of services that are planned or envisaged to enhance the usage of the library. The issues that influence the usage hinge upon how the information needs are gauged and the methods that are adopted to identify those needs. Some of the other major issues identified are:

- Focus of the parent organisation
- Information collection
- Information processing
- Information search in the Internet era
- Information dissemination
- Information barriers

The workshop offered a set of simple but effective steps to increase the library use with suggestions like involvement of users in procurement of literature, client based services etc., The other major recommendations include:

- The book selection and acquisition are both important and modalities like participatory practices have to be followed;
- User education and user services have to be frequently conducted by the library to improve the interaction between users and the library personnel;
- A brochure on the library highlighting the library collection, cataloging and classification system followed and the services offered would be more useful;
- Immediate computerization of all activities of library;
- Creation of new services like abstracting, alerting service, reference and making digests on specific topics etc.,
- Augmentation of facilities for document supply and other physical facilities like proper sign boards, stools to reach higher shelves, etc., and

- Strengthening of the resource sharing at the local level.

These recommendations were taken seriously as they were particularly important in the over all development of the library utilization. Fortunately, most of the suggestions would be implemented with a telling effect on the positive response of the readers.

LURE – II

After a gap of nearly two years, CORD thought of again reviewing the library utilization with the completion of library automation. Accordingly, in 1993 a second programme on LURE was conducted. This time with a difference. The impetus came from the management of parent organization. There was a constant refrain from the management that with automation is there any improvement in the utilization of library resources? How many faculty are visiting the library? What is the ratio between faculty and participants of various training programmes that visit the library? What special arrangements were made to familiarize the participants with the new automation etc.,

These were a few of the questions that were bothering the management. Also, with computerization of library procedures, a new barrier is likely to be perceived by the users. Such 'Automation anxiety' may have to be taken into consideration in designing training programmes on library initiation.

Accordingly, the participants were chosen from not only the users of the library but also the participants of the then running courses, besides other librarians of neighbouring institutions. The programme was conducted in 3 sessions. In these sessions several papers based on cases illustrating the circulation facility, visitors register, pattern of usage of library on different dates and use of various information products of CORD were presented. These studies provided a picture of the pattern of library usage after the automation which appeared to be promising and provided the guidance as to how to increase awareness and access to information. Several suggestions emerged based on the discussions and some of which are as follows:—

- **Information Products:**
  - The coverage of indexing and abstracting services done through CORD Index and CORD Abstracts is found to be satisfactory. However, emphasis may have to be given to the immediate interest of the faculty members depending on their research and training programmes.
  - The journals that are covered in CORD Alerts may have to be displayed at a designed place for their immediate location and identification of articles given in the service.
- **Maintenance:**
  - Upkeep and maintenance of various sections will provide the necessary incentive for the users to browse.

  - Library staff should be trained and motivated to assist the readers.
- **User Studies:**
  - Though the faculty members are patronising the library, there is a scope for improvement.
  - Visitors to the Library are not always recording their visits in the prescribed register and so it did not reflect the total visits made by the academic staff in comparison with non-academic staff. A strict vigil on the visitors register may have to be maintained to satisfy the management.

The other major recommendations include:

- Promotion of library with a professional image is essential;
- Library staff should be trained in inter-personnel communication skills;
- There is a need to display current journals in more attractive and useful manner like displaying latest issues at a prominent place, rearranging of primary journals in alphabetical sequence, etc.,
- NIRD publications should be displayed prominently for outside visitors.
- A marketing approach to its library and information products is essential. For this purpose Library counters and surrounding areas should be used for display of not only for acquired publications but also NIRD publications.
- There are about 3000 participants in a year coming to NIRD to participate in the training programmes, who should be given orientation tour to the library for better appreciation of the resources. Also, a session on information resources, and information management relevant to the theme of any course wherever possible should be arranged apart from display of the publications pertaining to the training programme.
- A faculty directory, user manual, training of staff on information technology etc., are other suggestions that emerged from the programme.

After LURE-II in 1993 there was marked improvement in the appreciation of library services, the physical facilities and the environment in the library. Non-book material like CD-ROMS, videos, electronic journal have slowly started to show their presence. In the mid 90s internet opened gates to the Information sources world wide, and made possible access to information from a remote location. As a result it has become more important to look into the problems of transforming a traditional library into an information clearing house.

LURE – III

Against this backdrop a 3rd LURE programme was conducted in the year 1998 after a gap of 5 years. This learning programme was made into a National Workshop inviting papers from all over India on various themes such as library utilisation; techniques of readership enhancement; evaluation of library services; internet and changing role of the librarian etc. Participants from several parts of the country made their presentations based on their own back-home experience in user education and identification of user needs. This workshop revealed various kinds of experiments that are on-going in several parts of the country by innovative librarians and demystifying the Internet for the librarian and the user. Information search in the Internet era has totally changed the way the readers look for information. Searching Internet should become a matter of routine in any special library, to make the expression "Internet is Librarianship" truly applicable. Some of the other major recommendations of the workshop were:

- Continuous study of user needs.
- Development of communication skills of the library personnel.
- Role of parent organization in recognising the contribution of their libraries and supporting their activity.
- Design and update of user manual in the fast changing information technology environment.
- Change of attitude of librarians to the market driven economy and interact with the users more closely and make users appreciate the library services.
- A thematic approach to all the library services have to be *i.e.*, the information products of the library like CORD INDEX, CORD ABSTRACTS should follow the themes identified for the research and training of the institute.
- The Selective Dissemination of Information (SDI) service can perhaps be concentrated on a faculty or a discipline at a time. Once a faculty is studied for a period of 6 months or so as a focussed group the impact on the group and its activities perhaps be quantitatively measured.

CORD is giving continuous training to the Library staff in the above areas in order to serve the clientele for effective use of Library Resources. They are also deputing the staff to other training programmes to get trained in these as well as new emerging areas. Simultaneously providing training and support to the users for better utiliztion of the resources without any barriers. Thus a new era emergd where information driven activities gained importance which will hopefully energize the users as well as information specialists to come together and work for the better uilization of information following the best practices in information dissemination through regular training programmes.

TRAINING AND DEVELOPMENT: CONCEPT, IMPORTANCE AND METHODS OF TRAINING

Changes in technology, especially information technology, generate knowledge spreading up at tremendous speed, as well as its quick obsolence.

In the period between 1900 and 1950, the amount of human knowledge doubled, and Since, then it has doubled every 5 to 8 years. Knowledge is becoming obsolete so quickly that all of us need do double our knowledge every 2 to 3 years in order to keep up with the changes. On the other hand, the increasing complexity, turbulency and uncertainty of the environment requires different and greater knowledge. Modern business requires more and more knowledge and skills that are still inadequatly present in the formal school education, *i.e.*, the gap between business reqiurements and the knowledge acquired at school is growing.

The period of mass producing is over and the customers are very selective. Increased consumer demands require new solutions and knowledge. Due to increasing competition, the organisation is required to constantly revise its product and service mix, managerial methods, and to increase productivity. Modern conditions of dynamic competition, sophisticated information technology, knowledge economy, market globalisation, has changed the relation to importance of human resources in organisation. These conditions actualise the human capital as the strategic resource of every organisation. Differences between the organisations exist exactly due to the differences between human capital, *i.e.*, the organisations human resources, ways of their management and development.

In a more and more global, complex and turbulent environment, knowledge is the only reliable source of competitive advantage. Traditional factors of manufacturing as the soil, Labour and capital did not disappear, but their significance is not primary anymore. Knowledge is viewed as the key of realisation of a competitive advantage. And therefore the question of where the corporative knowledge is located, how to release it and develop to achieve organisational goals has become very important.

Since, the organisational knowledge is largely located inside the human mind, *i.e.*, the head of employees, as carriers of knowledge and activities, human resources are becoming the key factor of business success. Organisational development is always conditioned by human knowledge and skills. That is why, contemporary organisations pay more and more attention to the development of their emplozees. Thus, employee education and training are becoming an optimal answer to complex business challenges, and the management of human resources is taking central role in modern management.

Through the process of employee training and development, the management of human resources provides constant knowledge innovation, creates conditions for mutual knowledge and experience exchange and proactive behaviour, in this way contributing to competitive advantage and satisfaction of all participants in business procedures. As a consequence of these procedures a learning organisation has formed. The aim of this chapter is to point to the fact that education and development of human potential are the basic factor for creation of basis for transformation from traditional to a learning company. Learning organisation is organisation that promotes learning of all of its members and it transforms permanently. Individuals and societies that do not have enough knowledge are in inferior position, compared to societies and organisations that have it and even permanently acquire new knowledge. That is the reason why we say that success is not among the educated but among those that are learning permanently, and everything changes except knowledge acquirement, which is constant.

EMPLOYEE TRAINING AND DEVELOPMENT

Understanding the phenomenon of employee training and development requires understanding of all the changes that take place as a result of learning. As the generator of new knowledge, employee training and development is placed within a broader strategic context of human resources management, *i.e.*, global organisational management, as a planned staff education and development, both individual and group, with the goal to benefit both the organisation and employees. To preserve its obtained positions and increase competitive advantage, the organisation needs to be able to create new knowledge, and not only to rely solely on utilisation of the existing. Thus, the continous employee training and delopment has a singnificant role in the development of individual and organisational performance.

The strategic procedure of employee training and development needs to encourage creativity, ensure inventiveness and shape the entire organisational knowledge that provides the organisation with uniqueness and differentiates it from the others. Education is no longer the duty and privilege of those in higher positions and skilled labour, but it is becoming the duty and need of everyone. The larger the organisations, the more funds they spend on education and provide their employees with greater and diverse possibilities of education and development.

Understanding the tremendous significance of education for the modern organisation and confident that it represents a good and remunirative investment, present day organisations set aside more and more resources for this activity. Most of the organisations invest 3 to 5 per cent of their revenue into adult education. It is estimated that the organisations that desire to keep the pace with changes need to provide their employees with 2 per cent of total annual fund of working hours for training and education. Thus, it is necessary to accept the model of permanent, continuous learning.

That truth has been known for more than two centuries. Denis Diderot, a French philosopher and literate of the Age of Enlightment, wrote the following: "Education shouldn't be finished when an individual leaves school, it should encompass all the ages of life... to provide people in every moment of their life with a possibility to maintain their knowledge or to obtain new knowledge". The only way for present day organisations to survive is the imperative to innovate or perish.

Since, this depends on the knowledge the organisation possesses, this imperative could be read as: learn faster than competition. The logical sequence is: knowledge creation – innovation – competitive advantage. If knowledge is good, is it not true that the more knowlegde we have, the better we are? Many organisations which consider knowledge as a good thing are trapped into the pitfall of gathering as much knowledge as possible. Knowledge that is not necessary is exatly what it is: unnecessary. And the efforts to obtain it are wasted efforts.

The only important knowldege is the knowledge with strategic importance to the company, knowledge that helps to increase the value of the company, knowledge with significance to the strategy of the company. It is not about knowledge for the sake of knowledge, but rather knowledge according to the needs, applicable knowledge, knowledge to create innovation and competitive advantage. Obtaining knowledge, learning, education, all could have a real effect on the quality of labour only if they are harmonised with the needs of a particular organisation, its goals and the goals of its employees.

The further choice of educational contents and educational methods, and the efficiency of educational effectiveness control depend on clearly defined educational goals and needs, answers to the questions of which knowldege is necessary to realise the strategy and the survival of the organisation in general, which employees need to possess this knowledge and will this knowledge solve certain problems. Employee training and development does not imply only obtaining new knowledge, abilities and skills, but also the possibility to promote entrepreneurship, introduce employees to changes, encourage the changes of their attitude, introduce the employees to important business decisions and involve them actively in the process of decision making.

To precisely define expectations and attract skilled workforce, more and more employment advertisings offer a certain number of annual hours or days for education. The most wanted resources are the people with particular knowledge, skills and abilities. Managers must learn to manage them, and the organisations to employ and retain them. Knowledge based organisations must preserve their competitive advantage by retaining skilled workforce, workers of knowledge, strengthening their motivation and improving the reward and compensation systems according to the workers' performances.

Within the context of learning organisation, it is not sufficient for the worker only to add value to the organisation based on his knowledge, but he also has to receive knowledge. He gives as much knowledge as he receives. For the present day employees the wage by itself is not a sufficient incentive, but they also need investment into themselves in a sense of investing in their knowledge. Empolyees no longer work for money alone, nor can they be influenced by traditional attractive financial packages.

CONCEPT OF A LEARNING ORGANISATION

Every individual should appreciate lifelong learning, and every successful organisation has to become a permanently learning organisation. Many successful organisations describe themselves as learning organisation or one of their strategic goals is to become such an organisation. Companies such as Coca-Cola, Motorola, General Electrics and Cisco have assigned vice presidents for knowledge, learning or intellectual capital whose task is to create knowledge management systems that enable them to quickly adopt development tendencies, influencing in that way the customers, competitors, distributors and suppliers.

The organisation is not only the user of knowledge, but also its creator. Peter Senge described in the book named "The Fifth Discipline", the learning organisation implies free flow of knowledge, *i.e.*, lifting of all barriers on developing knowledge and new ideas at the very beginning. In the future it will not be possible to "unthread things from above" and for all the others to follow the "big brother's" instructions anymore. The top organisations of the future will be distinguished by their knowledge about how to encourage engagement and develop the learning potential on each organisational level. Peter Senge's model of a learning organisation is very interesting Since, it recognises the organisation as a whole, *i.e.*, in his organisation, through their functions and sectors within the organisation, all the employees influence the course of business procedures, and the knowledge creation, consequently the creation of new values both for the organisation and its customers. With this definition, Senge has made significant qualitative progress compared to the classical organisation, Since, he emphasised the necessity of ability development through the process of learning.

Besides Senge, Chris Argyris was a great populariser of a learning organisation as well. In his book "Teaching smart people how to learn", he says: "Any company that aspires to succeed in the tougher business environment must first resolve a basic dilemma: success in the marketplace increasingly depends on learning, yet most people don't know how to learn.

What's more, those members of the organisation that many assume to be the best at learning are, in fact, not very good at it. I am talking about the well-educated, highpowered, highly committed professionals who take up key leadership positions in the modern corporation." Organisations learn only through the learning individuals. Individual learning does not guarantee organisational learning. But without it there is no organisational learning as well. The ablity to learn faster than the competitors may be the only sustainable competitive advantage.

Thus, the learning organisation is the organisation that learns and encourages people to learn in the organisation. It motivates information exchange between employees and creates staff with different knowledge. Chris

Argiris explains this: "On the other hand, there is a problem of existence of individuals within the organisation who know how to learn, but that doesn't create automatically conditions for the organisation to learn as well. This is due to the indisputable view that knowledge is still the only private property the man owns. This means that individual learning, and even learning of all the employees, doesn't imply the existence of a learning organisation. To have a learning organisation, it is necessary to know how to transfer individual into organisational knowledge, *i.e.*, into organisational learning." The starting point of knowledge management concept is in the fact that power does not come from knowledge, but from the exchange of knowledge.

It starts from the synergic effect. By exchanging knowledge, combining individual knowledge, we get much more qualitative knowledge than the individual knowledge. Obtaining and sharing knowledge is the core of the learning organisation. The reasons to become a learning organisation are the following: people are developing (greater motivation, flexibility of employees, people are more creative, improved social interaction), better working teams and groups (knowledge sharing, mutual dependence), benefiting organisations (greater work productivity, more qualitative products/services/ procedures, competitive advantage, profit).

APPROACH TO TRAINING AND DEVELOPMENT WITHIN OUR ORGANISATIONS AND NEED FOR TRANSFORMATION

Unfortunately, the procedures of employee training and development within our organisations are undeveloped. They are mainly performed occasionally, and not connected with organisational strategy, nor do they have some strategic significance. They are mostly enforced when such business problems occur or are perceived that are considered relievable or solvable by organising a training, course or seminar for some of the employees. Employees view the training as an imposed obligation, rather than a way to maximise their potential and they do not realise that by improving their performances and innovation of their knowledge they may contribute to better business results of the organisation they belong to. Unfortunately, top managers do not realise this as well. From their relationship with the employees it is plain to see that the employees are still treated as an expense, rather than an investment worthy of investing. In our organisations there is no culture of obtaining and sharing of knowledge. Many of our managers are under the influence of prejudices such as: training is expensive, training is an expense burdening the current business, it is not rewarding, training is for the young, etc., Knowledge is expensive, but ignorance is even more expensive.

Human possibilites to learn are unlimited, unless idviduals do not limit their abilities within their minds. Many studies have shown that investing in employee training and development has larger business effects than investing in equipment and other material resources. Our organisations must harmonise their approach to employee development with the changes. Employee training and development has to be connected with the organisational goals and strategy, they need to fulfil the new reqiurements of the environment.

Employee training and development needs to become a managerial function. It is a managerial challenge to consider the employees of the organisation from a strategic perspective (future orientedness) and constantly monitor and encourage the development of new skills and knowledge as the foundation of organisational development. This is not about assigning the employees to appropriate jobs, but rather about the constant dynamic of encouraging and discovering new possibilities. This is a new type of leadership, significantly different from the classical model of organisational management.

The leaders are no longer expected to be all-knowing bosses and supervisors, but rather moderators and inspirators. Since, people do not share the information which is the source of their power instictively, the leaders need to recognise, attract and release knowledge in the organisation. One of the main challegnes of modern organisations therefore is how to manage the process of knowledge transfer. "The answer is that wisdom, just because it is the most important, doesn't need to be located inside a tall building where the chief executive and his main assistants hang their hats (and soon their heads as well – unless they join the revolution of the mind). This pictoresque answer of Tom Peters refers to decentralisation and substantivity of employees (turning every workplace into business), which implies a high degree of employee competence and orientation Towards the participative style of management.

The process of democratisations, transitions, opening towards the EU, privatisations and arrival of foreign companies and praxis contributed considerably to transformation of approach to employee training and development within our organisations, from the *ad hoc* processes that originate from the goals and strategies, to a modern approach where human resources and their knowledge are gaining more and more significance.

IMPORTANCE OF TRAINING AND DEVELOPMENT

- Training and Development helps in optimising the utilisation of human resource that further helps the employee to achieve the organisational goals as well as their individual goals.
- Training and Development helps to provide an opportunity and broad structure for the development of human resources' technical and Behavioural skills in an organisation. It also helps the employees in attaining personal growth.
- Training and Development helps in increasing the job knowledge and skills of employees at each level. It helps to expand the horizons of human intellect and an overall personality of the employees.

- Training and Development helps in increasing the productivity of the employees that helps
  the organisation further to achieve its long-term goal.
- Training and Development helps in inculcating the sense of team work, team spirit, and inter-team collaborations. It helps in inculcating the zeal to learn within the employees.
- Training and Development helps to develop and improve the organisational health culture and effectiveness. It helps in creating the learning culture within the organisation.
- Training and Development helps building the positive perception and feeling about the organisation. The employees get these feelings from leaders, subordinates, and peers.
- Training and Development helps in improving upon the quality of work and work-life.
- Training and Development helps in creating the healthy working environment. It helps to build good employee, relationship so that individual goals aligns with organisational goal.
- Training and Development helps in improving the health and safety of the organisation thus preventing obsolescence.
- Training and Development helps in improving the morale of the Workforce.
- Training and Development helps in creating a better corporate image.
- Training and Development leads to improved profitability and more positive attitudes towards profit orientation.
- Training and Development aids in organisational development, *i.e.*, Organisation gets more effective decision making and problem solving. It helps in understanding and carrying out organisational policies
- Training and Development helps in developing leadership skills, motivation, loyalty, better attitudes, and other aspects that successful workers and managers usually display.

IMPORTANCE OF TRAINING OBJECTIVES

Training objectives are one of the most important parts of training Programme. While some people think of training objective as a waste of valuable time. The counterargument here is that resources are always limited and the training objectives actually lead the design of training. It provides the clear guidelines and develops the training Programme in less time because objectives focus specifically on needs. It helps in adhering to a plan. Training objective tell the trainee that what is expected out of him at the end of the training Programme.

Training objectives are of great significance from a number of stakeholder perspectives:

- Trainer.

- Trainee.
- Designer.
- Evaluator.

Trainer

The training objective is also beneficial to trainer because it helps the trainer to measure the progress of trainees and make the required adjustments. Also, trainer comes in a position to establish a relationship between objectives and particular segments of training.

Trainee

The training objective is beneficial to the trainee because it helps in reducing the anxiety of the trainee up to some extent. Not knowing anything or going to a place which is unknown creates anxiety that can negatively affect learning. Therefore, it is important to keep the participants aware of the happenings, rather than keeping it surprise. Secondly, it helps in increase in concentration, which is the crucial factor to make the training successful. The objectives create an image of the training Programme in trainee's mind that actually helps in gaining attention. Thirdly, if the goal is set to be challenging and motivating, then the likelihood of achieving those goals is much higher than the situation in which no goal is set. Therefore, training objectives helps in increasing the probability that the participants will be successful in training.

Designer

The training objective is beneficial to the training designer because if the designer is aware what is to be achieved in the end then he'll buy the training package according to that only. The training designer would then look for the training methods, training equipments, and training content accordingly to achieve those objectives. Furthermore, planning always helps in dealing effectively in an unexpected situation. Consider an example; the objective of one training Programme is to deal effectively with customers to increase the sales. Since, the objective is known, the designer will design a training Programme that will include ways to improve the interpersonal skills, such as verbal and non- verbal language, dealing in unexpected situation, *i.e.*, when there is a defect in a product or when a customer is angry. Therefore, without any guidance, the training may not be designed appropriately.

Evaluator

It becomes easy for the training evaluator to measure the progress of the trainees because the objectives define the expected performance of trainees. Training objective is an important to tool to judge the performance of participants.

TRAINING AS CONSULTANCY

Training consultancy provides industry professional to work with an organisation in achieving its training and development objectives.

Estimation of Training Outsourcing

It has been estimated that 58 per cent of the emerging market in training outsourcing is in customer education, while only 42 per cent of the market is in employee education. The training consultancies offer various benefits such as:

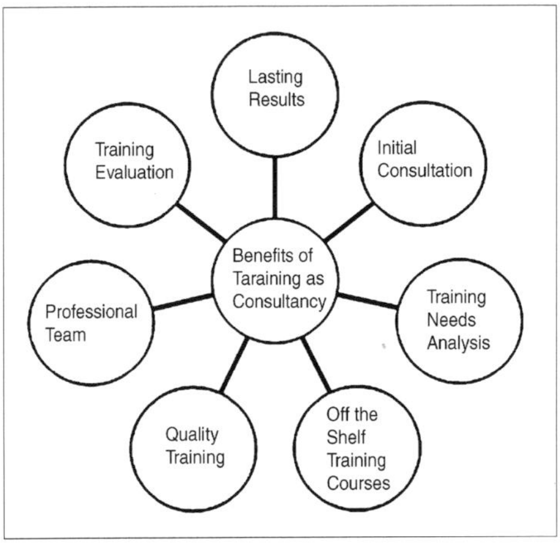

Training Courses that Consultancies Offer

- Business Training Courses:
  - Management Development:
    a. Conflict Management;
    b. Managing Diversity;
    c. Project Management;
    d. Stress Management;
    e. Time Management; and
    f. Senior Management Workshops.
  - Sales:
    a. Negotiation Skills; and
    b. Sales Technique.
  - Customer Care:
    a. Customer Care Training; and
    b. Managing Customers.
  - Human Resource:
    a. HR Administration;
    b. Induction Training;
    c. Recruitment and Selection; and

d. Successful Appraising.
- Personal Development Courses.
- Workshops on:

a. Assertive Skills;
b. Building Confidence;
c. Coping with Change;
d. Interview Techniques; and
e. Maximise Potential.

- One to One Coaching:

a. Focused entirely on personal objectives;
b. Move forward at individual pace;
c. Material used in tailor made to specific development Need; and
d. A strict code of confidentiality.

Importance of Training Consultancies:

- It helps in enhancing company's image.
- It helps in strengthening the team spirit.
- It helps in applying knowledge, developing core competencies, and reducing work load.
- It helps in improving the work relations.
- It helps in developing focused and inspired staff.
- It leads to greater chances of success.

Consultants can provide help on following areas:

- Management Development.
- Team Building Leadership.
- Health and Safety Training.
- Interpersonal Skills.
- Sales Training.

TRAINING AND HUMAN RESOURCE MANAGEMENT

The HR functioning is changing with time and with this change, the relationship between the training function and other management activity is also changing. The training and development activities are now equally important with that of other HR functions. Gone are the days, when training was considered to be futile, waste of time, resources, and money. Now a days, training is an investment because the departments such as, marketing and sales, HR, production, finance, etc. depends on training for its survival. If training is not considered as a priority or not seen as a vital part in the organisation, then it is difficult to accept that such a company has effectively carried out HRM. Training actually provides the opportunity to raise the profile development activities in the organisation.

To increase the commitment level of employees and growth in quality movement (concepts of HRM), senior management team is now increasing the role of training. Such concepts of HRM require careful planning as well as greater emphasis on employee development and long term education. Training is now the important tool of Human Resource Management to control the attrition rate because it helps in motivating employees, achieving their professional and personal goals, increasing the level of job satisfaction, etc., As a result training is given on a variety of skill development and covers a multitude of courses.

Role of HRD Professionals in Training

This is the era of cut-throat competition and with this changing scenario of business; the role of HR professionals in training has been widened. HR role now is:

- Active involvement in employee education
- Rewards for improvement in performance
- Rewards to be associated with self esteem and self worth.
- Providing pre-employment market oriented skill development education and post employment support for advanced education and training.
- Flexible access, *i.e.*, anytime, anywhere training.

MODELS OF TRAINING

Training is a sub-system of the organisation because the departments such as, marketing and sales, HR, production, finance, etc depends on training for its survival. Training is a transforming process that requires some input and in turn it produces output in the form of knowledge, skills, and attitudes (KSAs).

THE TRAINING SYSTEM

A System is a combination of things or parts that must work together to perform a particular function. An organisation is a system and training is a sub system of the organisation.

The System Approach views training as a sub system of an organisation. System Approach can be used to examine broad issues like objectives, functions, and aim. It establishes a logical relationship between the sequential stages in the process of training need analysis (TNA), formulating, delivering, and evaluating.

There are four necessary inputs, *i.e.*, technology, man, material, time required in every system to produce products or services. And every system must have some output from these inputs in order to survive. The output can be tangible or intangible depending upon the organisation's requirement. A system approach to training is planned creation of training Programme.

This approach uses step-by-step procedures to solve the problems. Under systematic approach, training is undertaken on planned basis.

Out of this planned effort, one such basic model of five steps is system model that is explained below. Organisation are working in open environment, *i.e.*, there are some internal and external forces, that poses threats and opportunities, therefore, trainers need to be aware of these forces which may impact on the content, form, and conduct of the training efforts.

The internal forces are the various demands of the organisation for a better learning environment; need to be up to date with the latest technologies.

The three model of training are:

- System Model.
- Instructional System Development Model.
- Transitional model.

SYSTEMATIC MODEL TRAINING

The system model consists of five phases and should be repeated on a regular basis to make further improvements. The training should achieve the purpose of helping employee to perform their work to required standards.

- *Analyse and identify the training needs*, *i.e.*, to analyse the department, job, employees requirement, who needs training, what do they need to learn, estimating training cost, etc The next step is to develop a performance measure on the basis of which actual performance would be evaluated.
- *Design and provide training to meet identified needs*. This step requires developing objectives of training, identifying the learning steps, sequencing and structuring the contents.
- *Develop* - This phase requires listing the activities in the training Programme that will assist the participants to learn, selecting delivery method, examining the training material, validating information to be imparted to make sure it accomplishes all the goals and objectives
- *Implementing* is the hardest part of the system because one wrong step can lead to the failure of whole training Programme.
- *Evaluating* each phase so as to make sure it has achieved its aim in terms of subsequent work performance. Making necessary amendments to any of the previous stage in order to remedy or improve failure practices.

TRANSITIONAL MODEL

Transitional model focuses on the organisation as a whole. The outer loop describes the vision, mission and values of the organisation on the basis of which training model, *i.e.*, inner loop is executed.

- *Vision*—focuses on the milestones that the organisation would like to achieve after the defined point of time. A vision statement tells that where the organisation sees itself few years down the line. A vision may include setting a role mode, or bringing some internal transformation, or may be promising to meet some other deadlines.

- *Mission*—explain the reason of organisational existence. It identifies the position in the community. The reason of developing a mission statement is to motivate, inspire, and inform the employees regarding the organisation. The mission statement tells about the identity that how the organisation would like to be viewed by the customers, employees, and all other stakeholders.
- *Values*—is the translation of vision and mission into communicable ideals. It reflects the deeply held values of the organisation and is independent of current industry environment. For example, values may include social responsibility, excellent customer service, etc.

INSTRUCTIONAL SYSTEM DEVELOPMENT MODEL (ISD) MODEL

Instructional System Development model or ISD training model was made to answer the training problems. This model is widely used now-a-days in the organisation because it is concerned with the training need on the job performance. Training objectives are defined on the basis of job responsibilities and job description and on the basis of the defined objectives individual progress is measured. This model also helps in determining and developing the favourable strategies, sequencing the content, and delivering media for the types of training objectives to be achieved.

The Instructional System Development model comprises of five stages:

- This phase consist of training need assessment, job analysis, and target audience analysis.
- This phase consist of setting goal of the learning outcome, instructional objectives that measures Behaviour of a participant after the training, types of training material, media selection, methods of evaluating the trainee, trainer and the training Programme, strategies to impart knowledge, *i.e.*, selection of content, sequencing of content, etc.
- This phase translates design decisions into training material. It consists of developing course material for the trainer including handouts, workbooks, visual aids, demonstration props, etc, course material for the trainee including handouts of summary.
- This phase focuses on logistical arrangements, such as arranging speakers, equipments, benches, podium, food facilities, cooling, lighting, parking, and other training accessories.
- The purpose of this phase is to make sure that the training Programme has achieved its aim in terms of subsequent work performance. This phase consists of identifying strengths and weaknesses and making necessary amendments to any of the previous stage in order to remedy or improve failure practices.

The ISD model is a continuous process that lasts throughout the training Programme. It also highlights that feedback is an important phase throughout the entire training Programme. In this model, the output of one phase is an input to the next phase.

METHODS OF TRAINING

There are various methods of training, which can be divided in to cognitive and Behavioural methods. Trainers need to understand the pros and cons of each method, also its impact on trainees keeping their background and skills in mind before giving training. Cognitive methods are more of giving theoretical training to the trainees.

The various methods under Cognitive approach provide the rules for how to do something, written or verbal information, demonstrate relationships among concepts, etc., These methods are associated with changes in knowledge and attitude by stimulating learning.

The various methods that come under Cognitive approach are:

- Lectures.
- Demonstrations.
- Discussions.
- Computer based training (cbt).
  - Intellegent tutorial system(its).
  - Programmed instruction (pi).
  - Virtual reality.

Behavioural methods are more of giving practical training to the trainees. The various methods under Behavioural approach allow the trainee to Behaviour in a real fashion. These methods are best used for skill development.

The various methods that come under Behavioural approach are:

- Games and simulations.
  - Behaviour-modeling.
  - Business games.
  - Case studies.
  - Equipment stimulators.
  - In-basket technique.
  - Role plays.

Both the methods can be used effectively to change attitudes, but through different means.

Another Method is Management Development Method

- The more future oriented method and more concerned with education of the employees. To become a better performer by education implies that management development activities attempt to instill sound reasoning processes. Management development method is further divided into two parts:
- The development of a manager's abilities can take place on the job.

The four techniques for on the job development are:

1. Coaching.
2. Mentoring.
3. Job rotation.
4. Job instruction technique (jit).

OFF THE JOB TRAINING

There are many management development techniques that an employee can take in off the job.

The few popular methods are:

- Sensitivity training.
- Transactional analysis.
- Straight lectures/ lectures.
- Simulation exercises.

DEVELOPMENT OF IT SKILLS FOR INFORMATION PROFESSIONALS

As a result of Information explosion the libraries and information centers (LICs) have become a necessity. A continuous flow of information in all the sectors of human activity through research and innovation has brought drastic changes in the present society. At present age Knowledge and information are strategic inputs in all walks of life, along with the traditional ones of man, money and materials. Knowledge and information will continue to play a significant role in the socio-economic development. Hence there is expansion of the employment market for library and information professionals. But despite increase in the number of jobs, the total market demand for LISc professionals at present is far less than the total output. Moreover, the quality of output is not fully compatible with the requirements of the expanding job market. Librarianship today has arrived at the information age where the role of information is increasingly emphasised as an economic resource, a marketable commodity and as a social wealth. In this context the role of librarian is very much important. He/ she will have to act as a facilitator, advisor, consultant, instructor, navigator, searcher, researcher, evaluator, organiser, preserver, promoter, communicator, technical expert, as well as a manager, leader, entrepreneur and visionary.

And for the success of library and information centers as effective communication system, the development of manpower to do such work is vital. One of the important aspects of manpower development in this connection is improved education system for library and information science. Mangla 'Library and Information Science programmes should be so designed as to equip the student:

- With knowledge and techniques to handle the immediate job requirements in an efficient manner; and

- "To develop programmes, procedures and services on modern lines in future where the use of various modern techniques, computers etc., could provide better, quicker and efficient service".

Skill in Information Technology (IT) can be gained only when one gets hands-on training and experience in laboratories under simulated conditions or in real life situations. The graduates and post graduates turned out by library schools of West Bengal do not possess adequate skill and expertise to interact confidently with IT specialists, evaluate what is recommended by them and full fill their requirements.

NECESSITY FOR PRACTICAL IT TRAINING

New Information Technology

Technological innovations have given rise to new ideas relating to collection, processing and dissemination of information. These innovations and ideas including Artificial Intelligence, Robotics, Speech Synthesis, Electronic mail, CD-ROM, CD Networking, Barcode systems, Electronic publishing, Hypermedia, Multimedia, Tele facsimile, Radio data paging, Networks etc. share a common technology revolving around electronics, computers, Telecommunication, Printing and Reprography, popularly known as Information Technology.

Futurist Alvin Toffler has rightly predicted that computers will enhance our 'mind power' just as the industrial revolution has enhanced our 'muscle power'. At least complete practical knowledge of computer applications in LICs is essential for a LISc professional. LIS being an information collection, organisation, and dissemination agency, technological innovations especially in the field of IT, have implications both for LIS, and the workforce required to service information users and their needs. Development in educational technology and the changing pattern of education and learning also indicate challenges for the library and information community to upgrade their IT skills.

Revolution Concept of Library

The LIS education aims at providing trained manpower to manage different types of libraries, information and documentation centers which, over a period of time have undergone changes in terms of needs, functions, types and range of services offered, as well as tools and techniques being used when offering the services. Application of information and communication technologies has revolutionised the whole concept of libraries, the system of information storage and retrieval and ways to access the information. Therefore, the objectives of LIS education also need to be redefined. The students need to be more practical oriented and should be equipped with intensive and extensive knowledge on the use of IT in libraries. Application of technology has opened up new vistas and thus, all LIS schools should think seriously in terms of the changing context.

Students need to be given adequate knowledge of computers (including hardware), computer and communication technologies, networking, operating systems, Internet concepts, and database management systems, with adequate practical exposure to handle these technological devices.

Table. Traditional Library Concepts and Modern Concepts of Information Science

Traditional Concepts	Modern concepts
History and Development of Libraries	Library Automation, Library Application Software
Preservation and conservation of Library Materials	Multi-media information sources
Cataloguing of Books	Online Public Access Catalogue
Library Systems and services	Design and development of Databases; Database Management Systems
Library Orientation	Computerized Information Retrieval; Online Search and Retrieval of Information; e-journals & e-books
User needs and user surveys	Internet basics etc.
Inter Library Loan	Networking & Resource Sharing; Consortia

Areas of Practical IT Skills Developments in LISc Curriculum

LISc courses offered by Indian library schools in different universities have become partially irrelevant since long. The debate about changing the LISc curricula has been going on for the last few years, but nothing concrete has yet been done at the national level, except for some cosmetic changes.

Dominance of Practice

The issue of the relationship between theory and practice is not properly addressed in the Indian context. An expert once stated that we are drowning in theory at library schools and not giving enough exposure to practice. The dilemma lies in the choice between teaching students the knowledge and skills needed in their first posts to which meet the immediate needs of employers and instilling principles from which they can expand their skills and knowledge base as their career develops. It is also seen that during the challenge of managing the complex and diverse new environment, some of the schools have been merged with different disciplines like information management and technology, information studies and mass communications. Given the pace of change in the nature of library and information services, there is a still need to not only in preparing library professionals but also in establishing practitioners, a commitment to lifelong learning because the circumstances are demanding greater professional and technical awareness.

As professional obsolescence becomes a real and ever present danger, only a systematic continuing education provides a method of combating such obsolescence. In the western countries many schools have made a thorough revision and development of course programmes and also introduced new courses to meet the needs of employers in industries, and the public and private sectors. The introduction of new programmes should therefore be seen too some extent as reflecting the 'Pull-Push Effect' of recognising the increasing need for the professional workforce to match the growth and significance of information industry and the expanding higher education system to provide the appropriate workforce. To design a model curriculum for a dynamic inter-disciplinary subject like Library and Information Science on the national level is quite difficult, and such attempts will raise awkward questions regarding inclusion or exclusion of particular topics and the emphasis to be given to individual topics. Hence, relevant topics, which are already implemented in LIS education emphasis on both theoretical and practical aspects but the information professionals are not getting hands-on training and experience in laboratory under simulated conditions or in real life situations (*i.e* trouble shooting).

Networking

- *Node failure:* In an automated library all the work station should be connected through LAN to the server, if the application is not being accessed from any of the work station then this situation is called node failure.
- *How to detect this problem:* Using of 'ping' command from run, if 'request time error' is coming then there must be an issue with the connectivity.
- *Syntax:* ping 'IP address of the work station' -t
- How to resolve issue:
  - Make sure the computer is turn on
  - Check the local area connection must be enable
  - Check the Ethernet cable must be plug in
  - Check other end of that Ethernet cable should be plug in into a network switch.
  - Check the IP address should be in the same class compare to the server IP if DHCP server is not there.

Database

- *Information retrieving/updating/deleting error:* In a server based library, application library software will be running in which all the information will be stored into the database. Sometimes we face a problem at the time of retrieving, updating and deleting records.
- How to resolve the issue:
  - Make sure the database are running
  - Make sure the database path is correct
  - Make sure that there is no issue with the front end application
  - If needed you can restore the database from database back up taken in every alternative minutes through 'database attachment'

Printing

- *Error:* Printer is not working.
- First needs to check the type (network/desktop shared) of printer, if it is a network printer then the following steps are:
  - Check printer is properly connected to the LAN switch through an Ethernet cable. RJ45 connector is working or not.
  - Check Power is turned on
  - Check the IP address, Subnet and default gateway of that printer by using network command in the printer's display. Also check the port details.
  - Check Printer's IP is pinging or not.
  - Check that is there any issue like paper jam, no paper in the tray etc.
  - Make sure that work station's 'printer spooler' service is running by using a command 'services.msc' from run.

Therefore, it is right time to inject some practical IT training with proper resources *i.e* Library Open Source Soft ware, Database, Servers and Network equipments etc. and fine tune the LIS courses accordingly. It will make the LIS courses consistent with the Job market.

9

The Beginning of Research in Library and Information Science

The roots of research in our profession are not very deep. Research in library science is a twentieth century occurrence ushered in by the library school of the University of Chicago in mid-1920s. The visionary efforts of the Chicago School bore abundant fruit and offered leadership to the world in library science research.

The pace of library research is picking up everywhere today due to social pressure as well as inspiration. In justifying the Ph.D. programme in our profession, it has been urged that "if librarianship aspires to become a profession, it should depend upon research to develop its knowledge base and its theoretical framework".

THE INDIAN CONTEXT

In India following British tradition and American precedent as established by Asa Don Dickinson, Librarian, Panjab University, Lahore, 1915-1916, library schools for advanced professional education have remained attached to universities. The growth of universities in Independent India ensured their constant growth. In a university, apart from teaching, a teacher is expected to do and guide research. The third function of a university, namely service and consultation, has always remained weak in India despite many newly established universityindustry linkage programmes.

RANGANATHAN'S WORK

The credit for the formal institution of the doctoral degree programme in library science in India goes undeniably to Dr. S.R. Ranganathan. In 1951, he started one at the University of Delhi surmounting many difficulties and facing personal ridicule. The University of Delhi awarded the first de jure degree in library science in 1957 to D.B. Krishan Rao who worked on a faceted classification for agriculture. Doctoral research remained in the wilderness when Ranganathan shook the Delhi soil off his feet in 1955. The *Documentation Research and Training*

Centre (DRTC) in Bangalore, founded by Ranganathan in 1962, is technically not empowered to award the Ph.D.

Therefore, for the rest of his life, from 1962 to 1972, Ranga-nathan only advocated solo and team research with stress on quality, relevance and basics. No big research projects were taken up at DRTC though individual teachers and students maintained both the quality and the tempo of research. Since the death of Ranganathan almost the entire DRTC faculty has earned Ph.D.s from other Indian universities on topics of research relevant to DRTC. Now the DRTC teachers are approved Ph.D. guides in many Indian universities, and they have already produced many Ph.D.

GROWTH OF DOCTORAL RESEARCH IN INDIA

Elsewhere in India other individual librarians and library science teachers eager to earn doctorates were hampered by the non-existence of programmes. In the 1960s and 1970s some doctorates on library-related topics were earned by library professionals from some other faculties such as sociology, history, law, economics, management, and the like.

The mantle of reviving and furthering doctoral research facilities was assumed by J. S. Sharma, then the university librarian and head of the library science department of the Panjab University, Chandigarh. Under his guidance the second *de jure* Ph.D. in library science was awarded in 1977 after a gap of full two decades. Thereafter, there was no looking back. Many universities followed with mostly individual efforts and enthusiasm. Doctoral research got a fillip in the 1980s. India maintained its Third World leadership in library research as well as in library education and literature. Ph.D. programmes have rather mushroomed even despite the lack of facilities or adherence to standards.

FACILITIES FOR RESEARCH

A conscientious university teacher is always in a dilemma over how to divide the time between teaching and research. Teaching is a primary compulsive and urgent duty to be performed. Students expect their teachers to give them time and personal attention. There may be appreciation in good teaching but the rewards lie in research. The university expects its teachers to do research for its prestige and fame lie therein. But when it comes to supporting of research many universities in India are neither generous nor unambivalent.

Ordinarily piecemeal research, especially in social sciences, is not supported financially. Internal support for research trickles through a tedious and off-putting bureaucracy and political manoeuvring. Colleagues are unsupportive. They are unappreciative, intolerant and jealous. Library facilities are poor. Thus most of the teachers are driven to the passivity of guiding doctoral research instead of doing postdoctoral work.

THE DETERIORATION OF STANDARDS

The University Grants Commission (UGC) preconditions for faculty employment and promotions have prompted many library professionals to acquire Ph.D. degrees, though many may not have the aptitude and the intrinsic ability to do research. Standards have not only been diluted but have been kept at abeyance. Supervisors and the examiners have become obligingly compromising. The cut-off date of December, 1992 for obtaining the Ph.D. degree to get an exemption from the national level test for teaching jobs in universities/colleges has done incalculable damage to research standards.

An eminent academician has corroborated the ill effects of this policy:

> "They were required to submit their theses before the deadline regardless of the date of registration. Some of the candidates on whom Ph.D.'s were conferred were not fully acquainted with the contents of their dissertations. In some cases even the supervisors were innocent of any knowledge of what the theses were about. The incitement came from the UGC".

Programmes for Ph.D. research have been introduced and expanded mindlessly. As a result, there has been a bit of doctoral boom – a spectacular rise in Ph.D. awarding universities and awardees – though many institutions lack utterly the resources of people or material or both. A 1987 bibliography listed 41 Ph.D. theses written from 1957 to 1985. In a recently published bibliography of doctoral dissertations in India from 1950 to March 1997 about 340 titles have been listed. This record of 340 dissertations, though not wholly authentic, is reliable by and large. In productivity the Panjab University, Chandigarh, led up to the mid-1980s. Thereafter, it lost the number game to the universities of the south.

The universities that have so far awarded up to ten degrees are ranked below:

- Karnatak University, Dharwad 44
- Jiwaji University, Gwalior 27
- University of Rajasthan, Jaipur 26
- Andhra University, Visakhapatnam 25
- University of Delhi 17
- University of Pune 16
- Gulbarga University 15
- Utkal University, Bhubaneswar 11
- University of Burdwan 10

The universities in Bangalore, Banaras Hindu University in Varanasi, and Nagpur University are picking up in research.

RELEVANCE OF RESEARCH

In a developing country like India, there could not be a dearth of research problems to be investigated. But there seems a lack of perception to visualise and identify valid problems for research. A cursory glance of the topics worked on will at once reveal that the topics chosen do not have a problem or hypothesis but merely survey the state of the art or the existing conditions. The popular areas for research have been, in order of popularity: university libraries, bibliometrics, library use and user studies, information seeking behaviour, information systems, classification and indexing, special libraries, library history, reference service and sources, and library science education.

Document selection and procurement, cataloguing, and experimental designs in library management are the least popular topics — though these seem practical and relevant to present day needs. That basic research is the most neglected area is endorsed by other surveys of doctoral research. Library automation, library software, networking and information technology are just emerging. There is need to revive research in classification especially in context of OPACs, information networks and the electronic information environment in general. The Curriculum Development Committee (CDC) on Library and Information Science of the University Grants Commission rehashed the importance of research, though it did not dwell at length on this aspect in its report.

The blue document listed some areas for research, which are no less broad than the current courses being taught at the Master's level:

- Structure and development of knowledge.
- Classification, cataloguing and indexing.
- Infometric studies.
- Computer applications.
- Historical studies.
- Social and economic aspects of librarianship.
- Library and Information management and systems analysis.
- Applications of techniques of library and information science to evaluate other disciplines.

The list could have been more specific. Though not much revered, the report rightly lays emphasis on standards in research. It uncompromisingly asks for a clear declaration from Ph.D. candidates that the "work is based on the discovery of new facts by the candidate or the new relations of facts... and how the work tends to the general advancement of know-ledge". While it is normally expected of every completed piece of research, yet it rarely happens. The evaluation process, however formal, is easily manipulated without qualms. Examiners are obliging on a reciprocal basis.

In a small profession like ours this interplay of mutual usability comes in easily. It is often said jocularly that the degree is recommended more for the supervisor than for the candidate. We must admit that the library profession has failed to lure the best brains and even more to retain them. Mediocrity thrives; hypocrisy reigns. But this is not to overlook the genuine research and researchers. Apart from not so relevant topics, theses have contributed little towards pushing the frontiers of knowledge; few are models of methodology. Indian library research seems to have no moorings in the prevailing realities.

Topics are ideal, superficial and bookish. Even experi-enced librarians keen on earning the Ph.D. degree rarely come with an important problem for research. The supervisor who shies from controversial topics usually suggests the topic. Criticising individuals in formal black-and-white mode or exposing harmful tendencies of a class are not for them. Even a mild and healthy criticism is not tolerated in India. Feudal norms still lie deep in the Indian social ethos.

In addition, there is a dire paucity of data archives and reference works. Collecting data and information is considered a satisfactory end to the job — the goal of the research exercise. It is very difficult to collect data by questionnaire in a vast country like India. Each researcher has a bag full of woeful tales to tell. Library associations at all levels seem to have washed their hands of the research responsibility. These do not even collect and compile statistics of the professional activities pertaining to their areas. Their libraries are poor. They have no research budget. For quite a time professionals have been talking, writing and conferencing about library education and research in India.

Every year the Indian Association of Teachers of Library and Information Science (IATLIS) holds a seminar on topics of library education and research. That it is the most popular topic with the teachers and librarians can be gauged from the fact that the FID/ET seminar was the largest of all the 49th FID pre-conference seminars held in India. The literature on library education and research is enormous, though repetitive and inflated. We have given lip service to the change of curricula and the raising of standards of research. But the needed change has not come through. The blame is wholly put on the lack of infrastructure and unavailability of funds. That is not the entire reason. The lack of effective collective efforts to safeguard the standards seems no less major cause.

THE CONTRIBUTIONS MADE BY RESEARCH

Contrary to expectations, dissertations are not fountain heads of the rest of the literature to grow and mature. These primary sources of information are distanced from relevance. The National Social Science Documentation Centre systema-tically procures one copy of each research dissertation in social sciences to preserve and make them available to researchers for consultation within the premises of its library. Retro-spective bibliographies of LIS dissertations in India are available.

The latest information on theses awarded, Ph.D. degrees and Ph.D. research in progress is available in the featured column of the weekly

University News of the Association of Indian Universities, New Delhi. It is a major source to keep track of the dissertations awarded Ph.D. degrees by Indian universities in all disciplines. In spite of availability, other researchers do not adequately use these dissertations; nor are these works cited or quoted by teachers or textbook writers.

Working librarians rarely use research results to solve their professional problems. There is no precedent of a library inviting a library school to do research on a problem confron-ting them. At the risk of calling attention to a red herring, it is worthwhile to have this idea corroborated from a veteran library leader.

Professor P.N. Kaula candidly observed:

- That LIS departments have little or no understanding and cooperation with the central library... The problem is more psychological than academic... Much harm has been done to the teaching of library science by the disharmony....

Librarians go in for local, *ad hoc* and *pro-tem* solutions for their practical problems. Researchers consult a teacher or a fellow researcher for a topic of research rather than a practitioner. It is not only true in India but elsewhere too. Thus research has become divorced from reality–a theoretical exercise at best. This seems a universal phenomenon in our profession. Carl Keren doubting the value of research in information science daringly suggests that “It would be worthwhile to find out how much of it has really contributed to our body of knowledge and to the methods used by practitioners.” He himself understands that “As suggested, probably be rather disappointed”.

American teacher Margaret Steig endorses this notion:

- Research done by library and information science educators seems to receive little respect from professionals, and if they do not find it of value one has to wonder who will.

MANAGEMENT INFORMATION SYSTEMS

Researcher has defined a Management Information System as:

- the process and structure used by an organisation to identify, collect, evaluate, transfer, and utilise information in order to fulfil its objectives. It is a system that provides management with information to make decisions, evaluate alternatives, measure performance, and detect situations requiring corrective action.

The implementation of performance assessment in academic libraries is an essential part of good management practice. Although she had reservations about the current Management Information Systems in university libraries because, for example, few academic libraries had produced a statement of their objectives, she still believed that Management Information Systems could contribute to effective management of library activities.

The four main objectives for Management Information systems have been defined as:

1. To facilitate the decision making process in the library by providing the managers with accurate, timely, and selective information that assists them in determining a specific course of action.
2. To provide for the objective performance measurement and assessment of selected relevant areas of the library. The areas are to be determined during strategic planning.
3. To provide pertinent information about the library's internal and external environments.
4. To provide information on alternative strategies and contingency plans.

The purposes can only be implemented if people look upon Management Information Systems as an integral part of the framework of management in the academic library and not as a peripheral system which has been installed for the benefit of an individual or a single department.

- There may be subsystems within the larger system, which may be branch libraries, or departmental divisions such as cataloguing, acquisitions or circulation, but they must still be seen as integrated parts of the whole, and must function as such. In the systems approach, however, the library organisation must be seen as an organic whole, with information as its lifeblood and in which each part of the system is integrated by the flow of information throughout.

An integrated Management Information System is very important because it can be used to provide supporting information to determine:

- *Efficiency*: is the library doing things right.
- *Effectiveness*: is the library doing the right things.
- *Competitiveness*: is the library heading in a direction which is consistent with the environment.

Any discussion of the Management Information System must lead to consideration of the inputs data, processing data and the outputs data. Inputs to the management information system consist of both internally and externally generated library data. External information covers factors such as legislation, politics, trends in society, changes in technology, user demand, and comparative statistics for other, similar institutions. Internal data is that derived from administrative routines and transactional information. Administrative routines include those related to personnel, finance, acquisition, cataloguing, processing of materials, binding, building services, maintenance services, etc.

Output measures will include data of circulation, general user satisfaction, etc. All service points will need to be monitored so that internal performance comparisons can be made and the contribution of each service point are the overall objectives of the organisation assessed. In term of library managers' needs, a variety of inputs is evidently needed. It may be necessary to process information in different ways for different levels of decision-making needs, and different types of output reports will be needed to meet those different needs.

Selection of appropriate data elements for inclusion in a Management Information System assumes that:

- Clear goals and measurable objectives have been developed for the library,
- For each data element there is rationale for how it will be used or in what combinations with other data elements it can be used to determine success towards the accomplishment of objectives, overall library effectiveness, or performance measures for specific library services/operations, and
- The library can, in fact, collect reliable and valid data for a particular data element.'

The data in a management information system also needs to be processed to turn it into meaningful information for library management. For this reason, management information systems require an appropriate data processing system. Data processing is the capture, storage and processing of data for the purpose of transforming it into information useful for decision making.

In recent years, data processing for management information systems in business and industry has increasingly been undertaken by computers:

- A modem MIS will always rely to some extent on computer technology, although a computer is not a requirement. The reality of the 1980's would indicate that a computer is a necessity for the most sophisticated systems.

In libraries, in contrast, the development of the use of computer has been:

- Modular, in the sense that it is based on a single library operation such as acquisitions, serials, control or cataloguing. The more general applications of management information lay hidden, as it is often seen only as a departmental resource.

This need not necessarily have been so. An early prediction of the advantages of information produced by computers was made in 1979 by Tague, who suggested that computers should produce information for control at both macro and micro level in libraries.

However, in 1986, Brophy, having analysed eight large computer systems used in British libraries, noted that:

- Automated library systems seem to be primarily about control at the micro level. Moreover, they produced management information which was relatively crude, highly structured and very much a system by-product.

The needs of individual managers tended to be overlooked, especially when the design of MIS was in the hands of computer personnel.

- Too often, management information has been produced as an afterthought following computerisation. Most computerised issue systems, for example, were never designed to produce management information although librarians have often struggled over the data generated by these systems in an attempt to derive some meaningful information about issue patterns.

Technological changes have helped to ease this problem. As opposed to the use of mainframe and mini-computers, 'the advent of the microcomputer now provides an alternative to the dependence on large-scale centralised computer systems. Computer power can now be deployed cheaply to different parts of an organisation to allow for local processing of data.'

Computers should be easily able to provide four types of report: periodic reports, exception reports, on demand reports, and predictive reports. Periodic reports provide routine, statistical information in detailed or summarised form. Exception reports highlight areas requiring managerial attention and would focus on those that have been overlooked. On demand reports provide a response to a particular non-standard question. Predictive reports give forecasts and provide comparisons based on statistical manipulation of data.

The principal requirement of the outputs of academic library management information systems is that they should be of interest to:

- The relevant committee - the members wish to know how the library service is performing and whether the institution, is getting value for money.
- The chief financial officer - his role is primarily custodial, and he wants to be assured that there is no overspending and that money is used for the purpose intended.
- The chief librarian - who wants to know how services under his control are performing in accordance with plans, targets and budgets.
- The managers of individual sections or services—who want to have data on the operations and performance with plans, targets and budgets.
- Outside organisations requesting library perfor-mance data on a regular basis.

In these ways, the outputs of management information systems become information for decision making.

In general, management information is:

- 'The right information in the right form at the right time, so enabling the manager effectively and effici-ently to do his/her job.'

The value or quality of management information is determined by three factors. They are:

1. The content of information: Information is the substance of communication, but to be information rather than data or noise, it must be meaningful, relevant and new to the receiver.

2. The form or presentation of the information: Information should be presented in a style and format readily understandable by the manager. This means that the producer of information must be aware of the recipient's knowledge of technical terms, numeracy/literacy levels, his individual characteristics, the characteristics of the group with which he works and so on. These and other factors help the information producer to form an idea of the perception level of the manager and increase the likelihood of producing understandable information capable of being used which, it will be recalled, is the only way information can create value.
3. The timing of its presentation: Information which is produced must be communicated to the manager in time to be used. Delays in data gathering, processing or communication can transform potentially vital information into worthless waste paper.

In the planning process, information should support the decision making process. Since one of the major problems facing academic libraries is the impact of changes in available financial support, the Colleges of Further and Higher Education Group (CoFHE) of the Library Association has been considering the categories of management information required for making decisions concerning the budget.

They concluded that these are:

- Information about the institutional identity of the library.
- Information about the target group.
- Information about the collection resources.
- Information about the financial resources.
- Information about library personnel.
- Information about facilities and equipment.
- Information about various programmes and functions.

CoFHE also considered the requirements for collecting management information, and suggested the following guidelines:

- The information sought must be worth the costs of collecting it - direct and indirect.
- Consider sources of information already available within the institution before setting up mechanisms to collect it.
- Keep the collection of information relevant, *i.e.*, remember the purpose - 'to support the budget request.'
- Remember to consider qualitative and quantitative data as both can be relevant.

CHANGES IN LIBRARY AND INFORMATION CENTRE MANAGEMENT

Due to fast-paced technological change and new skill requirements, information professionals are increasingly required to renew their skills and practice in order to gain an awareness of technological advances. As a result, the profession itself exists in a state of flux alongside these emerging technologies, with traditional roles being increasingly subsumed by new skills and working environments, and, therefore, job descriptions. Thus, information professionals are now expected to be aware of and capable of using and demonstrating emerging ICTs. There is a need for additional training to augment the traditional skill and knowledge base with a competency in ICT use. Information professionals must be flexible, and adopt traditional skills to incorporate the requirements of technological advances.

Given the current situation, wherein ICTs are being continuously updated or introduced and traditional formats are being replaced or supplemented by digital formats, it seems likely that there will continue to be a need for regular training for information professionals. There is also an increased focus on communication skills, with more people involved in the electronic information environment. Information professionals are being called upon to work closely with ICT users and providers - including IT staff - and to work in collaboration with others in the profession. Some groups of users lack the necessary IT skills to obtain quality information and information professionals will therefore be called upon to act as both educators and intermediaries.

Given these circumstances, information professionals are required to have additional teaching and communication skills. Thus, it is vital for those in management positions to recognise the imperative of *continuing professional development* (CPD) and ensure that the staff is proactive in maintaining up-to-date levels of expertise. The significance of CPD in this milieu has been acknowledged by both the United Kingdom's *Chartered Institute of Library and Information Professionals* (CILIP) and the United States' *American Library Association* (ALA).

Certain active roles are necessary for change management to:

- *Establish the quality goals of the library:* Library and Information Centres (LICs) should aim to establish the quality goals for qualitative service to its user community.
- *Provide the resources to their library:* LICs should provide all necessary resources suitable in the ICT era to manage the LICs in a better way.
- *Provide the quality-oriented training to the library staff:* New generation library staff are almost trained with ICT applications to LICs but old staff and others who are novices in such applications need quality training because without quality training library staff are unable to provide automated services.
- *Stimulate quality improvement in the day to day activities of library:* This is the age of competition. Like other organisations, to survive the LICs, top management should stimulate the staff for quality improvement in the day to day activities of LICs.

- *Review progress of the library activities:* Higher management should review the progress of library activities to maintain the quality and quantity of assigned job to the staff.
- *Give recognition to library staff:* Top level management should recognise the operational level library staff for quality performance, without which they will be demoralised to perform the job in a better way.

With the change in environment the objectives need to be revised to face the challenges of future. Over a period of time, due to the impact of technological advances, research and development, economic, social and political factors, the objectives also tend to change. To adopt these changes, it is essential to state objectives and functions of information system in changing context. For this purpose the following steps should be followed.

Structure Related Changes

The structure related changes in libraries and information centres may include:

- *Change in the work design:* The work design of a traditional library is not similar to modern automated library, so a change in the work design is compulsory for the success of automated library.
- *Change in the basis of departmentalisation:* There are various departments in university and research libraries. In case of automated library, book acquisition, classification and cataloguing, circulation, serial control assignments are being done through computer with specific software instead of doing manually. Besides these departments, modern library has other departments like barcoding, RFID tagging, OPAC/web-OPAC, e-journals, e-books, CD-ROM, digital library, touch screen kiosk, server maintenance etc.
- *Change in the number of operation levels to perform various activities, routine work of library staff:* As there is a major change in the processing and service departments a change in the number of staff in the lower level or operational level management has become essential.
- *Change in the plans, programmes, policies and procedures to and improving integration among various sections:* Due to changse in the pattern of service; plans, programmes, policies and procedures and integration within various departments it is very essential to cater to the service in a better way.
- *Change in the span of management and levels of management for effective co-ordination mechanism and flow of task:* Since the nature of job of modern automated library is more complex than traditional library, it is very difficult to manage large number of operational level staff under

one middle level manager. In view of this span of management should be narrow and levels of management should be changed because top and middle level management have to be directly linked with every department to perform each department's functions in a better way as well as for effective co-ordination mechanism with every department.

- *Change in line-staff and functional authority, work group relations between people and functions to improve their ability:* Line positions are responsible for accomplishing the organisation's primary objectives; they have final authority to make decisions. Staff positions, on the other hand, provide suggestions and advice for the line positions but cannot, theoretically make decisions for the line positions. An organisation seeks to keep authority for decision making in the positions accountable for results and to preserve a clear chain of command from the top to the bottom of the organisation. But in the automated library system there should be no hurdle between line and staff position because anyone who is aware about a particular system can give his advice. It helps to improve the work group relation as well as the ability of the all levels of management.

Structural changes affect relationships among the organisational positions and in the interactions among internal departments, the reporting mechanism, interactions of all sections in the library and the functional relationships.

Changes for Technological Advancement

The technology refers to the sum total of human knowledge providing ways to do the things in a better way with the help of techniques. It may include inventions and techniques affecting the ways of doing things.

Thus, technology related changes may include:

- *Use of new machines and equipments for developing new services or modifying existing services:* Many new machines and equipments, *e.g.*, computer, server, barcoding equipments, RFID tools are necessary for developing new services or modifying existing manual services. So the awareness about the use of new machines, equipments and tools is very essential.
- *The procedure of doing things which may result in change of work process:* The methods and procedures of doing new tasks should be changed in context of old library system. So that the work process is not disrupted.
- *Introduction of technological devices like computers and computer related technologies:* Introduction of technological devices like computers and computer related technologies is necessary for automated library. Without computers and related technologies, we are unable to cater to services in automated library system.

- *Change in the existing techniques for making or doing the things in effective way or adoption of new techniques for creative work:* Automated library is ICT oriented and some technique is involved in every work. So existing techniques of traditional library management should be changed and adoption of new techniques is very essential to carry out every task and service in automated library environment.
- *Change in the methods of using new tools equipments and products:* In the traditional library system, there are only a few equipments like fumigation chamber, catalogue cabinet, book rack, cardex, journal display rack, etc. But now computer terminals, server, barcoding equipments, RFID tools, etc., equipments and products are being used, so it is very natural to change the methods of using new tools, equipments and products.

The change in the technology affects the nature of work and activities, organisational structure, the processes and the people's behaviour.

Task-related Changes

Technology related changes determine the ways to complete the task effectively and efficiently. Task related changes helps to achieve major gains in terms of cost, service and time.

Task related changes may include:

- *Identifying the steps involved in performing tasks:* It is very necessary to organise meeting with library staff at all levels to identify the steps to perform the tasks effectively.
- *Task identification:* Every task should be identified to depute the staff who is efficient in that work. So, proper task identification is the key factor to perform the task properly and to serve the user community in a better way.
- *Significance of task related changes in attaining the organisational and institutional objectives:* As the nature of library has been changed so it is very significant to change the task which is relevant in changed atmosphere to attain the organisational and institutional objectives.
- *Identifying the skills and abilities required for the changed task:* It is very natural to identify the skills and abilities required for the changed task and to assign the specific job to the specific staff that is suitable for that particular job.
- *Improving both quality and quantity of work/ service:* For the satisfaction of our customer we should improve our quality as well as quantum of day to day work/service.
- *Bringing cost-effective solutions through maximum use of available resources:* Cost-effectiveness is concerned with the value. It asks, "This is what the service costs. Is it worth it?" So effectiveness of the resources is the key to maximum use of available resources.

- *Improving the work performance:* Quality training of staff is very essential to aware the task of each and every personnel effectively which improves the work performance.

People-related Changes

Change in any factor has an impact on human resources and human behaviour.

In the context of Library and Information Science, the people-related categories include:

- *The library staff:* In case of library staff, it requires the corresponding changes to be made in the skills, abilities and the performance of the employees.
- *New investment in training and development activities so that employees acquire new skills and activities:* New skills and activities are required in automated library system so new investment in training and development is essential. Library can get the fund from UGC for this purpose by making a systematic and comprehensive proposal
- *Socialising employees into the organisational structure so that they learn the new routines on which organisational performance depends....':* Top management should meet with middle and operational level management to become aware about the every bit of work with theory and practical and to assign the job to every personnel as well as time required for this purpose. Through socialising the employees organisational efficiency can also be increased.

Accordingly the change may also include –

- *Change in skill levels of the workforce:* Skill levels of each and every employee should be changed to cope up with new task.
- *Change in the training programmes to improve performance levels:* Training programme should be organised in a scientific way to sensitise the employee about every practical aspect of work and service. So change in training programmes is essential to improve performance levels of the staff.
- *Change in attitude and values:* Change in attitude and values is a must for better performance in work and service in the changed library environment.
- *Change in behaviour and interaction pattern:* As the library scenario has changed from traditional to automated one, behavioural and interaction pattern regarding work and service should also be changed.
- *Change in technology requires different skills of the operator:* Presently, library is technology controlled. To cope up with this change, the library personnel requires different skills to carry out their own task because it is very difficult to work properly for a unskilled staff.

- *Change in the structure requires change in their position, their authority, responsibility, etc.:* Due to shift from traditional to automated library, structural change is required. For this purpose positional, authoritative and responsibility change is necessary for better performance.
- *The readers:* Readers/users/customers are our prime focus. To serve the right user to the right information at the right time, we have to organise our resources systematically through which they can collect their information himself/herself. Such a systematic arrangement helps us to work and serve the users with less human resources.

Any change in the processes demands that it should be communicated to the readers to enable them to adjust to these changes. Readers are ultimately getting the benefits of all the technological advances, procedures, services, activities as well as other resources for their satisfaction in the libraries and information centres.

Changes in Library Policies

Change in the objectives and functions of the library and information system by the planning body would directly impact the existing plans and policies of the library. Accordingly, change in plans and policies become essential. The developmental plans and policies should be in conformity with the objectives and functions of library and information system as well as the institution it serves.

Changes in Objectives and Functions of Information System

The information system in the changed environment shall aim at:

- *Ensuring maximum use of all available resources:* Top management should ensure maximum use of all available resources through cost-effective solutions.
- *Promotion and development of all units in the library:* In the automated library, to cater the service to the users in a right way, it is very essential to develop all units in a proper way.
- *Better communication of ideas to achieve the objectives in an ever changing environment:* To communicate every new ideas to all levels of management is essential to achieve the objectives in constantly changing environment of library work and service.
- *Minimising the time, cost and efforts involved in all the activities, processes and functions:* Top level management should plan with with staff at middle and operational level for proper coordination of every function with minimum time, cost and efforts because duplicity of activities, processes and functions increases the time, cost and efforts.

In order to achieve the newly stated objectives as per the requirement of changing circumstances, certain functions are to be carried out. These functions may relate to adoption of latest technologies, use of modern tools and techniques, updating professional skill, ability and knowledge through education and training, future prospects of change in goals, objectives and functions, etc.

Librarians will need to be ready for competition and prepared to find new ways to make their skills and services distinct from those offered by the competition from media companies, publishers, internet companies, intermediary service providers and also from technologists parking on traditional library territory with technical names for old fashioned library ideas.

DISTRIBUTED SEARCH ACROSS OF DIGITAL LIBRARIES

The peer-to-peer (P2P) approach allows handling huge amounts of data of digital libraries in a distributed and self-organising way. These characteristics offer enormous potential benefit for search capabilities powerful in terms of scalability, efficiency, and resilience to failures and dynamics. Additionally, such a search engine can potentially benefit from the intellectual input of a large user community.

However, recent research on structured P2P architectures is typically limited to exact-match queries on keys. This is insufficient for text queries that consist of a variable number of keywords, and it is absolutely inappropriate for full-fledged Web search where keyword queries should return a ranked result list of the most relevant approximate matches. This stage builds upon the MINERVA system architecture presented in and brings current challenges to ultimatively making distributed search across digital libraries feasible. MINERVA provides ranked search on data and an efficient query mechanism that adheres to reasonable space and bandwidth limits. Unlike the approach criticised in, we do not spread inverted lists across the directory, but use only pointers to promising digital libraries as compact metadata and utilise these pointers to efficiently answer multiple-keyword queries. We leverage the extensive local indexes to incorporate features that are impossible in the approach studied in, such as phrase matching or proximity searches. Our bandwidth requirements are well within the postulation that a query should send no more data than the size of the documents ultimatively retrieved.

RELATED WORK

Recent research on structured P2P systems, such as Chord, CAN, Pastry, or P-Grid is typically based on various forms of distributed hash tables (DHTs) and supports mappings from keys to locations in a decentralised manner such that routing scales well with the number of peers in the system. We briefly discuss some prior and ongoing projects towards P2P Web search. Galanx is a P2P search engine implemented using the Apache HTTP server and Berkeley DB.

The Web site servers are the peers of this architecture; pages are stored only where they originate from. PlanetP is a publish subscribe service for P2P communities, supporting content ranking search. PlanetP distinguishes local indexes and a global index to describe all peers and their shared information. The global index is replicated using a gossiping algorithm. The system appears to be limited to a few thousand peers. Odissea assumes a two-layered search engine architecture with a global index structure distributed over the nodes in the system. A single node holds the complete, Web-scale, index for a given text term. Query execution uses a distributed version of Fagin's threshold algorithm.

The system appears to cause high network traffic when posting document metadata into the network, and the presented query execution method seems limited to queries with at most two keywords. The paper actually advocates using a limited number of nodes, in the spirit of a server farm. The system outlined in uses a fully distributed inverted text index, in which every participant is responsible for a specific subset of terms and manages the respective index structures. Particular emphasis is put on minimising the bandwidth used during multi-keyword searches. considers content-based retrieval in hybrid P2P networks.

The peer selection for forwarding queries is based on the Kullback- Leibler divergence between peer-specific statistical models of term distributions. In addition to this recent work on P2P search, prior research on distributed IR and metasearch engines is also potentially relevant; see for overviews. However, their work has assumed a relatively small number of digital libraries or databases and a fairly static configuration.

SYSTEM DESIGN

As a detailed description of the system design has already been given in, we only present a brief overview here and refer the interested reader to this prior work. We view every library as autonomous. A conceptually global but physically distributed directory, which is layered on top of a Chord-style dynamic hash table (DHT), holds only very compact, aggregated information about the peers' local indexes and only to the extent that the individual peers are willing to disclose. Every peer is responsible for a randomised subset of the global directory. The global directory consists of aggregated information (Posts) that contains contact information about the digital library who posted this summary together with statistics to calculate IR-style relevance measures that try to estimate the relevance of a particular digital library to a query. These measures are used to support the peer selection process, *i.e.*, determining the most promising libraries for a particular query. If, at query time, the local query result is considered unsatisfactory by the user, a library retrieves a list of potentially useful libraries. Using collection selection methods from distributed IR and metasearch, a number of promising libraries for the complete query is computed from these PeerLists. In we have studied promising and efficient techniques for this purpose. Subsequently, the query is forwarded to these libraries and executed based on their local indexes.

The results from the various libraries are combined at the querying peer into a single result list; this step is referred to as result merging. The goal of finding high-quality search results with respect to precision and recall cannot be easily reconciled with the design goal of unlimited scalability, as the best information retrieval techniques for query execution rely on large amounts of document metadata. Posting only compact, aggregated information about local indexes and using appropriate peer selection methods to limit the number of peers involved in a query keeps the global directory manageable and reduces network traffic. We expect this approach to scale very well as more and more peers jointly maintain the moderately growing global directory.

CHALLENGES

Our work is driven by the question of how a collaborative search across digital libraries can benefit from the unique nature of the P2P paradigm. We want to address the shortcomings of centralised search engines and further benefit from the intellectual input of a large user community.

Democratic Community Search

To overcome the danger of the infiltration of a centralised index by (commercial) interest groups we leverage the indexes from potentially thousands of digital libraries, making it harder to bias the final query results.

Implicit User Feedback

Additionally, we want to incorporate the fact that every library has its own local index, *e.g.*, by executing all queries first locally at the initiating library and using implicit-feedback techniques for automated query expansion.

User Recommendations

We want to incorporate local user bookmarks into our query execution. Bookmarks represent strong recommendations for specific documents. Also, user bookmarks can be considered as compact samples of peer indexes that describe their fields of interest. Queries could be exclusively forwarded to thematically related libraries with similarly interested users, to improve the chances of finding subjectively relevant pages.

Replication

In order to achieve service levels comparable to today's search engines and in order to actually benefit from the infrastructural advantage of a distributed system, we are going to introduce a certain degree of replication to the directory. Currently, as dictated by the DHT-style maintenance approach, a peer gracefully leaving the system forwards its share of the global directory to another peer.

Analogously, a library entering the system asks for its appropriate share of the directory.

While one approach to ensure a valid, complete, and up-todate directory is to simply rely on the libraries to regularly re-send their Posts to the directory, it is also necessary to replicate parts of the directory to avoid data loss as libraries ungracefully leave the system. Also, replication can serve as a load-balancing measure, relieving the burden from peers that host popular parts of the directory, and increases data availability. Adaptive, self-tuning strategies for choosing appropriate degrees of replication and placing replicas are an open issue in our ongoing work.

Caching and Proactive Dissemination

To further enhance query efficiency, statistical summaries and also the results of queries from across the network may be cached in a way that allows other peers not only to instantly benefit from the existing query results but also to benefit from click streamst that were recorded on the occasion of similar queries. Statistical summaries may also be disseminated proactively among thematically related peers. Finding good strategies to this end is a widely open issue.

Overlap-aware Query Routing

Peer selection has been a research issue for years. Most of the existing literature estimates the expected result quality of a collection, typically using pre-computed statistics, and ranks the collections accordingly. We believe that this is insufficient if the collections overlap, *e.g.*, in the scenario of digital libraries that share an arbitrarily large fraction of documents. We argue for the extension of existing quality measures using estimators of mutual overlap among collections.

Preliminary experiments show that such a combination can outperform popular approaches based on quality estimation only, such as CORI. Taking overlap into account during collection selection in this scenario can drastically decrease the number of libraries that have to be contacted in order to reach a satisfactory level of recall, which is a great step towards the feasibility of distributed search across digital libraries.

Benefit/Cost Optimisation

Ultimatively, we want to introduce a sophisticated benefit/cost ratio when selecting remote libraries for query forwarding. For the benefit estimation, it is intuitive to consider such measures. Defining a meaningful cost measure, however, is an even more challenging issue. While there are techniques for observing and inferring network bandwidth or other infrastructural information, expected response times are changing over time. One approach is to create a distributed Quality-of-Service directory that, for all peers, holds moving averages of recent response times.

INTERNET ON LIBRARY AND INFORMATION SERVICES

Perhaps no other recent innovation has impacted the library profession to such a great extent as Internet. Not only is our world becoming an interconnected global community, but this early use of the Internet has changed the fundamental roles, paradigms, and organisational culture of libraries and librarians as well, which created profound impact on LandIS by offering new modes of information delivery and a vast information source.

There is a continuing evolution of the roles and functions of libraries and librarians, which appears to parallel the growth of acceptance and use of the Internet by library professionals. The innovative use of Internet technologies enable us to reach both local and distant users much more easily and effectively than hither to possible.

Technologies such as e-mail and Web provides tremendous opportunities for library and Inf. Scientists to deliver the information to the desktops of our users. Web offers significant advantage by integrating different library and information services with a common user interface offered by Web browsers. Realising the potentials, many libraries are rushing to getting the connectivity. The following listing will give an idea of which various functions of libraries may take advantage from Internet and Web technologies.

Acquisition:

- Correspondance with Book seller and Publisher.
- Reminders, Price verification
- Biblographic details and downloading of bib. records etc
- Ordering, billing
- Bookshops are on-line, *e.g.,* amazon.com

Classification:

- Network resources
  - — Available on the net
  - — Subscribed or free or trial basis
- Dewey Online
- Maths. Classification System
- Engineering Electronics Lib. Classification
- Search engines – such as yahoo use DDC.

Collection Development:

- Ownership vs Access
- Subscribe in print or e-form
- Subscribe in print as well as in e-form
- Pay-per-use
- Consortial approach

Cataloguing:

- Cataloguing of network resources

- Online Catalogues
- WorldCat (OCLC)
- WebOPAC – web sites
- MARC adds 856 field
- OCLC Scorpian project- MARC and AACR2
- Metadata standards- Dublin core

Circulation:

- Remote login
- Status check
- OPAC access
- Reminder to users
- User requests
- Direct borrowing
- ILL

Resource Sharing:

- Union Catalogue
  - Access, adding, downloading
- Access to databases over networks
  - Ohionet, ILLINET, WLN, OCLC, BID (UK)
  - Full text journals access,etc.

Services:

- ILL
- Document Delivery Service, *e.g.,* Ariel
- Reference/ Inf. Services
- CAS
  - Recent additions,
  - Contents pages
- SDI
  - From library collection
  - Databases
  - Internet Sources
- OPAC
- Database access
  - Bibliographical
  - Full text
  - Many vendors and organisations are moving to Internet (web) access

Subject Lists/ Gateways:

- Internet Public Library
- *EEVL* – Engineering
- *SOSIG* – Social Science
- *OMNI*- Medical
- *ADAM* – Arts, Design,etc.

User Education:

- Through E-mail
- Through Web
- Setting Intranet

Preservation and Storage:

- The Internet is also a medium for the preservation and storage of information. In past, libraries were seen as the main storage facility of information. As society becomes increasingly more digital and more information resides on the Internet, the focus on storage and preservation is shifting. For example, some academic libraries are now faced with the problem of whether or not to purchase serials that can be just as easily accessed on – line. Preservation of these same media also becomes an issue of economics, not the 'just in case' preservation ideology of the past paradigm. Co joined to the function preservation is the destruction of information. Because the Internet can be seen as a medium for preserving information, the process of destruction of information also is affected. As more and more information is created and stored on the Internet, the capacity to store this information is also decreasing.

RETRIEVAL OF INFORMATION

Directories, Search Engines, Meta Search Engines and Information Gateways/Virtual Libraries etc are widely used to retrieve relevant information from Internet.

Search Engines:

- They are also called Meta crawlers or multi search engines
- Do not crawl the web compiling their own searchable databases
- Search the databases of multiple sets of individual search engines simultaneously from a single site and using the same interface.
- They function as intermediary
- Present the results of their searches in two ways
  - — Single lists
  - — Multiple Lists.
- There are three types of meta search engines,
  - — Listing
  - — Options
  - — Automatic
- While you query, options less
- Cover all major search engines
- Do not return all results retrieved, they take only top ones from the list.
- They are very fast.
- Use them when you are in a hurry

- Helpful when you want to have quick overview on a subject and/or unique term.
- Use them when you are,
  — Conducting a relatively simple search
  — Not having any luck pulling up documents in your search.

RESOURCES AVAILABLE ON THE INTERNET

The advent of IT and other communication technologies changed all means of information services and sources. The Internet has given the world numerous easy-to-use and inexpensive research tools. Internet is changing the way we view information sources. Information bundled in World Wide Web in the form of structured and Non-structured sources create huge problem for professionals who are dealing with information. The shift in publication process takes place as individuals, institutions, publishers, professional associations, business houses and many others are publishing information on Internet.

Electronic publishing is considered as the speedy, accurate and effective way of communication among academia and research community, and becoming a favorite idea among information professionals to experiment with. The library and information professionals have a vital role to play in organising the information and bridging the *information gap*. Internet has become a part of library environment today. Internet for reference work in the library is gaining popularity. It can be successfully utilised for providing short-range and long-range reference service because various primary and secondary sources of information are available online from many sites. As information professionals, we can arrange the sources on net as we come across, in a structured manner.

These can be;

- E-journals
- E-books
- Standards
- E-TDs
- Preprints
- Library catalogue
- Bibliographical Tools
- Share wares
- Old books
- News papers
- Dictionaries
- Magazines
- Encyclopaedias
- Databases
- Directories
- Films
- Maps

- Technical reports
- Audio/Video
- Proceedings
- Patents
- Web sites of Companies, Institutions, Organisations, Associations,etc.

Here the relevant question is that *'What is not available on Internet?'*

Evaluation of Information Sources

When we access or retrieve something on the Web, we need to decide whether the information is useful, reliable, and appropriate for our purposes. The resources identified can also occasionally contain inaccurate and misleading information. The nature of the Internet and WWW makes it easy for almost anyone to create and disperse information.

People also have considerable freedom and variety in the formats with which they publish information on the Web. We have to double -check the facts before giving it to users. Here we need to use some general guidelines or criteria when evaluating information sources. We should ask the following questions about whatever information we found.

- Who is the author or Institution?
- How current is the information?
- Who is the audience?
- Is the content accurate and objective?
- What is the purpose of the information?
- How easy to use it?

More than that, we can consider coverage, presentation and arrangement of information in the sources to find out its value. The tremendous increase in online information sources made the searching difficult, where organising skill is required for library and information professionals. Libraries role is also enhanced where they will have to adapt to changing environment. The scope is only limited to the imagination of information professionals, where they have to acquire thorough understanding of changes in their profession. Willingness to take up the challenges in information resource management is the need of the hour for us.

WEB SITE FOR A LIBRARY

The roles of libraries and the Internet in providing information in the 21st century are firmly intertwined. It behooves any librarian working today to understand not only how to find things on the World Wide Web, but to have a basic understanding of how it works. Librarians will be called on to become information architects, to be able to create Web sites with clearly stated goals, that are aesthetically pleasing and filled with relevent content and functionality.

As more and more libraries set up comprehensive Web sites, there becomes an increasing demand for librarians who have an understanding of HTML, as well as other types of Internet programming skills such as javascript, SQL, CGI, ASP, and Cold Fusion. Librarians should know the principles of setting up an efficient information resource. As the Internet becomes more interactive, there is a push Towards making databases accessible online; the best example of this is the library card catalog. Other interactive options include e-mail and bulletin board service, and moving from CD-ROMs to online subscriptions.

A library Web site is not merely establishing a presence on the Internet. It can be a virtual addition to the existing library structure, reaching out to patrons around the clock and providing valuable information resources. Additionally, a library's Web site is an important source of information about the library. The library's Internet policies, special programming, and new materials can all be made viewable at any time from the Web site. Libraries, too, should be designing their own Web sites that serve as portals to interesting sites that have been reviewed and annotated by professional librarians. Librarians will continue to play an important role as information professionals in the Information Age, well into the 21st century.

MARKETING OF LIBRARY SERVICES

In recent years, libraries of all types from all countries have found it necessary to compete for both money and clients as major changes have occurred. The Internet brings a whole new dimension of competition that public, academic, and special libraries are facing daily. Whereas budget problems have been around for some time, the recent competition from the Internet can translate into fewer users, despite the fact that the Internet is also a crucial tool used by librarians for research and marketing.

Because of all of these existing challenges and intensifying changes at least a handful of libraries have turned to 'tried and true' business models for improved planning and development, and that they are employing marketing plans as one method for moving forward. As time goes on, libraries must think about marketing of their services and resources to achieve goals. It is important to clarify what marketing means in a library environment.

Marketing is not so much about 'selling' information products to researchers, as it is more about spreading the word about potentially useful new tools. It is also about keeping users informed about library activities and involving them in collection development. It is more about integrating new research tools into existing, effective research processes, and in some way enhancing researchers' work, rather than selling the tool to users as an end in itself.

As librarians market new tools, they should know how the tools may offer clarity, and not simply contribute to noise for the users. Effective marketing can only occur when librarians understand, at least in a broad sense, what the scientists, professors, and graduate students are already doing to keep informed, and what their research projects are about.

WEB BASED LIBRARY SERVICE

A digital Library service manages and develops electronic services, the library Web sites and library staff. According to White, it can be defined broadly as 'an information access service in which users ask questions via electronic means, *e.g.,* e-mail or web forms'.

Library service on the internet requires many of the same qualities as traditional references: accuracy, promptness, courtesy, an understanding of the information need. It provides users with the convenience of accessing information in their own time, saving them traveling cost and time and new options for answering reference questions. The provision of these services is not constrained by the traditional opening hours but can be offered on a 24-hour, seven-days-a-week basis known as 24/7. And while there may be a disadvantage in not having a face-to face encounter, there are many advantages to this new medium and the greatest advantage is that many more users can be helped by using electronic library services. Advantages and disadvantages of electronic access over printed form access are showed in table. Web based services are established due to the following reasons.

- Ensuring the needs of users and the accessible information sources are suitable matched at all times.
- Delivering those information sources to the user in a timely and appropriate fashion.
- Ensuring the information provided is high quality, accurate and appropriate.
- Assisting the user in interpreting the materials, if necessary.
- Promoting user awareness of new services and information sources as they develop.
- Providing users with individualised guidance and support as they build their information search and application skills.

DIFFERENT RESOURCES FOR WEB BASED LIBRARY SERVICES

Today, users may have access a variety of textual information resources. There are different kinds of webbased reference resources and services for accessing information from libraries such as OPAC, Gateways, Portals, Subject Portals, Electronic Journals, Online Databases, Subject Directories and Search Engines. These resources overlap considerably in the type of information they cover, and sometimes it is difficult to distinguish between some of them. A library should have a good collection of these resources like selected Web links, subscription resources, and library materials in well-organised pages for serving better services to their users.

Many libraries and organisations are providing digital reference service through collaborative services. Existing library consortia are adding digital reference to current shared services, and networks of libraries. Some regional library consortia are offering member libraries the opportunity to share reference questions with each other using the Internet and other technologies.

OPAC

OPAS's - On Line Public Access Catalogues, form an important part of many digital library's collections. It allows users to search for the bibliographic records contained within a library's collections. Now days, some OPAC also provide access to electronic resources and databases, in addition to the traditional bibliographic records.

GATEWAYS

A gateway is defined as a facility that allows easier access to network based resources in a given subject area. Gateways provide a simple search facility and a much-enhanced service through a resource database and indexes, which can be searched through a web based interface. Information provided by gateways is catalogued by hand. Gateways cover a wide range of subjects, through some areas, such as music and religious studies, currently lack subject gateways. Some well-known gateways are as follows:

- Internet Public Library (IPL),
- Bulletin Board for Libraries (BUBL),
- National Information Services and Systems (NISS),

PORTALS

In the library community, portals may be defined as an amalgamation of services to the users where the amalgamation is achieved through seamless integration of existing services by using binding agents such as customisation and authentication services, search protocols such as Z39.50, loan protocols such as ISO10161, and e-commerce.

The result is a personalised service which allows the individual to access the rich content of both print-based and electronic systems. Portals are either commercial or free web facilities that offer information services to a specific audience. The facilities include web search to communication to e-mail to news,etc.There are three kinds of portals; Consumer (or horizontal), Vertical and Enterprise.

- Consumer portals are aimed at consumer audiences and offer free e-mail, games, chat,etc., Examples are Yahoo!, MSN and AOL.
- Vertical portals, target a specified audience, such as a particular industry, and offer many of the consumer portal features. Example includes VerticalNet.

- Enterprise portals on the other hand are similar to consumer portals, but they are offered only to corporations or similar organisations. Examples include Epicentric and Corporate Yahoo! These portals can be best understood as electronic pathfinders for users, pulling together in one place in a web site selected links to subjects or interest-oriented resources located on the WWW.

SUBJECT PORTALS

Web Search Engines had been developed initially by computer scientists, by borrowing techniques from information retrieval search such as best match searching and relevance ranking. Information professional are increasing bringing their skills to help organise the growing wealth of Internet resources.

A good example of their influence is the development of subject-specific web search engines known as subject portals, where evaluation of material covered is a major concern.

Two prime UK subject portals are SOSIG Social Science Information Gateway, covering social science resources and OMNI Organising medical networked information covering medical resources. Subject portal sites can be very helpful, but they should be used with care. Users should bear the following points in their mind:

- The aim of the subject portal is to list and review the most important sites on the web relevant to that subject. The sites are usually constantly peer-reviewed to ensure that the site is relevant and up to date.
- New sites are appearing all the time. Relying on a subject portal site to find everything users require may mean that they miss an important site that has recently appeared and has not yet been reviewed by the producers of the particular subject portal.
- A subject portal is a one stop shop for information on the topic it covers. Users don't have to carry out extensive Internet searches in order to find the information require. They can simply go to the required subject portal site.
- Subject portals save users having to have long lists of bookmarks (saved addresses of web pages), which are often, cumbersome and time consuming to arrange and keep up to date. However, if users do prefer to use bookmarks they can arrange them in an order to suit the way they work and not have an order forced on them by the subject portal.
- A subject portal site is only as good as the reviewers who peer-review the site listed. The reviewers need to have a policy of keeping the portal sites up to date and of constantly reviewing the sites they list,

to make sure that they are still relevant and still contain good, timely information.

- A subject portal may be available to everyone who needs to use it to only certain groups of users. A good portal should be publicly available to anyone who needs it.

ELECTRONIC JOURNALS

Electronic journals form a large part of the collection of a library for providing web based services. Today many journals are available electronically - some are full text and some contain only bibliographic information with abstract. Major advantage of electronic journals is that they are constantly updated and easy to access but disadvantage is that breaching of copyright law is very easy.

They are available as bitmaps, PostScript, PDF, ASCII, SGML and HTML. Library services may be delivering to users on CDRom, through e-mail or through web. Some international societies and associations have developed their own digital libraries through which users can get access to all their publications. Services are available to the members of society or associations through subscription.

ONLINE DATABASES

These are large collections of machine-readable data that are maintained by commercial agencies and are accessed through communication lines. Many libraries subscribe to them for easy access and use of current information. The disadvantage is that only bibliographic data is presented and not full text. The information cannot be accessed when the system is down for any reason. Examples Ei Compendex, SciFinder Scholar, Web of Science, Current Contents, etc.

SEARCH ENGINES

Search Engines are huge databases of web page files that have been assembled automatically by machines where as the subject directories are human-compiled and maintained. Search engine indexes every page of a Web site and subject directories linked only homepages.

Search Engine is the popular term for an information retrieval (IR) system. A search engine is computer software that searches a collection of electronic materials to retrieve citations, documents, or information that matches or answers a user's query.

The retrieved materials may be text documents, facts that have been extracted from text, images, or sounds. A query is a question phrased so that it can be interpreted properly by search engine. Depending on the type of software, it may be a collection of commands, a statement in either full or partial sentences, one or more keywords, or in the case of Non-text searching, an image or sequence of sounds to be matched.

SUBJECT DIRECTORIES

Subject directories differ from search engines in that search engines are populated by robots that finds and index sites whereas humans making editorial decisions that populate subject directories. Subject directories are basically index home pages of sites and can be classified as general, academic, commercial or portal.

Among the well known subject directories are the Argus Clearinghouse and Yahoo. Strengths include relevance, effectiveness and relative high quality of content. Weaknesses are that they lack depth in their coverage of the subjects.

FUTURE OF WEB BASED SERVICES

Library Web services will continue to spread out, offering more full-text electronic journals and indexes that do not now include full text will begin to do so, or link to external resources. Bibliographic access to full-text periodicals either through cataloging, databases, or vendors will be in improved form. There will be more Web forms for user feedback, and perhaps a virtual librarian who interacts in real time chat or video conferencing. More Document delivery services to distance education or users and Savings on Interlibrary Loan and user convenience are incentives. Information resources through creative consortia purchasing will be popular.

A well-developed user education modules or tutorials, especially to support independent exploration of library and Web resources. Somebody will have to figure out how to keep Word users from saving print documents as XML, without thinking in terms of Web, not print, space. XML will be embraced as a way to control page appearance and Behaviour, but it will take a while for people to figure out how to use it well and there will be trends we haven't thought of yet.

The standards for organising web-based resources are still in the early stages of development, and librarians are forced to utilise standards for print resources that were not designed for electronic resources. Additionally web-based information resources are volatile in the sense that may be moved from one site to another or may be removed altogether from web. Web-based library services will become more widespread and sophisticated as the web becomes common place throughout the world, and to be successful players in the E-world. Libraries must continue to address the web design and implementation issues.

As we actively transfer library services, our central purpose remain the same, to serve and teach users to find, evaluate, and use information effectively.

The librarians should be expert to hold the hands of the users who are moving towards new communication paradigm a shift from face to face human contact to human machine interaction, from paper to electronic delivery, from text centered mode to multimedia and from physical presence to virtual presence. Despite these changes in communication technology, the reference interview will remain at the heart of the reference transaction. To meet these challenges the librarians may play a leadership role in providing better Web Based library Services facilities to their current techno savvy users.

Bibliography

Aadhavan Omesh : *Development of Digital Library*, Oxford Book Company, Delhi, 2010.

Alimohammadi Dariush : *Operations Research for Library and Information rofessionals*, Ess Ess Publications, Delhi, 2010.

Arora Kanu : *University Library System : Centralization and Decentralization*, Regal, Delhi, 2008.

Atkinson, P.: *Imagining the Digital Library in a Commercialized Internet*, New York: Oxford: Pergamon Press, 2003.

Ballabh, Anand : *New Approaches to Library Administration,* Rajat, Delhi, 2002.

Boyle, J: *Privacy: The Next Challenge*, England: University Press, 2006.

Buckland Michael : *Book Availability and the Library Users,* New York: Perga-mon Press, 1975.

Chan, L.M.: *Library of Congress Subject Headings: Principles and Application*, Colo, Libraries Unlimited, 1995.

Cohen, M.: *Maintaining the Privacy of Library Records*, London: Waverly Book Company, 2003.

Dean, R. G.: *The Transparent Society: Will Technology Force us to Choose between Privacy and Freedom*, London: Smith College Studies in Library Science, 2002.

Denzin, N.: *Privacy in the Information Age*, Chicago: American Hotel Register Company, 2004.

Dos John Passos : *Tom Paine:The Living Thoughts Library*, Rupa Pub, Delhi, 2002.

Drisko, J.: *Issues in the Information Age, Library Science Education*, 2003.

302 Handbook of Library Security Giorgi, A.: *Computerized Monitoring and Online Privacy*, Duquesne University Press, 2005.

Glaser, B.: *Confidentiality in the Use of Library Materials*, Mill Valley, Sociology Press, 2001.

Gopal, Krishan : *Technological Future of Library and Information Science*, Authors Press, Delhi, 2001.

Guba, E.: *RSS for Non-Techie Librarians*, San Francisco: Jossey Bass Press, 2003.

Harris, Michael H. : *History of Libraries in the Western World,* Metuchen, N.J.: Scarecrow Press, 1984.

Hyde, C.: *Online Resources for Adaptive Information Technologies*, Boston: William J. Nagel Company, 2001.

Jackson, Sideny L.: *Libraries and Librarianship in the West: A Brief History,* New Yokr: McGraw-Hill Book Company, 1974.

Kapoor S.K. : *Library Science Education and Mass Communication*, Cyber Tech Publications, Delhi, 2010.

Kumbhar Rajendra : *Thesaurus of Library and Information Science Terms*, Ess Ess, Delhi, 2004.

LeCompte, M.: *Computers in Libraries*, San Diego: Academic Press, 2004.

Mahapatra, Rabindra K.: *Capacity Building and Restructuring of Library and Information Centres*, Ess Ess Pub, Delhi, 2010.

Mishler, E.: *Accessibility in the Virtual Library*: London: Harvard University Press, 2002.

Padgett, D.: *Information Technology and Libraries*, New York: University Press, 2000.

Rastogi K.G.: *The Functions of Cataloguing in Library Science*, Alfa Publications, Delhi, 2006.

Singh P K: *Current Trends and Techniques in Library and Information Science*, Shree Pub, Delhi, 2007.

Strauss, A.: *Assistive Technology in Special Libraries*, San Francisco: Harper Bowling Green State University, 2000.

Van Maanen, J.: *Library Assistive Technology: Predictions and Trends*, Chicago: The Hotel Monthly Press, 2006.

Verma Kusum: *Computer Applications to Library*, Vista International Pub, Delhi, 2008.

Vygotsky, L.: *Adaptive Technology Equipment for the Library*, New York: Columbia Press, 2001.

Zweig Arnold: *Baruch Spinoza :The Living Thoughts Library*, Rupa Pub, Delhi, 2003.

Index